Entrepreneurship, Dyslexia, and Education

The development of entrepreneurial abilities in people with dyslexia is a subject of great interest. It has gained increasing importance in economically difficult times because of its potential for the development of new business opportunities. This book brings together contributions from researchers, educators, and entrepreneurs with dyslexia, investigating this subject from many perspectives.

Is there something different in the profile of a person with dyslexia that supports the development of entrepreneurship? This book aims to draw out key themes which can be used in education to motivate, mentor, and create the business leaders of tomorrow. It offers a fundamental text for this area of study with a comprehensive, international examination of its topic. It includes views by new and established international writers and researchers, providing up-to-date perspectives on entrepreneurship, dyslexia, and education. It is accessible to read, to understand, and to learn from and is suitable for recommended reading for graduate and postgraduate students.

The diverse views and perspectives demonstrated in this book make it as relevant as possible for a wide group of readers. It informs study in the fields of business and dyslexia, and will be of interest to educators, researchers, and to anyone interested in the overlap of entrepreneurship and dyslexia.

Barbara Pavey is an independent dyslexia and special educational needs and disability specialist and author, focusing on Dyslexia-Friendly principles and techniques, and with a particular interest in entrepreneurship.

Neil Alexander-Passe is a special educational needs and disability coordinator in primary and secondary schools and an expert inclusion adviser to the UK's Department of Education, and his focus is the emotional impact of dyslexia.

Margaret Meehan is a specialist tutor in higher education, previously directing tutor support, and a former chartered chemist and chartered science teacher. As an author she is concerned with researching the holistic impact of dyslexia and other learning attributes.

Routledge Studies in Entrepreneurship

This series extends the meaning and scope of entrepreneurship by capturing new research and enquiry on economic, social, cultural and personal value creation. Entrepreneurship as value creation represents the endeavours of innovative people and organisations in creative environments that open up opportunities for developing new products, new services, new firms and new forms of policy making in different environments seeking sustainable economic growth and social development. In setting this objective the series includes books which cover a diverse range of conceptual, empirical and scholarly topics that both inform the field and push the boundaries of entrepreneurship.

A History of Enterprise Policy
Government, Small Business and Entrepreneurship
Oliver Mallett and Robert Wapshott

New Frontiers in the Internationalization of Businesses
Empirical Evidence from Indigenous Businesses in Canada
Fernando Angulo-Ruiz

Contextualizing Entrepreneurship Theory
Ted Baker and Friederike Welter

Entrepreneurial Marketing and International New Ventures
Antecedents, Elements and Outcomes
Edited by Izabela Kowalik

Entrepreneurship, Dyslexia, and Education
Research, Principles, and Practice
Edited by Barbara Pavey, Neil Alexander-Passe, and Margaret Meehan

For a full list of titles in this series, please visit www.routledge.com/Routledge-Studies-in-Entrepreneurship/book-series/RSE

Entrepreneurship, Dyslexia, and Education

Research, Principles, and Practice

**Edited by Barbara Pavey,
Neil Alexander-Passe, and
Margaret Meehan**

Routledge
Taylor & Francis Group

NEW YORK AND LONDON

First published 2021
by Routledge
52 Vanderbilt Avenue, New York, NY 10017

and by Routledge
2 Park Square, Milton Park, Abingdon, Oxon, OX14 4RN

Routledge is an imprint of the Taylor & Francis Group, an informa business

Library of Congress Cataloging-in-Publication Data
Names: Pavey, Barbara, editor. | Alexander-Passe, Neil, editor. | Meehan, Margaret, editor.
Title: Entrepreneurship, dyslexia and education: research, principles and practice/edited by Barbara Pavey, Neil Alexander-Passe and Margaret Meehan.
Description: New York, NY: Routledge, 2021. | Series: Routledge studies in entrepreneurship | Includes bibliographical references and index.
Identifiers: LCCN 2020032789 (print) | LCCN 2020032790 (ebook) | ISBN 9780815396468 (hardback) | ISBN 9781351036900 (ebook)
Subjects: LCSH: Entrepreneurship. | Dyslexics—Intellectual life.
Classification: LCC HB615.E577883 2021 (print) | LCC HB615 (ebook) | DDC 338/.04071—dc23
LC record available at https://lccn.loc.gov/2020032789
LC ebook record available at https://lccn.loc.gov/2020032790

ISBN: 978-0-8153-9646-8 (hbk)
ISBN: 978-0-367-54210-8 (pbk)
ISBN: 978-1-351-03690-0 (ebk)

Typeset in Sabon
by Apex CoVantage, LLC

This book is dedicated to the memory of
Professor Robert (Bob) Burden (1940–2014)
Whose scholarship and research in education created
an important appreciation of the emotional impact of dyslexia

Contents

**Conclusion: The Experience of Entrepreneurs
With Dyslexia** 255
BARBARA PAVEY, NEIL ALEXANDER-PASSE
AND MARGARET MEEHAN

Acknowledgements

As editors, we would like to thank all of the contributing authors who gave their time and expertise to provide input for this book. Their chapters have enabled us to present a wide panorama in exploring different aspects of the topic of entrepreneurship and dyslexia, and we are enormously grateful for their support of the project.

We would also like to thank the many individuals who provided context and detail for us in approaching our subject. These include the students and entrepreneurs who donated their time so that we could interview them, and also the independent business people and sole traders with whom we had informal conversations about entrepreneurship and dyslexia.

Where research was carried out within the purview of Swansea University, we would like to thank Adele Jones, Disability Office Manager, and Sandy George, Director of the Centre for Academic Success, for their support of the research project, and also Sara Griffiths and Caroline Kneath for their help in transcribing the interviews. In addition, we would like to thank Paul Adkins, who at that time was a member of the staff of Harper-Adams University, for reviewing two of the chapters about entrepreneurship.

Regarding resources, we would like to acknowledge that the table comparing principles of Universal Design for Instruction and Dyslexia-Friendly principles, shown as Appendix One, appeared first in *Asia Pacific Journal of Developmental Disabilities* in 2015. It appears here by kind permission of the journal's editors.

Finally, we would like to thank the editorial team who guided us at Routledge, particularly Brianna Ascher, Mary del Plato and Naomi Round Cahalin for their patience and support. We would also like to acknowledge, with gratitude, the unfailing patience of our copy editor, Gilbert Rajkumar Gnanarathinam and his team.

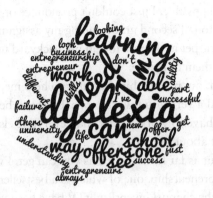

Foreword

Stephen Key, has dyslexia and is the author of *One Simple Idea* and a cofounder of inventRight. He has lectured at the University of Newcastle on 'How to launch a product without starting a business.'

I was delighted to be asked to write the foreword for this interesting book. It is an impressive achievement, combining as it does the fields of entrepreneurship, dyslexia and education in a way that illuminates a topic which has caused great interest.

The chapters provide an eclectic mix, approaching the topic from different perspectives and through their cumulative impact, contributing to a better understanding of why entrepreneurs who experience dyslexia might be in a particular position that encourages success.

The theme of the book interests me because I am an entrepreneur who experiences dyslexia, and who also lectures in the Higher Education (HE) sector. That puts me in a particular position to appreciate this volume. Like others described in these pages, I too had a difficult time in education when I was young.

Life is full of surprises. Growing up, school was truly a nightmare for me. Never in a million years did I imagine that I would become an educator, let alone grow to love teaching others.

My favourite part of grade school was recess, because that's where I felt safe. I remember staring out of classroom windows constantly, praying and hoping I wouldn't be called upon. That was my biggest fear—that I'd be asked to read aloud or have to spell. I knew something wasn't quite right, because for my classmates these tasks were effortless. For me, they were nearly impossible. I just couldn't pronounce or spell words the right way. I began to fail second grade, hiding my assignments from my parents under the carpet in the tree fort in my backyard until the lump grew too large for them to ignore.

Very concerned, my parents hired a tutor to help me, but to get by I also developed a very good work ethic. To not to be found out, I realized I would have to work harder than everyone else. At an early age, I learned a lot about hiding.

Today, I'm about as far from hidden as you can get. I've authored four books about entrepreneurship, one of which is a bestseller. Videos on my educational YouTube channel inventRightTV have been viewed nearly three million times. Over the past decade, I've published 1,000 articles about commercialising product ideas online, primarily for business magazines including *Forbes*, *Inc.*, and *Entrepreneur*. My inventing coaching company, inventRight, has 20 employees. In 2018–2019, I was nationally recognized as an American Association for the Advancement of Science-Lemelson Invention Ambassador.

As it turns out, you don't need to be able to spell to write. But you absolutely do need to be able to overcome obstacles to become a successful entrepreneur. Before my dyslexia was diagnosed, I always felt confused, insecure and less than. I was ashamed. I did not want to be discovered. Now I look at my dyslexia as a blessing.

I can see things others cannot see. I notice the smallest details. I'm always looking ahead so that I can identify and overcome any obstacles in my way. These skills are a huge part of my professional success.

I wasn't diagnosed with severe dyslexia until my 40s, which meant I hid my learning disability for decades. I had a lot of time to cultivate these skills, in other words. Because I was terrified of being exposed, I was always pre-planning. In every situation, I carefully considered the smallest of details, with an eye for an exit. It wasn't until I turned 50 that I really, truly began to embrace how I'm different.

Because of this particular problem, I learned to never give up. Like I said, my learning disability taught me very early on that I would have to work twice as hard as everyone else. Today, my work ethic is my greatest strength. Most people give up way too early and are afraid to make mistakes. Not me. I've been failing my entire life! For me, failure is a friend. I'm willing to put myself in situations where I don't know what I'm doing because I have enough confidence in myself that I'll figure it out.

Fundamentally, having dyslexia taught me how to look at situations differently so I could overcome obstacles. There's always another way of doing something. You just have to identify that alternative path. My skillset as an entrepreneur is a direct reflection of the roadblocks I've had to get around. These days, I don't even think of problems as roadblocks—really, they're just opportunities to shine. I'm able to accept what I don't know and move forward quickly.

I apply my powers of observation all the time by studying the landscape of any business opportunity extremely closely. I look at all the angles, including strengths and weaknesses. I'm very curious. I know that by asking the right questions, I can find the answers.

Ultimately, dyslexia and entrepreneurship are inextricably linked for me. Because I had such difficulty spelling, I assumed no one would ever hire me and that I would need to create my own job—so I did. I began working with my hands, discovered that I loved it and made developing new products and bringing them to market my career for decades. Now I teach others how to do the same, including sharing my ten-step process for licencing ideas with university students around the world.

My dyslexia used to be such an embarrassment to me. But in truth, it's been the biggest gift I could have ever received. For someone who is creative, being able to examine fine details and brainstorm alternatives could not be more helpful. Everywhere I look, I end up finding different opportunities.

I think we need to do a better job of celebrating people who are different. We need to give students who have some type of learning disability other opportunities to shine, not merely label and relegate them to certain classes. When they're older, their problem-solving skills are going to come in extremely handy. They need role models and important problems to solve so we can all celebrate their successes.

This book offers the reader a huge opportunity to better understand both dyslexia and entrepreneurship, and how education has a vital part to play in the development of entrepreneurs of the future.

The book begins by looking at Sharon Hewitt, an entrepreneur like myself. She struggled at school but found her unique ability was that she could offer the business world new insights, as Richard Branson and others have done, by bringing new products to market.

Lockett (in Chapter 6) also understands that dyslexia brings abilities and not disabilities, and that there is scope for innovation in society if one is open to embracing difference. I very much agree with the idea that dyslexia may be a 'superpower!'

Looking at Singapore, Hewes and Shantha Ram's chapter help us understand how a forward-looking society can embrace dyslexia at all levels of society; raising awareness certainly is a noble cause. Interestingly, the chapter by Sefotho documents the reality that entrepreneurship may offer the only choice for many with dyslexia, due to their difficulties working in mainstream work environments. I personally relate to this.

Sepulveda and Nicolson's chapter suggests the use of positive psychology in understanding successful individuals with dyslexia. The investigation by Smith, Conley and Manning into the high levels of individuals with dyslexia in UK farming demonstrates why many with dyslexia may be drawn to farming professions—a practical and vocational career. The numbers turning to such career choices makes this an interesting topic to read about.

The chapter by Fawcett offers a novel understanding as to why entrepreneurs like myself can be creative in their approach and offer 'blue sky' divergent thinking or solutions to problems that most linear thinkers would not see. The trauma and traits for success as noted in Alexander-Passe's chapter suggest my own struggles are commonplace among those with dyslexia, in that they allow for the ability to take risks in life, as failure is a means to an end and not just an end.

Gyarmathy's chapter looking at multi-sided dyslexia offers readers a breather to conceptualise if dyslexia is part of the next evolution of mankind, where a perceived weakness in one sphere can be an advantage in another. Maybe we really are moving towards valuing creative problem-solving at all levels of society? I hope.

Looking to the chapters on education, I can see my own path of supporting learners to be entrepreneurial in their thinking, especially those who may struggle in traditional university learning settings. My own course at the University of Newcastle is one such means to enhance the understanding of entrepreneurship. Pavey's chapter, which features a study that asked entrepreneurs with dyslexia what they would have liked when studying at university, reflects a desire for a greater awareness of needs and greater accommodations.

The innovative approach to education in Wales, in that all courses must include a module in entrepreneurial career choices, opens up the ability for those with learning difficulties and different genders to be empowered. The term 'Dyspreneur' offers a new way to describe entrepreneurs with the ability to think differently. This is reflected in the later chapter that questions how business courses are offered at university for those with dyslexia or other learning differences, and if computer software simulations are a means to offer the visual-kinaesthetic experience that many with learning difficulties strive for so that they can experience success in their studies.

Alexander-Passe's chapter on post-traumatic growth resonates with my own thinking that only through the trauma of school have I been able to be successful in life; that my gut intuition and openness to failure and risk have come from working through failure to get to success. A very hard journey, but a road less travelled, as Robert Frost's poem notes, is more productive, richer and makes all the difference. The question is must those with dyslexia suffer in school to be successful? I hope this book helps change the mindsets of educators, aiding them in recognising dyslexia earlier and valuing the unique skills and abilities of such individuals.

Stephen Key

Chapter Summaries

Introduction

Entrepreneurs With Dyslexia: Challenge and Achievement in the Business World by Barbara Pavey

Research has indicated that a higher than expected proportion of entrepreneurs experience dyslexia, when compared with corporate managers. This chapter provides an overview of concepts underpinning entrepreneurship, dyslexia and entrepreneurship education, in relation to entrepreneurs who experience dyslexia. Current understandings of entrepreneurship and dyslexia are described, and the relevance of the concept of 'bricolage' is discussed. The chapter considers the intersection of entrepreneurship and dyslexia as described by the book's authors, and points the way to deeper considerations of the 'space' where entrepreneurship, dyslexia and education meet.

Entrepreneurship

Chapter 1: An Award-Winning Entrepreneur: Sharon Hewitt by Neil Alexander-Passe

This chapter investigates a successful female entrepreneur who experiences dyslexia. Tracking her life's journey from school to employment helps to understand the personal experience of dyslexia and how an individual can overcome a learning difficulty to become an award-winning entrepreneur. This chapter investigates how UK mainstream schools in the 1970's and 1980's struggled to understand students who were intelligent verbally but who, when it came to transferring such ideas to paper, were seen as lazy and stupid, with a knock-on effect to the young individual's self-esteem. This narrative tells of how post-school an individual with traits associated with dyslexia can use their strengths and abilities to overcome perceived literacy barriers, and that through creating a support structure an individual with dyslexia can reach career heights that their school careers advisors could only dream of.

Chapter 2: Documenting the Role of UK Agricultural Colleges in Propagating the Farming-Dyslexia-Entrepreneurship Nexus by Robert Smith, Gillian Conley and Louise Manning

It is now acknowledged that the incidence of dyslexia in farming and land-based industries is significantly higher than in the average population, albeit there are no definitive statistics available. This chapter expands upon and updates previous work by the authors on the topic and extends our knowledge base into the equine industry. There is a paucity of serious academic studies into the phenomenon, and much of what we know is based upon self-reporting by farmers and students and the anecdotal experience of staff at Agricultural Colleges and Universities in dealing with students with dyslexia. Additionally, this chapter provides conceptual and theoretical purchase by synthesising the established literature on farmers as entrepreneurs and the entrepreneurship-dyslexia nexus. Using anecdotal evidence, case studies and data from preliminary qualitative interviews with respondents, a clearer picture of the incidence and scope of the phenomenon emerges. The discussion raises awareness of dyslexia in rural industries at a time when there is increasing demand for support services to enable those in industry to complete everyday tasks which can involve literacy and numeracy skills.

Chapter 3: Dyslexia, Entrepreneurship and Education in Singapore by Deborah Hewes and Geetha Shantha Ram

In the past decade, there has been a clear shift in what dyslexia means in Singapore's educational, political and socio-cultural conversations. Officially, the nation is clear that dyslexia is not seen as a stigma, and government level efforts have increased the awareness of dyslexia among its people. Yet, while on the surface it is apparent that dyslexia should not be stigmatised, beneath the surface there is a fragmented understanding of dyslexia; many do not know how to understand, and deal with, dyslexia holistically. The 'Embrace Dyslexia' campaign launched by the Dyslexia Association of Singapore (DAS) aims to promote the positive aspects of dyslexia. Entrepreneurs with dyslexia contributed their personal stories, showing that success was achievable in spite of dyslexia; some of these stories are shared in this chapter. While much is known about supporting children, Singapore continues to develop awareness about adults with learning differences such as dyslexia. It is evident from entrepreneurs' stories that adults with learning differences can and do make a significant contribution to the Singaporean community and economy.

Chapter 4: Entrepreneurship, Dyslexia, and the Modern World: A Positive Psychology Approach by Poliana Sepulveda and Roderick Nicolson

It can be argued that the key focus of the entrepreneurial world in the twenty-first century will be attention to specific traits, specifically those which could help a person to become an entrepreneur. Interestingly there appears to be a link between entrepreneurship and dyslexia, but this has not been widely explored using empirical techniques. In earlier research by Sepulveda, a qualitative study was carried out to identify the themes that clustered around entrepreneurial traits, traits associated with dyslexia and those which were more generic traits for entrepreneurs. 11 themes were identified, which were communication skills, resilience, delegation/team-work/shared tasks, vision, proactivity, risks with precaution, empathy, freedom, entrepreneur family, asking for help/modesty and control. These traits can be compared with those found in the work of Logan (2009). Further exploration of the traits of entrepreneurs who experience dyslexia, as described in this chapter, lead to a wider understanding of those characteristics and an appreciation of how the experience of dyslexia can lead to traits, strategies, skills and entrepreneurial action.

Chapter 5: Dyslexia, Entrepreneurship and Transition to Decent Work by Maximus Monaheng Sefotho

This chapter explores entrepreneurship, dyslexia and the transition to decent work. Generally persons with disabilities, in particular those with dyslexia, find it difficult to enter the world of work. Youth with dyslexia face the dilemma to transit to decent work due to lack of understanding of how people who experience dyslexia perceive and interpret the world.

In order to understand dyslexia from indigenous knowledge perspectives, this chapter benchmarks the interpretation of dyslexia from the Basotho ontology of disability. The chapter anchors dyslexia, entrepreneurship and transition to decent work on Basotho paremiography as a premise for meaning. This creates space for voices from the South, which are less represented in discourses on dyslexia on the global stage. The Basotho ontology of disability mirrors positive perspectives which allow for the empowerment of youth with dyslexia to enter and participate in entrepreneurship and decent work.

Chapter 6: Towards a Dyslexia Superpower: Reflections on the Year in the Life of a Dyslexic Professor of Entrepreneurship by Nigel Lockett

This chapter consists of extracts from 52 weekly blogs entitled *The Dyslexic Professor*, posted by Nigel Lockett, Professor of Entrepreneurship, between December 2016 and December 2017 at www.nigellockett.com. These blogs explored the personal challenges and organisational advantages of dyslexia. They advocated the seismic shift from portraying dyslexia as a disability through learning difference to advantage or superpower. To retain the sense of unfolding self-awareness, the sequence of the blogs is retained. In essence, this is a story of disclosure, which resulted in the author's liberation and determination— liberation from the disability label and determination to do something to extol the positive advantages of dyslexia, and ultimately neurological diversity, for organisations.

Dyslexia

Chapter 7: Dyslexia and Entrepreneurship: A Theoretical Perspective by Angela Fawcett

This chapter outlines recent developments in Nicolson and Fawcett's theories of dyslexia, focusing on delayed neural commitment. This theoretical perspective provides a natural explanation based on delays in acquiring automaticity in dyslexia. This can provide a rationale for the creativity and 'blue skies' thinking that characterise entrepreneurs. The chapter is illustrated with case studies of adults and children that the author has worked with over the years, who have themselves demonstrated aspects of this entrepreneurial flair. The chapter indicates some of the major opportunities identified by the positive dyslexia movement in ensuring success for those with dyslexia in any field.

Chapter 8: Dyslexia, Trauma and Traits for Success by Neil Alexander-Passe

This paper investigates school-based trauma and the life-long post-school effects of such trauma, creating successful/unsuccessful individuals in society. Three studies were investigated:

1. A study of 20 successful individuals with dyslexia, many in business and the charity sectors
2. A study of 29 adults with dyslexia, many indicating depressive symptoms
3. A study of 88 adults using a screening measure to indicate severity, looking at gender and degree-education, with profiles created to aid understanding

School-trauma was found in all. Successful individuals enjoyed higher parental-child support, sports and non-academic subject success. As adults, they were more willing to take risks, saw failure in a positive light and frequently were self-employed, allowing a focus on strengths rather than weaknesses. Unsuccessful adults were prone to doubt their own abilities, self-blaming, pessimistic and getting upset when things go wrong.

School is a crucial environment that provides a melting pot in the life of a young learner with dyslexia. It is an environment in which they learn how society works and whether they can succeed or fail, setting them on a path for life. Both successful and unsuccessful people who experience dyslexia agree that their educational experiences were mostly terrible and in most cases traumatic, but each group has taken different lessons from their time at school.

Chapter 9: Multi-Sided Dyslexia: The Age of the Entrepreneurs With New Reading Abilities by Eva Gyarmathy

Due to the plasticity of the human brain, the environmental changes at the turn of the twenty-first century have caused changes in human abilities. Similar changes happened 4,000–10,000 years ago with the turn towards a farmer lifestyle and subsequently with the advent of hieroglyphs; this was followed by the appearance of phonological letter-to-sound-based writing. Another profound literacy-related change is happening today, noticed so far only by few, but causing multiple diagnoses of dyslexia and other neurologically based achievement difficulties. However, a weakness in one given culture can be an advantage in another. Highly achieving entrepreneurs who experience dyslexia are a sign that the environment has become advantageous for this kind of atypically developing brain. Reading and writing modes of successful people with dyslexia may reveal the ability changes characterising the beginning of the twenty-first century and, accordingly, provide hints for the development of education.

Education

Chapter 10: Entrepreneurship Education and Dyslexia: Pedagogies and a Pilot Study by Barbara Pavey

This chapter describes the growing importance of entrepreneurship education in the context of economic constraint. It considers the corresponding growth of policy focus upon entrepreneurship education. An examination of the field reveals its difficulties including agreed purpose, professional doubt and pedagogical uncertainty. The chapter discusses reviews of entrepreneurship education provision, as they progress towards the detailed recommendations of the Entrepreneurship Competence Framework (EntreComp), identifying links with life skills that are evident in broader conceptualisations of entrepreneurship. A pilot study, asking entrepreneurs who experience dyslexia for their views about school and Higher Education (HE) provision for young learners with entrepreneurial interest or potential and also with dyslexia, reveals concerns that courses should offer more intensified pedagogical opportunities. Courses also need to display and respond to a greater awareness of the specific learning needs of people who experience dyslexia, and should manifest a greater willingness to accommodate them.

Chapter 11: Developing Entrepreneurs With Dyslexia Through Higher Education (HE) in Wales by Matthew Armstrong and Margaret Meehan

As the Welsh education system is devolved, legislation regarding disability is not the same as in other areas of the UK, notably England. However, Wales has recognised the importance of entrepreneurship and the necessity of encouraging entrepreneurs at all stages of education and beyond for its economic growth. The Global Entrepreneurship Monitor identifies resilience and self-determination as characteristics of successful entrepreneurs. However, rather than considering 'what' an entrepreneur is, the question 'who' is an entrepreneur is asked. Currently, more female students are present in Welsh HE Institutions (HEIs), heralding a possible change in the gender balance of entrepreneurs. The characteristics of successful entrepreneurs as well as successful individuals who experience dyslexia have been explored, and the overlap between the two is coined in the term 'Dyspreneur.' The numbers of students who experience dyslexia and pursue nursing is investigated and the parallels between the characteristics needed by nurses and entrepreneurs are explored. Controlling the internal Welsh market is the arena in which Wales has influence and one way to promote entrepreneurship is to support young Dyspreneurs.

Chapter 12: Post-Traumatic Growth (PTG): A New Way of Understanding the Experience of Successful People with Dyslexia by Neil Alexander-Passe

This chapter looks at the origins of success in adults who experience dyslexia, using both an online survey to locate successful adults with dyslexia and a sub-group of 20 interview participants to understand the nature and motivation of success in adults with dyslexia. School trauma was a focus of the study using the theory of 'Post-Trauamtic Growth' as a means to understand how individuals can have a traumatic and humiliating schooling but gain success post-school through the positive use of trauma. The 30-item online survey reflected the 8-main item investigative interview script, so that both quantitative and qualitative data could be studied. The items looked at were: personality descriptions by others, supportive parents, trauma at school, avoidance at school, excellence in non-academic subjects, leadership qualities, team-building, delegation, gut intuition, use of mentors, motivation, Unique Selling Points (USPs), risk, failure, pursuit of passions, creativity and entrepreneurship. A consistency of response was found between the two groups researched, with comments from the interview study enriching the responses from the online survey to present a coherent picture of success. The interview study indicated that school trauma could become a positive force in creating successful and resilient individuals with dyslexia.

Chapter 13: Dyslexia and Entrepreneurship Education: What Do Students Who Study in Higher Education (HE) Say? by Margaret Meehan, Paul Adkins, Barbara Pavey and Angela Fawcett

This chapter presents some of the preliminary results of a small-scale pilot study involving 17 students, from two universities, who experience dyslexia and study business as their main degree or as modules accompanying their main discipline. Responses were analysed from semi-structured interviews regarding the development of entrepreneurship skills and the ways in which educational opportunities may be improved for them. The focus here was on two questions related to how universities help entrepreneurs who experience dyslexia, and whether business simulation games proved useful. Many shared themes emerged, and some interesting unique themes were expressed. The main shared theme was that universities need to provide a more practical/applied course. Some students thought business games could be helpful if they mimicked real business scenarios.

Conclusion

The Experience of Entrepreneurs With Dyslexia— by Barbara Pavey, Neil Alexander-Passe and Margaret Meehan

The concluding chapter brings together the findings and perceptions generated by the exploration of the book's topic. It begins by focusing on how the concept of disability may be more nuanced and variable where dyslexia is concerned and continues by discussing the difficulties of the workplace when people experience dyslexia, asking whether self-employment and/or entrepreneurship present better options for some. The position of HE in supporting potential entrepreneurs with dyslexia is discussed. The chapter considers whether individuals with dyslexia are uniquely skilled to be entrepreneurs, answering this question with a qualified 'yes,' based on the view that selected behaviours become successful strategies, leading in turn to traits that support entrepreneurial endeavours and possible entrepreneurial success. The chapter looks at the potential for further research and includes a brief discussion of how an inclusive pedagogy can address the recognised concurrence between entrepreneurship and dyslexia.

Reference

Logan, J. (2009). Dyslexic entrepreneurs: The incidence; their coping strategies and their business skills. *Dyslexia*, *15*, 328–334. https://doi.org/10.1002/dys.388

Introduction: Entrepreneurs With Dyslexia
Challenge and Achievement in the Business World

Barbara Pavey

The real-life experience of entrepreneurs with dyslexia has become more widely recognised following the research of Julie Logan (2009). This indicated that, in both the UK and USA, a greater than expected proportion of entrepreneurs showed traits consistent with dyslexia, when compared with corporate managers. The introduction of dyslexia into the entrepreneurship narrative has attracted interest, as more people acknowledge their own dyslexia and describe the ways in which they have transcended their learning differences. Increasingly, successful entrepreneurs with dyslexia who are in the business, entertainment, creative and sporting worlds have come forward with their personal testimonials. People across different fields now seem to be more willing to acknowledge their learning differences and difficulties, whereas previously these might have remained private matters.

The chapters of this book build upon the interest and stimulation generated by existing research, to explore the topic and to extend discussion about how young people with dyslexia and entrepreneurial flair might be encouraged and supported in education. They include psychological, sociological, experiential and narrative perspectives, and embrace a range of international contexts, including those of Singapore,

Wales and Southern Africa. Together the chapters describe some of the theoretical and personal aspects clustered at the intersection of entrepreneurship, dyslexia and education, never forgetting that beyond any abstract considerations there are individual lives, struggles and stories.

Foundational Concepts of Entrepreneurship

The interest in entrepreneurship has existed for centuries, and the growth of commerce and the generation of new business are of enduring interest. As ideas about entrepreneurship became formalised during the twentieth century, an entrepreneur generally was viewed as someone who usually operated on their own, challenging but also conforming to the norms of business (De Clercq & Honig, 2011). Over time entrepreneurship developed as an area of research interest inside the subject of business studies, itself a branch of economics, with considerable efforts being made to define and refine its epistemology. The 1980s saw an increasing focus upon entrepreneurship, being described as '[t]he onset of the entrepreneurial age' by Becker, Knudsen and Swedberg (2012, p. 920). Attempts were made to identify the conditions and characteristics that led to successful entrepreneurship and the generation of successful new ventures. Accordingly, the development of entrepreneurship in individuals has been a subject of considerable research.

The efforts to capture and facilitate conditions for the development of entrepreneurship have gained increasing importance in times of economic recession, because of their potential for the development of new business opportunities. These efforts have included a drive towards entrepreneurship education. Entrepreneurship and enterprise have become topics of global interest in primary, secondary and Higher Education (HE), in government initiatives and in policies.

Entrepreneurship itself remains an imprecise concept, with some deep epistemological and ontological issues. It is open to challenge regarding its traditional discourse of opportunity, competition, growth, power and success measured by material means. Consequently, there has been a considerable amount of literature discussing the nature of entrepreneurs and entrepreneurship. Associated with this there has been literature about how, and indeed if, entrepreneurship can be taught (see for example Marram, Lange, Brown, Marquis, & Bygrave, 2014). Entrepreneurship concepts and definitions continue to be analysed and criticised, giving rise to publications which seek to challenge pedagogies and to offer alternative curricular structures for entrepreneurship education.

Entrepreneurship offers the prospect of hope and success, through its potential for the generation of wealth through individual effort. It supports the concept of a creative flowering of skills and abilities, leading to individual and social goods. The concepts of human and social capital are seen as important for entrepreneurial activity, to the point where social capital is suggested as a foundational theory for entrepreneurship (Gedajlovic, Honig, Moore, Payne, & Wright, 2013), reflecting the social contexts in which entrepreneurial activity takes place. However, an understanding of entrepreneurship is subject to the definition being used. In parallel with discussions of dyslexia, entrepreneurship can be found described in terms of both narrow and broad definitions.

Defining Entrepreneurship

The descriptions and understandings of entrepreneurship have been contested areas. Definitions have varied from broad views that include individual activity in the arts and in sports to definitions suggesting that only a person who develops a successful business should be called entrepreneurial.

Later twentieth and early twenty-first century understandings of entrepreneurship have tended to separate it from self-employment and from enterprise (Bolton & Thompson, 2004), with entrepreneurs being considered separately from owner-managers and from self-employed individuals working in traditional trades. Furthermore, there has been a difference between more stringent views originating from US and a wider, European view which linked entrepreneurship competencies with qualities similar to those for life skills or transferable skills. The USA took a robust position in the white paper, 'Embracing Innovation: Entrepreneurship and American Economic Growth' (Ewing Marion Kauffman Foundation, 2000). This defined entrepreneurship as providing: '[m]ore jobs, better quality of life, success in global markets and reinvestment of new wealth' (NCOE, 2000, p. 8).

Similarly, the Global Entrepreneurship and Development Index 2018 (GEDI) challenged a conceptualisation of small business owners as entrepreneurs (Acs, Szerb, & Lloyd, 2017). Acs et al. consider that people working for themselves are not necessarily entrepreneurs unless they plan 'scalable, high-growth businesses' (p. 18). However, while their definition is restricted, these authors feel that it can also be considered as broad because it applies to entrepreneurial efforts anywhere in the world and within any social group. Gompers, Kovner, Lerner, and Scharfstein (2008), too, refer to entrepreneurial success in terms of businesses that go public, that is businesses that provide the public with the opportunity to invest in the company. The authors suggest that being considered a successful entrepreneur is something of a self-fulfilling prophecy, since being successful would be the factor that resulted in this label being applied to an individual.

In contrast, European entrepreneurship initiatives have been concerned with increasing quality of life and the social good. The route to economic well-being for individuals has been seen as residing in the increase of their human capital and social capital (Healy & Côté, 2001), with a policy focus upon social inclusion, the fight against poverty and the creation of opportunities to overcome youth unemployment. In 2016, the European Commission published the Entrepreneurship Competence Framework, known as the EntreComp (Bacigalupo, Kampyis, Punie, & van den Brande, 2016). This document identified entrepreneurship as being relevant across the entire spectrum of daily life, rather than focusing upon generating new businesses.

It saw entrepreneurship as covering wider social territory:

> [f]rom nurturing personal development, to actively participating in society, to (re)entering the job market as an employee or as a self-employed person, and also to starting up ventures (cultural, social or commercial). It builds upon a broad definition of entrepreneurship that hinges on the creation of cultural, social or economic value.
>
> (Bacigalupo et al., 2016, p. 6)

Within this broad definition, the EntreComp did not restrict 'value' to financial effects and it embraced individual efforts to build sole-trader businesses.

In 2018, the UK's Quality Assurance Agency (QAA) followed this definition by issuing enterprise and entrepreneurship education guidance for UK Education (HE) providers. The document reviewed and built upon an earlier, similar publication, the authors noting that between the dates of the two publications, interest and practice in entrepreneurship, and also entrepreneurship education, had increased significantly. The QAA guidance saw 'enterprise' as related to 'employability' and suggested behaviours, attributes and competencies which would lead to both employment and entrepreneurship:

> **Behaviours** include: 'Taking initiative, taking responsibility, reflecting, risk management, networking'
>
> **Attributes** include: Curiosity, open mindedness, proactiveness, determination and resilience, together with 'self-efficacy'
>
> **Competencies** include: The ability to identify and solve problems creatively, the ability to be a negotiator, influencer, and leader, and the capacity to be 'business and finance aware.'
>
> (QAA, 2018, passim)

Together these suggest that entrepreneurship educators should embrace a learning culture that comprises both autonomy and teamwork, fostering a 'can-do' attitude. These characteristics are to be combined with flexibility, resilience and a range of skills, including practical skills, which are all directed towards problem-solving in the real world.

Entrepreneurship Policy

Interest in entrepreneurship as a means of creating new business had already generated international attention, in both academic and non-academic arenas. However, the economic crisis following 2008 triggered a renewed interest in entrepreneurship and the conditions in which it might be encouraged to develop. Entrepreneurship became a matter of national and global policy interest.

The *Entrepreneurship 2020 Action Plan: Reigniting the Entrepreneurial Spirit in Europe* included entrepreneurship among eight key competencies for lifelong learning. It discussed the importance of cultivating an entrepreneurial outlook that includes, 'creativity, initiative, tenacity, teamwork, understanding of risk and a sense of responsibility' (European Commission, 2013, p. 6), in addition to knowing about the world of business. As with other sources, the document called for practical experience for learners and opportunities to interact with established entrepreneurs.

One country that rose early to this challenge was Wales. The Welsh government created and implemented the *Youth Entrepreneurship* strategy (Welsh Assembly Government, 2002), promoting it with resources and materials. Even with this degree of support, evaluation of the strategy called for greater focus on education in enterprise and entrepreneurship (National Assembly for Wales Business and Enterprise Committee, 2013, p. 25).

In a subdued economy, the Welsh entrepreneurship policy sought to create an educational and business climate that fostered attitudinal and practical changes towards self-employment and entrepreneurship. The 2013 review of the strategy and action plan found that it was difficult to be certain if, or how far, the changes might be effective due to the length of time between entrepreneurship input and the actual starting of new businesses, and also due to the difficulties of identifying a clear relationship between input and start-up. Nevertheless, the Welsh commitment to enterprise and entrepreneurship continues in all phases of education, acknowledged in the Welsh government economic action plan, *Prosperity for All: The National Strategy* (Welsh Government, 2017).

The economic circumstances of the present time, combined with the potential for adding to quality of life, continue to support the development of entrepreneurship and entrepreneurship learning. To be effective, entrepreneurship education must be accessible. A rights-based approach, embodied in legislation, supports the view that people with learning difficulties and/or disabilities should not be denied access to education on account of their diverse needs.

With these factors in mind, a consideration of how learners with dyslexia and with entrepreneurial interests can be aided to develop and take advantage of their potential is timely. This goes beyond literacy learning; it means employing a pedagogy that is sympathetic to neuro-diverse learners, such as the 'Dyslexia-Friendly' approach originating with the work of Neil Mackay (2012) and Universal Design for Learning and for Instruction (see for example Black, Weinberg, & Brodwin, 2015; Scott, McGuire, & Shaw, 2003). Both of these approaches are summarised in Appendix One (Pavey, 2015).

Foundational Concepts in Dyslexia

In a similar development to entrepreneurship, dyslexia awareness experienced a growth in the 1970s and 1980s as researchers sought a comprehensive causal theory and debated over terminology. There have been bitter arguments as to whether dyslexia does, or does not, exist. Even where dyslexia is accepted as a cognitive characteristic in its own right, there are differences in the discourse. Some consider that dyslexia should not be seen as a deficit but as something exceptional that provides different, advantageous ways of thinking and information-processing. Additionally, there are people with dyslexia who refuse to be discounted on the grounds of their learning difference, and who insist that society needs to adapt and to take advantage of what they can offer. They point out that different ways of dealing with, and exchanging, information can be an advantage, and that the characteristics of dyslexia in a person need not necessarily be an impediment.

Defining dyslexia is, therefore, difficult. In the UK, the definition of dyslexia settled on, identified in the Rose report, was 'Dyslexia is a learning difficulty that primarily affects the skills involved in accurate and fluent word reading and spelling' (Rose, 2009, p. 30). In explaining the definition, the Rose report focussèd on six elements: Cognitive characteristics, prevalence 'across the range of intellectual abilities,' the existence and impact of co-occurring learning characteristics and difficulties, the reduced response to skilled teaching intervention and dyslexia's identity as 'a continuum, not a distinct category' (Rose, 2009, passim). This definition was augmented by the British Dyslexia Association, highlighting the significance of visual and auditory processing difficulties and pointing out the complications that combined learning characteristics can make for learners who experience dyslexia.

More recently, the *Diagnostic and Statistical Manual of Mental Disorders* (DSM-5) (American Psychiatric Association, 2013) and the *International Classification of Diseases for Mortality and Morbidity Statistics* (ICD-11) (World Health Organisation, 2018), which are the diagnostic manuals guiding psychologists and paediatricians, have had new editions. In the DSM-5, difficulty with reading is one of a number of conditions described as learning disorders; the term learning disabilities is also noted, although the two terms are not synonymous.

Spelling and written expression are listed as separate from reading, and the word 'dyslexia' is not used. In the ICD-11, intractable literacy difficulties are described as developmental learning disorders, with reading impairment described as one of these. Developmental dyslexia is shown as a term of inclusion, which means that it is either a synonym or it is not to be listed as a specific condition in its own right. It is evident that, as with entrepreneurship, agreed meaning for the term 'dyslexia' is hard to find.

Dyslexia: The Present Position

Dyslexia affects the interaction of verbal and visual cues in the recognition and expression of written language. Like entrepreneurship, dyslexia at present has advocates for both broad and narrow definitions. Wider conceptions of dyslexia include mathematical, musical, sequencing and memory difficulties and movement effects in conjunction with literacy difficulty. Research therefore continues to explore the question of whether dyslexia has a distinct identity and whether such other features are separate, intrinsic or overlapping (Wilson et al., 2015). In addition, for some researchers there is a cautious view that the term 'dyslexia' might be understood to describe the extreme end of the general range of reading acquisition, where literacy becomes most difficult and, for some people, disabling (Snowling & Melby-Lervåg, 2016), although this is not agreed upon by all.

The prevalence of dyslexia, as it is currently understood, is usually put at around 10% of the general population (Cramer, 2014), with about 4% experiencing dyslexia more severely (Kelly & Phillips, 2011), while some sources place the incidence of dyslexia at a higher figure. As Kelly and Phillips (2011) confirm, even the more conservative estimate suggests that in any non-selected class of 25-30 pupils, around three are likely to experience dyslexia, and, statistically, one of these pupils is likely to experience it significantly.

In spite of debate, there is some consistency in accounts of what we recognise as dyslexia, whether it is known by this term or by other terms such as reading disability, learning disability or specific learning difficulty. Pragmatically, dyslexia is the name given to an intractable difficulty in gaining literacy skills when there is no other reason to account for it, such as illness or poor educational experience. In spite of earlier reliance upon discrepancy definitions, dyslexia is not considered to be directly related to intelligence (Hatcher, 2000). So dyslexia is now generally understood to be a cognitive characteristic that causes literacy difficulty to those who experience it, exacerbated through a cultural and societal dependency upon literacy. It is located in cerebral connections and interactions, and research continues as to the actual nature and origin of these.

Dyslexia is described as a disorder in diagnostic manuals because of its unusual nature, which means that it does not reflect the type of cognitive processing in literacy that is experienced by the majority of the population. However, it is not a disease or, in itself, a mental illness or a psychiatric problem. Dyslexia can be mitigated, rather than 'cured,' by a dint of specific and effortful work, applied together with compensatory strategies, including technological strategies.

Dyslexia can be inherited, although there is no single dyslexia gene; some dyslexia-susceptible genes have been identified, but research continues (see for example Ramus, Altarelli, Jednorog, Zhao, & di Covella, 2018). If a child has a parent who experiences dyslexia, there is around a 50% chance of them inheriting dyslexia. However, dyslexia may also appear without an obvious specific, literacy-based learning difficulty showing in other family members. Whatever causal attributions are made, and whatever individual aspects of dyslexia may be manifested, there are shared characteristics of dyslexia and these are increasingly well-known and respected. They include an intractable difficulty in the acquisition and utilization of literacy skills, and a slower than usual speed of processing in literacy-related tasks.

Entrepreneurship and Dyslexia

Given the interest in both entrepreneurship and dyslexia, and growing disability awareness, it is understandable that there is an interest in entrepreneurs who experience dyslexia. Julie Logan's research provides the focal literature for this topic, continuing to be referenced widely. Other studies concerning dyslexia and entrepreneurship include Smith (2008), who drew on internet sources, taking his lead from Logan's 2001 PhD study, and Franks and Frederick (2013). While Smith focussed upon personal stories, Franks and Frederick explored the traits identified by Logan for entrepreneurs with dyslexia, as did Sepulveda (2014) and this volume.

Logan's (2009) article reported a study of entrepreneurs with dyslexia in the USA, which followed the methodology of her earlier study of entrepreneurs with dyslexia in the UK, enabling a comparison to be made. In her 2009 study, Logan found that:

> There is a much higher incidence of dyslexia in entrepreneurs than in the normal corporate management population in the US and the UK. The incidence of dyslexia in entrepreneurs is also much higher than the incidence in the population in general.
>
> (Logan, 2009, p. 344)

Logan suggested that a number of characteristics experienced by entrepreneurs with dyslexia were supportive of entrepreneurial activity. She considered that characteristics such as delegation, verbal communication, risk-taking and individual ways of approaching tasks could be coping strategies developed in the face of dyslexia. These were useful for starting and growing new businesses, with entrepreneurs who experience dyslexia growing businesses more quickly, owning more businesses and employing more people. Other authors have expressed similar views regarding the possible contribution of difficult learning experiences to the development of entrepreneurship in some people who experience dyslexia (Miller & Le Breton-Miller, 2017; Wiklund, Hatak, Patzelt, & Shepherd, 2018), a theme explored by Alexander-Passe in this volume.

Logan and Martin (2012) explored Logan's initial findings in more detail, interviewing a small group of successful entrepreneurs who also experienced dyslexia. The study explored the high incidence of dyslexia within the population of highly-effective entrepreneurs, seeking to explain the characteristics that supported their success. Logan suggested earlier that a number of characteristics experienced by entrepreneurs with dyslexia were supportive of entrepreneurial activity. Logan and Martin took this further, concluding that in support of earlier findings, 'We have found that entrepreneurs with dyslexia tend to acquire these skills early. Amalgamation of communication, leadership and delegation skills with the fourth attribute of thinking differently may well be what gives these entrepreneurs the edge in business' (Logan & Martin, 2012, p. 71).

It should be noted that a study by Hessels, Rietveld and van der Zwan (2014) challenges the possibility that there is a greater prevalence of dyslexia among entrepreneurs than is found generally in the population, as has been claimed by Logan (2013, citing her 2001 and 2009 studies). The authors considered that their findings showed no significant association between entrepreneurship and dyslexia in the two large samples of Dutch population that were studied (Hessels et al., 2014, p. 438). Their research did, however, find a weaker association. This book does not seek to adjudicate in this matter, but to focus upon the factors that may lead a person with dyslexia to become an entrepreneur and the issues and considerations that may arise when they do so. In the process, it is hoped that ways may be found of aiding young people with dyslexia, if they have an entrepreneurial interest. Accordingly, Logan's research provides a springboard for many of the authors in this volume.

A Matter of Bricolage

The concept of bricolage has been employed in both entrepreneurship discourse and educational research (Phillimore, Humphries, Klaas, & Necht, 2016). This originated with Claude Lévi-Strauss, in his efforts to understand patterns of thought among humans. He identified bricolage as one such pattern: 'The French word *bricoleur* describes a handyman or handywoman who makes use of the tools available to complete a task' (Kincheloe, 2001, p. 680). This would suggest the use of a somewhat random variety of tools and materials, embracing not only physical means and methods but also conceptual and experiential ones.

Lévi-Strauss' 1962 delineation of categories of thought (art, craft, engineering and bricolage) was challenged by Derrida. He considered bricolage to be incoherence, a kind of randomness that could not justify itself in classical/logical discourse, being action without a strong, clear scientific and philosophical foundation. However, Phillimore et al. point out that Derrida's criticism of Lévi-Strauss also extended the originator's concept. Derrida saw bricolage—borrowing earlier ideas and expressing them in new iterations—applying to every subject (Phillimore et al., 2016, p. 6.21, citing Derrida, 1967); if it was true for one discourse, it was true for all.

The 'ad hoc' nature of bricolage is no longer seen as necessarily lacking in conceptual rigour and, as such, ineffectual. Instead it may be viewed as a source of vigour and serendipity. A post-modern outlook sees bricolage as a way of coping with complex and uncertain situations, requiring a creative and innovative approach. Indeed, this repositioning, or recycling as we might now understand it, seems to bear a kinship to the approach of a number of entrepreneurs who experience dyslexia, as expressed in the 'different thinking' identified by Logan and Martin (2012).

In educational research, Kincheloe (2001) discusses bricolage as not only calling upon mixed methods but also upon diverse theoretical and philosophical positions. He sees it as a response to the disruption of traditional ideas and understandings resulting from post-modern attitudes towards traditional research concepts. Phillimore et al. (2016, pp. 10/20) note the view that researching in this way demands considerable rigour in order to understand the realities and complexities of real life. Confining the messy, lived experience of reality in order to fit a framework of traditional research epistemology is not, in this view, effective or justifiable.

In the world of business, Stinchfield, Nelson, and Wood (2013) consider entrepreneurship to be moving away from traditional definitions that focus upon resource and wealth generation. They suggest that, in times of economic constraint, the longevity of a business should be considered as success. Stinchfield et al.'s (2013) study of 23 entrepreneurs sought to re-examine Lévi-Strauss' categories, reviewing the concept of bricolage from a twenty-first century perspective; as a consequence, the authors added the concept of 'brokerage' to the original categories. Different entrepreneurial styles seem to generate different ideas of success for the entrepreneurs themselves; the authors considered that a bricoleur's aim is 'getting by.' This fits with the suggestion of ad hoc solutions characterised by bricolage.

Of particular interest for this volume is the authors' assertion that there seems to be causality involved, running from identity to behaviour; 'While our study does not directly address why certain types of behaviours are selected, interviews and observations suggest that an entrepreneur's behaviour is largely inseparable from, and heavily influenced by, their self-perceived identity' (Stinchfield et al., 2013, p. 913).

For entrepreneurs who experience dyslexia, this identity may have included some deeply problematic situations in their youth, giving rise to a need to generate both success and, as Smith (2008) suggests, a narrative of personal triumph over the odds in order to achieve a sense of agency in the world.

In a Changing World, Do the Old Rules Apply?

Developments in information and communication technology, together with improvements in connectivity, have supported inclusivity widely, across a range of social contexts. For entrepreneurs with dyslexia, it is now much easier to develop a business idea by commissioning someone to interpret it, design a website or page complete with a marketing and monetising facility and host it so that it enters the market speedily. The designer may be a person living on the other side of the globe, advertising their skills and their availability through a website. This links information and communication technology (ICT) and the gig economy, an approach which grew out of the Great Recession: 'Participants in the gig economy may be small-scale entrepreneurs' (Organisation for Economic Co-operation and Development (OECD), 2017, p. 8).

This approach, being less dependent upon the transfer of information through written language, also benefits entrepreneurs who experience dyslexia. Ease of Access functions within computer programs, and assistive technology in the form of both hardware and software, provide responses to equality legislation requirements which have now made their way into the mainstream. These support communication and make it easier to do business across countries and time zones. Information and communication technology, plus connectivity, have changed the social world to the extent where, in business entrepreneurship as in education, there is a question as to whether the 'old rules' still apply.

Changing perspectives in both entrepreneurship and education are expressed in the concept of 'superdiversity.' The term, originating in linguistics and anthropology, describes developments in language and its use that occur when people move between communities. These changes are accomplished through the frequent and widespread use of information and communication technology. The results make for socio-linguistic change (Blommaert, 2015).

Though the concept originates with human migration in the twenty-first century, it is tempting also to think of superdiversity in terms of the changes which have brought disabled people into the visible community in the last 50 years. These changes too are facilitated by widespread use of ICT, in many forms. Blommaert states: 'What superdiversity has provoked, I believe, is an awareness that a lot of what used to be qualified as 'exceptional', 'aberrant', 'deviant' or 'unusual' in language and its use by people, *is in actual fact quite normal*' (emphasis is the original author's, Blommaert, 2015, p. 83).

This shift in perspective is reflected in present-day disability principles, articulated in the social model of disability and in positive psychology; principles and perspectives which are reflected in this volume. Put simply, the social model of disability states that while people may have difficulties and differences, it is society that disables people through its attitudes and practices. Positive psychology, too, offers an alternative to a deficit-based view, and is discussed in detail in Chapter 5, by Sepulveda and Nicolson.

What Do the Chapters Tell Us?

Entrepreneurship takes place in different ways and in different settings, and approaches to dyslexia may be different in those settings; however, it is only when these characteristics are formalised that a discussion of entrepreneurship co-occurring with dyslexia emerges. In informal situations, there are likely to be many more people who have been unable to gain well-developed literacy skills despite educational opportunity. Nevertheless, they are engaged in using their ingenuity to conduct business that maintains themselves and their families.

In this respect, entrepreneurship is a concept that ranges from the most basic economic survival up to the development of a company that grows, develops employment, makes profit for shareholders and operates globally. If this is viewed as a continuum, as Lackéus (2015) suggests, then the chapters in this volume open windows upon a number of points along its length. These demonstrate real-life experiences that clarify what entrepreneurship means for some people with dyslexia, experiences that may resonate with others who are considering self-employment and entrepreneurship in the quest for meaningful, remunerative work.

Further chapters explore aspects of dyslexia theory in the context of entrepreneurship and challenge conventional, deficit-based interpretations of dyslexia. Adding context, chapters with an educational focus acknowledge the sometimes difficult and harsh impact of schooling on people with dyslexia who have, later, found ways to become entrepreneurs. However, for individuals with dyslexia who have entrepreneurial interests, post-school life can lead to opportunities recognised and taken, innovation applied and success achieved through individual perception and effort, although there is always a risk factor to consider. Within and beyond post-school settings there are likely to be young people with dyslexia who have entrepreneurial interest and potential. Some will be building their own businesses in an ad hoc fashion; others will be looking for knowledge acquisition and guidance via the academic framework.

Exploring the potential pedagogy of value creation, which represents the broader view of entrepreneurship, Lackéus, Lundqvist and Middleton (2016) identify two extremes of educational style within this framework; the traditional and the progressive. As a means of bridging these two poles, the authors recommend a socially constructed approach that, following Vygotsky, employs mediating tools (the involvement of adults, i.e. teachers, parents), the involvement of material tools and the use of psychological (conceptual) tools that aid thinking.

However, it can be seen from the responses of actual and potential entrepreneurs in the small-scale and qualitative research described in this book that what individuals who experience dyslexia want from entrepreneurship education is both approaches, the traditional and the progressive. They do not see entrepreneurship education as an either/or situation; they want access to all of it, available when they perceive it to be relevant and necessary. This perhaps creates an impossible standard, especially when there is a lack of clarity underpinning definitions and theoretical understandings of entrepreneurship as a subject area. Nevertheless, without challenging the programmes themselves, there is still much that can be done to aid young people who experience dyslexia but who have, also, entrepreneurial interest and flair.

Conclusion

This volume explores the overlap of entrepreneurship and dyslexia, and its expression in different contexts. It considers the implications for entrepreneurship education when learners who experience dyslexia may be potential entrepreneurs. The literature shows that each of the two domains, entrepreneurship and dyslexia, has both wide and narrow definitions, and that in each domain research continues. Meanings may not always be agreed. Nevertheless, the view that a greater than expected proportion of entrepreneurs experience dyslexia is a finding that is borne out by personal testimonials, anecdotal evidence and some, if not all, research.

The volume is itself an example of bricolage, calling upon traditional discourses of entrepreneurship and dyslexia in order to create and explore a deeper understanding of the role of individual entrepreneurs who also experience dyslexia. In this process, the book brings together experience, qualitative research, narrative and opinion. The book does not record a formal research project; nevertheless each chapter offers information and insight that illuminate the individual topics and the subject in general.

The variety of chapters presented in this volume broadens considerably the understanding of the concurrence between entrepreneurship and dyslexia. The contributions explore the implications for education, although they do not set out to provide definitive recommendations as to the structure of entrepreneurship education. Instead, the chapters address the processes and settings in which entrepreneurship education takes, or could take, place. In this way, they support efforts to improve access to learning and higher study for potential entrepreneurs who may experience dyslexia. Individuals with dyslexia may have had a very difficult school experience. Dyslexia can undermine confidence and cause people to modify their goals, even when they have reached a pinnacle in their field. However, personal accounts show that even negative experiences can have a positive effect, giving rise to resilience and self-knowledge that can aid learners, and inspire educators to find ways forward.

The chapters reveal both detail and context for the book's topic. Often, within these accounts, the key skills identified by Logan and Martin (2012) can be discerned. These include the abilities to communicate well, to lead successfully, to delegate effectively and to think innovatively about a chosen business, in ways that open up possibilities for a new product or a new approach in an existing market. 'Thinking differently' may or may not be a cognitive characteristic of dyslexia itself, and it is not always valued within conventional teaching and learning. Yet, it may also be the characteristic that differentiates the approach of entrepreneurs with dyslexia from that of others. Where these abilities are demonstrated as traits, this aspect of Logan's research is confirmed, and extended.

A picture emerges suggesting that individuals with dyslexia may have traits, interests or skills which go unrecognised in school, where there is a mandated emphasis upon core subjects, especially literacy and numeracy. Post-school settings may offer opportunities to recognise learners' strengths and abilities and to apply these to wider-ranging or practical tasks, where individuals with dyslexia can be recognised for the positive qualities they can offer. The many stories told within these pages testify to the numerous ways in which people with dyslexia have found their way into an entrepreneurial role.

References

Acs, Z., Szerb, L., & Lloyd, A. (2017). *The global entrepreneurship index 2018.* Washington, DC: The Global Entrepreneurship and Development Institute. https://doi.org/10.1007/978-3-030-03279-1

American Psychiatric Association (APA). (2013). *Diagnostic and statistical manual of mental disorders* (5th ed.). Arlington, VA: Author.

Bacigalupo, M., Kampylis, P., Punie, Y., & van den Brande, G. (2016). *EntreComp: The entrepreneurship competence framework for citizens* (No. JRC101581). Brussels, Belgium: Joint Research Centre, European Commission. Retrieved from http://publications.jrc.ec.europa.eu/

Becker, M. C., Knudsen, T., & Swedberg, R. (2012). Schumpeter's theory of economic development: 100 years of development. *Journal of Evolutionary Economics, 22*(5), 917–933. https://doi.org/10.1007/s00191-012-0297-x

Black, R. D., Weinberg, L. A., & Brodwin, M. G. (2015). Universal design for learning and instruction: Perspectives of students with disabilities in higher education. *Exceptionality Education International, 25*(2), 1–16. Retrieved from https://ir.lib.uwo.ca/

Blommaert, J. (2015). Commentary: Superdiversity old and new. *Language & Communication, 44*, 82–88. https://doi.org/10.1016/j.langcom.2015.01.003

Bolton, B., & Thompson, J. (2004). *Entrepreneurs; talent, temperament, technique* (2nd ed.). Oxford, UK: Butterworth-Heinemann.

Cramer, S. (2014). *Dyslexia's impact (The Duke report).* Developed in collaboration with the Centre for Child and Family Policy at Duke University USA. London, England: Dyslexia and Literacy International. Retrieved from www.dyslexia-international.org/

De Clercq, D., & Honig, B. (2011). Entrepreneurship as an integrating mechanism for disadvantaged persons. *Entrepreneurship & Regional Development, 23*(5–6), 353–372. https://doi.org/10.1080/08985626.2011.580164

Derrida, J. (1967). Structure, sign and play in the discourse of the human sciences. In J. Derrida (Ed.), *Writing and difference* (trans. Alan Bass, pp. 278–294). Paris, France: Editions de Seuil. Retrieved from http://hydra.humanities.uci.edu/derrida/sign-play.html

European Commission. (2013). *Entrepreneurship 2020 action plan: Reigniting the entrepreneurial spirit in Europe.* Brussels, Belgium: European Commission. Retrieved from https://publications.jrc.ec.europa.eu/

Ewing Marion Kauffman Foundation. (2000). *The role of entrepreneurship in the U.S. economy.* Boston, MA: Harvard Business School. http://dx.doi.org/10.2139/ssrn.1260355

Franks, K., & Frederick, H. (2013). Dyslexic and entrepreneur: Typologies, commonalities and differences. *Journal of Asia Entrepreneurship and Sustainability, 11*(1), 95–115. Retrieved from www.researchgate.net/

Gedajlovic, E., Honig, B., Moore, C., Payne, G., & Wright, M. (2013). Social capital and entrepreneurship: A schema and research agenda. *Entrepreneurship, Theory and Practice, 37*(3), 455–478. https://doi.org/10.1111/etap.12042

Gompers, P., Kovner, A., Lerner, J., & Scharfstein, D. (2008). Performance persistence in entrepreneurship. *Journal of Financial Economics, 96*(1), 18–32. https://doi.org/10.1016/j.jfineco.2009.11.001

Hatcher, P. (2000). Sound links in reading and spelling with discrepancy-defined dyslexics and children with moderate learning difficulties. *Reading and Writing, 13*(3–4), 257–272. https://doi.org/10.1023/A:1026486500271

Healy, T., & Côté, S. (2001). *The well-being of nations: The role of human and social capital.* Paris, France: Centre for Educational Research and Innovation, Organisation for Economic Co-operation and Development (OECD). Retrieved from www.oecd.org/

Hessels, J., Rietveld, C., & van der Zwan, P. (2014). Unraveling two myths about entrepreneurs. *Economic Letters, 122,* 435–438. https://doi.org/10.1016/j.econlet.2014.01.005

Kelly, K., & Phillips, S. (2011). *Teaching literacy to learners with dyslexia.* London, England: SAGE.

Kincheloe, J. L. (2001). Describing the bricolage: Conceptualizing a new rigor in qualitative research. *Qualitative Inquiry, 7*(6), 679–692. https://doi.org/10.1007/9789460913976_016

Lackéus, M. (2015). *Entrepreneurship in education: What, why, when, how.* Paris, France: Organisation for Economic Co-operation and Development (OECD). Retrieved from www.oecd.org/cfe/leed/

Lackéus, M., Lundqvist, M., & Middleton, K. W. (2016). Bridging the traditional-progressive education rift through entrepreneurship. *International Journal of Entrepreneurial Behavior & Research, 22*(6), 777–803. https://doi.org/10.1108/IJEBR-03-2016-0072

Logan, J. (2009). Dyslexic entrepreneurs: The incidence; their coping strategies and their business skills. *Dyslexia, 15,* 328–334. https://doi.org/10.1002/dys.388

Logan, J. (2013). Dyslexia and entrepreneurship. In A. Fawcett & K. Saunders (Eds.), *The dyslexia handbook.* Bracknell, UK: The British Dyslexia Association. Retrieved from www.researchgate.net/

Logan, J., & Martin, N. (2012). Unusual talent: A study of successful leadership and delegation in entrepreneurs who have dyslexia. *Journal of Inclusive Practice in Further and Higher Education, 4*(1), 57–76. Retrieved from www.brainhe.com/

Mackay, N. (2012). *Removing dyslexia as a barrier to achievement* (3rd ed.). Wakefield, UK: SEN Marketing.

Marram, E., Lange, J., Brown, D., Marquis, J., & Bygrave, W. D. (2014, March 25). Is entrepreneurship a teachable profession? An examination of the effects of entrepreneurship education and experience. *SSRN* (e journal). http://dx.doi.org/10.2139/ssrn.2412932

Miller, D., & Le Breton-Miller, I. (2017, January). Underdog entrepreneurs: A model of challenge-based entrepreneurship. *Entrepreneurship Theory and Practice, 41,* 7–17. https://doi.org/10.1111/etap.12253

National Assembly for Wales Enterprise and Business Committee. (2013). *Youth entrepreneurship (Report on the inquiry into youth entrepreneurship).* Cardiff, UK: National Assembly for Wales; A Support Document. Retrieved from www.senedd.assembly.wales/

Organisation for Economic Co-operation and Development (OECD). (2017). *Entrepreneurship at a glance.* Paris, France: Author. https://doi.org/10.1787/22266941

Pavey, B. (2015). The UK's Dyslexia-Friendly initiative and the USA's Universal Design movement: Exploring a possible kinship. *Asia Pacific Journal of Developmental Differences, 2*(1), 39–54. Retrieved from www.das.org.sg

Phillimore, J., Humphries, R., Klaas, F., & Knecht, M. (2016). *Bricolage: Potential as a conceptual tool for understanding access to welfare in superdiverse neighbourhoods* (IRiS Working Paper Series 14). Birmingham, UK: Institute for Research into Superdiversity, University of Birmingham. Retrieved from www.birmingham.ac.uk/

Quality Assurance Agency (QAA). (2018). *Enterprise and entrepreneurship education (Guidance for UK Higher Education providers)*. Gloucester, UK: The Quality Assurance Agency for Higher Education. Retrieved from www.qaa.ac.uk/

Ramus, F., Altarelli, I., Jednorog, K., Zhao, J., & di Covella, L. S. (2018). Neuroanatomy of developmental dyslexia: Pitfalls and promise. *Neuroscience & Biobehavioral Reviews, 84*, 434–452. https://doi.org/10.1016/j.neubiorev.2017.08.001

Rose, J., Sir. (2009). *Identifying and teaching children and young people with dyslexia and literacy difficulties*. Nottingham, UK: Department for Children, Schools and Families (DCSF). Retrieved from www.thedyslexia-spldtrust.org.uk/

Scott, S. S., McGuire, J. M., & Shaw, S. F. (2003). Universal design for instruction: A new paradigm for adult instruction in postsecondary education. *Remedial and Special Education, 24*(6), 369–379. https://doi.org/10.1177/07419325030240060801

Sepulveda, P. (2014). Dyslexics and their entrepreneur behaviours. In R. Dautov, P. Gkasis, A. Karamanos, T. Lagkas, A. Prodromidou, & A. Ypsilanti (Eds.), *Proceedings of the ninth annual south-east European doctoral student conference* (pp. 671–690). Sheffield, UK: South East European Research Centre, University of Sheffield. Retrieved from www.researchgate.net/

Smith, R. (2008). Being differently abled: Learning lessons from dyslexic entrepreneurs. In R. T. Harrison & C. M. Leitch (Eds.), *Entrepreneurial learning: Conceptual frameworks and applications* (pp. 291–312). Abingdon, UK: Routledge.

Snowling, M. J., & Melby-Lervåg, M. (2016). Oral language deficits in familial dyslexia: A meta-analysis and review. *Psychological Bulletin, 142*(5), 498–545. http://dx.doi.org/10.1037/bul0000037

Stinchfield, B. T., Nelson, R. E., & Wood, M. S. (2013). Learning from Levi-Strauss' legacy: Art, craft, engineering, bricolage, and brokerage in entrepreneurship. *Entrepreneurship Theory and Practice, 34*(4), 889–921. https://doi.org/10.1111/j.1540-6520.2012.00523.x

Welsh Assembly Government. (2002). *Youth enterprise and entrepreneurship; a strategy for Wales* (The National Assembly for Wales Enterprise and Business Committee 2013 Youth Entrepreneurship). Cardiff, UK: National Assembly for Wales. Retrieved from www.careerswales.com/

Welsh Government. (2017). *Prosperity for all: The national strategy*. Cardiff, UK: Author. Retrieved from https://gov.wales/

Wiklund, J., Hatak, I., Patzelt, H., & Shepherd, D. (2018). Mental disorders in the entrepreneurship context: When being different can be an advantage. *Academy of Management Perspectives, 32*(2), 182–206. https://doi.org/10.5465/amp.2017.0063

Wilson, A. J., Andrewes, S. G., Struthers, H., Rowe, V. M., Bogdanovic, R., & Waldie, K. E. (2015). Dyscalculia and dyslexia in adults: Cognitive bases of comorbidity. *Learning and Individual Differences, 37,* 118–132. https://doi. org/10.1016/j.lindif.2014.11.017

World Health Organization (WHO). (2018). *International classification of diseases for mortality and morbidity statistics* (11th Rev.). Geneva, Switzerland: Author. Retrieved from https://icd.who.int/browse11/l-m/en

Part I
Entrepreneurship

1 An Award-Winning Entrepreneur
Sharon Hewitt

Neil Alexander-Passe

Introduction

Over the last 20 years there has been a rise in awareness that dyslexia can bring both advantages and abilities as well as difficulties in a society that relies heavily on literacy and numeracy skills (West, 1997). The role of entrepreneurs who experience dyslexia has been spearheaded by Julie Logan with her work investigating both British and North American entrepreneurs. Other researchers have also investigated successful people with dyslexia (Gerber, Ginsberg, & Reiff, 1992; Goldberg, Higgins, Raskind, & Herman, 2003), and this study aims to build on such studies.

Empirical evidence suggests that growing up with dyslexia in mainstream education can be traumatic, especially in the 1970s and 1980s in the UK, where dyslexia and Special Educational Needs (SEN) were still in their infancy regarding understanding in schools. The lack of awareness in teachers (both then and more recently) has been found to cause low self-esteem and low self-confidence; individuals believed the labels of 'stupid' or 'lazy' that were given to them by teachers, peers and, at times, family. Such feelings have long-lasting manifestations which can be related to Post-Traumatic Stress Disorder (PTSD) according to Alexander-Passe (2015a, 2016).

However, whilst many individuals with dyslexia leave school feeling worthless with few paper qualifications to their name, fortunately many do not. Others, as indicated in this literature review, have been able to use their school trauma positively, to not only gain employment, but to succeed in the workplace. Some have also chosen to become self-employed and entrepreneurs, which not only demonstrates their strengths, skills and abilities, but offers unique services which (neuro-typical) individuals had never thought of. Entrepreneurs such as Sir Richard Branson and Sir James Dyson are two such examples where despite their dyslexia difficulties, they have created billion-dollar companies that are not only innovative but have reshaped their sector (airlines, music, and engineering and electrical products). The advantages of self-employment include the ability to concentrate on strengths (e.g. selling and creating) and to delegate areas of weakness to others (e.g. administration), which can be impossible when working in large organisations, especially where the employer struggles with the concept of dyslexia and how to support such individuals.

This chapter aims to develop this entrepreneurship theme by interviewing Sharon Hewitt, an award-winning entrepreneur with dyslexia who has redefined the property buying experience. It also looks at gender as a factor in Sharon's success and how she struggled to not only cope with her dyslexia and working in a male-orientated environment, but also to challenge gender stereotypes so that she could do more than take the expected role of a housewife, becoming an entrepreneur who brought an innovative approach to her chosen industry sector.

This Study/Methodology

This chapter investigated a single successful, female adult entrepreneur with dyslexia. A media search was conducted to identify such individuals in the UK and USA; one was approached. Confidentiality was assured at several points in the preparation for the interview, along with a brief overview of the book project for which the interview would be used. Before the interview took place, the participant was again asked to confirm that they were happy to proceed with the interview and for her name to be used in this publication.

Interview Results

Diagnosis

> At secondary school I was taken into a class for special lessons.

> I was assessed for two hours at school (with tests in e.g. reading out loud, completing forms, reading comprehension, and mathematic skills). This assessment was probably by a specialist teacher; after many tests, I was told I was dyslexic. I have no paperwork to support my diagnosis as a child.

Although Sharon does not believe she has been formally diagnosed with dyslexia, she is aware that the term was used when she was at school and that she received additional or special educational lessons. The two-hour assessment, which is still a strong memory in her mind, indicates more than a basic assessment, with both oral and written abilities tested.

Childhood (Home Life)

> I define my father as clearly dyslexic, but it was never discussed at home. He never wrote a word, he was a precision engineer, and learnt by watching. He would not even write on my mother's birthday card, he would give her a blank birthday card as he was afraid he would get her name wrong, and upset her. Apart from his signature, he would never write a thing in his life. Now you look back it's clear to say he was clearly dyslexic. My mother would just fill in the gaps where needed, when he needed to do things/write things and he signed it.

There seems to be a clear hereditary nature to Sharon's dyslexia, as her father had similar, if not more severe, symptoms of dyslexia. He developed advanced 'avoidance' coping strategies, not only with regard to the outside world but also with his own family and spouse. It would be fascinating to talk to Sharon's mother to understand at what point she was aware of his severe literacy difficulties. Sharon suggests her father's illiteracy was never discussed at home; however, it seemed clear that all their children demonstrated varying difficulties with reading and writing. Interestingly, only Sharon gained an assessment/diagnosis at school. The term 'we all just muddled through' is reflective of schooling in the 1960s to the 1980s where Special Educational Needs (SEN) were not discussed, were dismissed or were ignored.

The introduction of the UK Education Act of 1970 (Handicapped Children) led to The Warnock Report (Warnock, 1978), beginning our modern understanding of 'SEN' where the crucial figure 20% of young people was estimated to experience learning difficulties at least at some point in their educational career. The Warnock Report aimed to highlight that young people were struggling at school and that new inclusive education provision/legislation was needed, and future education acts have moved schools both physically (e.g. the need for wheelchair accessible toilets and classrooms) and academically (e.g. every class teacher is a teacher of SEN).

School (Primary)

It was immediately said when I started primary school 'that Sharon was not trying hard enough'. The reports would say 'if she worked harder, listened more'. The homework, I would work really hard but I would get red lines through it all. I would hand it in and I was told I had made no effort, I hadn't listened. It's all spelt wrong, you are not even copying correctly from the board into your text book. I could never do it quick enough, I could not spell it well enough and it looked messy and scruffy, and they just told me I was 'lazy' and that was like a lot of my primary schooling.

My writing was very small and scruffy as I thought if I write small they can't see if it's mis-spelt, and I just felt I was letting everyone down. The teachers thought I was just lazy; my mother was asking me 'why aren't you trying'? But I was trying really hard.

Primary school is often where many learners with dyslexia (and unidentified learners who experience dyslexia) first find out that they are different. Young people with dyslexia find that they can't do things and are often moved to the table with others that struggle, whilst others progress faster in class and gain praise and respect; causing a 'them and us' positioning, first in the classroom and then in the playground with social groups formation. The young learner who experiences dyslexia soon thinks of themselves as 'lazy and stupid' and this affects their ability to try and risk new learning in class, believing themselves to be second class citizens (as previously found in Alexander-Passe, 2010).

No matter how much Sharon tried, she felt ill-equipped to be at school and fell quickly into the same pattern. '*I felt I was letting everyone down*' indicates that her self-esteem was at rock-bottom and her mother and teachers were lost as to knowing what to do.

School (Secondary)

> Subjects I was good at? Languages were a nightmare for me. I was interested in using commas in my writing, and geography. Not great at maths. Not great at catching ball, hand eye co-ordination.

> Friendship wise, I had a core group, it was a group of the outcasts. I would stick up for the ones being bullied. We were part of the odd crowd.

> Did I feel stupid? That word!

> I had from teachers 'Sharon, you are so good verbally, you get what we are saying, you get our questions right, but when I see your homework it is like you hadn't listened. Why can you answer the questions in class and we think you understand it'. This written work is appalling I would say 'I just don't know why I can't do it, I just don't understand' and that was frustrating.

At secondary school Sharon suggests that there was a distinct difference between her oral and written work in class, with teachers even asking her why she was so good orally but unable to produce the same high results on paper. However, knowledge of dyslexia/learning difficulties was very poor then and no one referred her for further investigation.

Sharon recognised that school was an unfair environment to be in, with her peers and friends seemingly able to do what was being asked of them but sadly she could not. Even when she felt she was doing well and was moved to a higher ability class, she was quickly moved down again, which was a 'humiliating' experience and reinforced her low self-worth in her own eyes and that of her peers. When questioned about whether she felt 'stupid,' her reaction to this word had strong ramifications and she has now vowed to never use that word to her own children due to the traumatic effect it had on herself.

Initial Post-School Career

> *When it came to career guidance. This guy would just look at my qualification I had previous and said 'if I work really hard you could be a shop assistant in Boots' and that is okay to be a shop assistant, but if that was my goal to aim for, that was dreadful. There was more to me than working in a shop, why should that be it for me?*

> *I found I was really good with the customers, so began to spend more time with them than on reception. When someone complained to the boss he then said 'get someone in to do the receptionist job, I want Sharon with the sales team'. I then moved myself up to be the first female branch/ area manager in the business.*

Career guidance was very disappointing to Sharon, as they only looked at written abilities and ignored her strong verbal skills. She was not allowed to take O Levels and left school with few qualifications to her name—not enough to go to 6th form to study for A Levels for university entrance. College however was a possibility, starting at a very low level course. Of her family, none of them went to college and all left school at 16 years old for the workplace. Sharon's mother didn't think that she had much potential and thought that having a basic job (e.g. a cleaner) and being a housewife was all she was capable of.

Sharon was fortunate to gain an au pair position with a family, where she could demonstrate her many abilities without literacy being an impairment. When she wished to leave, she was offered a receptionist post in an estate agency run by the family where she was working as an au pair. This turned out to be the start of a long journey to the success she currently experiences. Again, without the impairment of reading and writing she was able to demonstrate her people skill abilities. Demonstrating her abilities to sell to customers and manage a team led her to become the first female branch manager of one of the UK's largest estate agency organisations, not only beating the men but challenging and breaking glass ceilings for women in her organisation. Such things were not recognised by her school career counsellor and it demonstrates that only looking at paper qualifications discounts the skills and abilities required in the workplace, especially when working with the public and managing teams.

My Family, Children

> *I have two children, we tested them for learning challenges at primary school. We took them to an educational psychologist and they said my son had mild surface dyslexic. He has done well in life, is now an architect and things are different now and school support better.*
>
> *When I brought my children up I would never allow my children to call each other stupid. That word is so painful to me as I was called that so often, it is a very painful word for me.*

The choices that many individuals with dyslexia have to make while bringing up children are wrapped up with so many emotions. Knowing that you had difficulties and traumas yourself at school, can make people who experience dyslexia wary of putting their own children through a system that was extremely cruel to them. Some even choose to not have any children for this reason. However, with time comes progress, and Sharon made sure that her children were tested at primary school. The hereditary nature of dyslexia can mean it can be passed down in families, mainly through males (Hales, 1994); however, this is not guaranteed. It turned out that her son was diagnosed with 'surface dyslexia'—this means that he can read and spell words that abide by reading rules but will struggle with exceptional words (e.g. island). Sharon also wished to be more involved with her children's education than her father, who avoided all things to do with school due to his own trauma, which may have been the result of unsympathetic and unfair treatment by teachers who misunderstood his difficulties.

This again demonstrated Sharon's resilience in overcoming her own literacy challenges, and her determination that her own children would not suffer at school by teachers who misunderstood their skills and abilities. She is very proud about her son's achievements in becoming an architect.

Going It Alone

> *I was frustrated at the (former) estate agency by the type of service I could offer clients; I wanted to introduce a finder's package that previously only larger, more global companies would offer to corporate customers so I went out and set up by myself to offer this personalised service.*

Failure in business always takes Sharon back to school emotionally, where: *I felt I was never good enough.*

My Team

> *I sometimes feel a fraud, always feeling that someone will find me out, discovering that I had no qualifications to do what I did.*
>
> *I am very aware some of my team are much more qualified than I am.*

Whilst being successful at work, Sharon began to question the perceived wisdom of how her sector worked with clients and questioned the level of service they should be offering. This is very much what Sir Richard Branson did when he challenged British Airways by creating the Virgin Airways brand. He wanted to enhance the customer experience and thought that the public would pay for an enhanced service.

Sharon began over 13 years ago with a small loan to set up a new type of estate agency, and has won several awards as a result of her innovative approach. Sharon sees her role as advocating for the buyer and not the seller, her service charges the buyer for a personalised package that understands their unique demands for a new home, and will hunt for homes that meet highly specified criteria for location to school catchment areas, transport links, parks, recreation and shopping facilities. The service she offered had only been available to corporate clients to date, but her unique selling point (USP) is local knowledge and customer service. Her clients now include both global corporate clients, who need tailored location services for their staff, and private clients.

Sharon's success has been based on her selling and people skills, her understanding of the needs of clients and her ability to use her gut reaction to find the right properties that tick her client's boxes. She has recruited a highly professional team, all with degrees, who are the logistical brains behind her success. However, she chuckles to herself that for many years they did not know they were employed by a person without a degree, who was once told that she was only good enough to work as a shop assistant in Boots. To begin with, and for many years, she felt she would be found out to be a fraud, as someone who was unqualified to be in her position, but slowly as the awards have come in she realised that she was not a fraud, and that her success, rewards and awards were justified and a true reflection of her ability and potential.

Sharon's success is very much based on gut reactions, believing her sixth sense of what is right, be it choosing a new team member or choosing the perfect property to show a client. Such skills and abilities cannot be taught at university, but develop over time—the ability to create divergent combinations which can be illogical at times. This divergent ability for business decision making has been found to be common in many successful people with dyslexia (Alexander-Passe, 2017).

Interestingly, Sharon created a team that supports her unique combination of strengths and difficulties. They complement her, and she has only in the last few years told them of her dyslexia and explained why she may do things in sometimes illogical ways (e.g. why she may avoid taking messages, work via Skype or want things stored in a certain format). However, sharing such information also gives her team a window into understanding why she is so successful and how apparently illogical decisions and hunches can be right for their clients. That questioning of perceived wisdom can reap benefits to help redefine the moving home experience.

Strategies

> *I write very curt, short emails, to the point and 'no nonsense' in style.*

> *I use Grammarly (software package) to check all my written letters and emails.*

> *I am very good at delegating tasks, and knowing the right person to do the right job–I found this out when working at (a former estate agency).*

Sharon seems very aware of her strengths and difficulties, but has developed a range of strategies to mitigate any difficulties, turning negatives into positives to create an award-winning brand. Alexander-Passe (2017) also found that understanding one's balance of abilities/difficulties allows you to put in place solutions and to create teams that complement an innovative leader. Early on, Sharon developed the skills to delegate roles to the most suitable person in her team; 'they' can do what they do best, so 'she' can do what she does best. Knowing this allows projects to be completed efficiently and to the highest standard.

Sharon's use of a writing software programme and then writing short, to-the-point emails and letters is typical of many successful people who experience dyslexia, in that they are effective in reducing complex information into short and punchy statements which are actionable.

Business Style

> I take a person-centred approach to business, emphasising customer service.

> Unique selling point: my company offers a tailored service for clients who are willing to pay for the right service, which includes someone looking out for them, someone that understands their unique needs (e.g. in relation to family, work, pleasure).

> My company has won several awards for the service it offers.

In deciphering Sharon's business style, it is important to appreciate why and how she has become a leader in her sector. She is very person-centred, understanding that in this era the need for excellent customer service is vital to success in today's marketplace. Customers are willing to pay for a service that saves them time and offers them a means to gain the perfect solution. Sharon's business charges the buyer and offers a tailored service with exceptional local knowledge, whereas traditional estate agencies charge the seller. Sharon also talked about avoiding failure at all costs, describing how any failure is taken personally and reverts her back to the feelings she once felt at school—that she was worthless and helpless in a world that values the abilities to read and write.

Do You Feel Successful, What is Success?

> Success is being happy and achieving your goals. It's not about money!

As 'a woman in business,' Sharon attributes success to personal features, and does not consider achievement being purely in financial terms. This concurs with the study of $N=25$ successful people with dyslexia

by Alexander-Passe (2015b), who also found that men and women
with dyslexia tend to value time (work-life balance) and happiness over
material worth. It could be argued that having struggled at school,
they believed there was more to life than just work, therefore rejecting
traditional values of success, and as a result they were less materialistic.
Sharon sees success as achieving personal goals and giving back; giving
back so that others can also achieve success—those whom schools would
normally write off due to the lack of paper qualifications.

Is it Hard and/or Different Being a Woman in Business?

> *I don't feel the need to explain my success to men I think it is quite clear*
> *the awards, longevity of business and the respect I have in the industry.*
> *I know this sounds big-headed but facts and stats click more in the male*
> *psychology, in my opinion.*

This study intentionally sought a female entrepreneur who experienced
dyslexia, as it aimed to understand if gender was a factor in how they
worked, their values and their concept of workplace success.

Sharon has said that she feels there are differences to how males
and females act in the workplace, interestingly that females feel more
threatened by other females than males.

> *I feel there are differences, I feel I need to prove myself amongst*
> *my female peers, such as have I achieved enough, and in a male-*
> *orientated world. The need to be successful both as a mother and as a*
> *business person in a male-orientated world, compared to a man who*
> *just needs to be successful in business.*

She feels that she is able to demonstrate her success in a male-
dominated business context through her many sector awards. Her view
is that women look at other factors, such as the ability to juggle both
business and home careers, and it's about finding the right balance.

When asked if any other person with dyslexia works in her
organisation, Sharon says no, but she does not rule out employing
someone with traits associated with dyslexia. However, she would
expect them to have overcome their difficulties and, like her, to have
survived the difficult school process as if overcoming our failed system

is a 'rite of passage.' She believes that like her, a team member with dyslexia would bring benefits:

> *I could see the value of employing a dyslexic, because the team would benefit from someone looking at issues from different angles, it's great for business growth. Also their interpersonal skills in general are better.*

Tips for Parents

> *Find out what they are good at (parents and school) and use these strengths to form a career, as a motivating force. What I mean is find out what your child is good at and encourage them, giving them confidence that they can achieve great things, and this will have a knock-on effect on their schooling.*

> *Schools now have more understanding of special needs, and will ask why a child is not learning.*

Sharon volunteers as a mentor for the Prince's Trust, which aims to offer opportunities to young adults who would traditionally be unable to gain funding to develop new business ventures—helping them to reach their potential and to challenge the 'no's' in society. Regarding young people with dyslexia, she suggests that schools and parents seek to find their strengths and abilities, encouraging them to locate their strengths and to 'reach for the stars' to aim for their potential. They should question the value of exam-based paper qualifications; schools should offer vocational opportunities and offer career guidance that recognises both oral and written abilities. Sharon recognises that today's schools offer more awareness of SENs such as dyslexia and that through this young people can gain the help that she once sought at school and be offered careers beyond working as a shop assistant.

Emotional Effects of School

> *I am motivated to prove that I have value in the world, and that I am not stupid. Failure is hard for me and I will do everything to avoid it, to avoid looking stupid, and to prove I am not a fraud in business.*

Previous research (Alexander-Passe, 2015c, 2017) indicates that adults who experience dyslexia can manifest long-term effects from their experienced school failure, both in perceived successful and less successful people with dyslexia. That experience can cause them post-school to develop a personality that protects themselves (emotionally) to avoid re-experiencing failure again, but also causes them to develop coping strategies to avoid failure (task-orientated coping) and to develop resilience and determination to prove to others that they have worth and value in the workplace. Sharon fits this profile, as the word 'failure' has strong emotional characteristics, and she will try hard to avoid looking like a failure in front of others (re-experiencing the failure she once experienced in the classroom at school and feeling helpless at the hands of others).

Discussion & Conclusion

Sharon's interview is interesting, as it gives a first-hand account of UK schooling in the 1970s and 1980s, and contrasts her own experience of being a parent in the 2000s– and 2010s. She was misunderstood at school, demonstrating clear difficulties, but while her experience with secondary school teachers suggests that they recognised a disparity between her oral and written schoolwork there was a lack of knowledge, commitment or expectation to investigate further.

Whilst dyslexia was first identified in the UK by Pringle Morgan (1896) and Hinshelwood (1917), schools have been very slow to recognise dyslexia in young children. Baroness Warnock's Report (1978) was an attempt to recognise the many learners in mainstream schools who might experience barriers to learning. Many researchers now point to the emotional effect of UK educational policies in the 1970's through the 1990's (see for example Burden, 2005; Riddick, 1996; Humphrey & Mullins, 2002). More recently, the author's own studies have indicated that adults with dyslexia can be successful despite, and not because of, mainstream educational policies, and this study adds to this evidence.

Sharon's dyslexia was discussed at several points, along with her motivation to prove her self-worth and to overcome her lack of formal education, to develop an award-winning business that reflects her strong people and sales skills and to offer a unique business opportunity to both high-income families and corporate organisations.

References

Alexander-Passe, N. (2010). *Dyslexia and depression: The hidden sorrow*. New York, NY: Nova Science Publishers.

Alexander-Passe, N. (2015a). *Dyslexia and mental health: Helping people identify destructive behaviours and find positive ways to cope*. London, England: Jessica Kingsley Publishers.

Alexander-Passe, N. (2015b). Perceptions of success in dyslexic adults in the UK. *Asia Pacific Journal of Developmental Differences, 2*(1), 89–111. https://doi.org/10.3850/S234573411500023X

Alexander-Passe, N. (2015c). Investigating post-traumatic stress disorder (PTSD) triggered by the experience of dyslexia in mainstream school education? *Journal of Psychology and Psychotherapy, 5*(6), 1. https://doi.org/10.4172/2161–0487.1000215

Alexander-Passe, N. (2016). Dyslexia, success and post-traumatic growth. *Asia Pacific Journal of Developmental Differences, 3*(1), 87–130. https://doi.org/10.3850/S2345734114000232

Alexander-Passe, N. (2017). *The successful dyslexic: Identify the keys for success to achieve your potential*. Rotterdam, The Netherlands: Sense Publishers.

Burden, R. (2005). *Dyslexia & self-concept: Seeking a dyslexic identity*. London, England: Whurr.

Gerber, P. J., Ginsberg, R., & Reiff, H. B. (1992). Identifying alterable patterns in employment success for highly successful adults with learning disabilities. *Journal of Learning Disabilities, 25*(8), 475–487. https://doi.org/10.1177/002221949202500802

Goldberg, R. J., Higgins, E. L., Raskind, M. H., & Herman, K. L. (2003). *Life success for children with learning disabilities: A parent guide*. Pasadena, CA: The Frostig Center.

Hales, G. (1994). The human aspects of dyslexia. In G. Hales (Ed.), *Dyslexia matters* (pp. 184–198). London, England: Whurr.

Hinshelwood, J. (1917). *Congenital word-blindness*. London, England: H.K. Lewis.

Humphrey, N., & Mullins, P. (2002). Personal constructs and attribution for academic success and failure in dyslexics. *British Journal of Special Education, 29*(4), 196–203. https://doi.org/10.1111/1467-8527.00269

Logan, J. (2001). *Entrepreneurial success: A study of the incidence of dyslexia in the entrepreneurial population and the influence of dyslexia on success* (Unpublished doctoral thesis), University of Bristol, UK.

Logan, J. (2009). Dyslexic entrepreneurs: The incidence; their coping strategies and their business skills. *Dyslexia, 15*(4), 328–346. https://doi.org/10.1002/dys.388

Pringle Morgan, W. (1896, November 7). A case of congenital word blindness. *British Medical Journal, 2*(1871), 1378. https://doi.org/10.1136/bmj.2.1871.1378

Riddick, B. (1996). *Living with dyslexia*. London, England: David Fulton Publishers.

Warnock, H. (1978). *Special educational needs: Report of the committee of enquiry into the education of handicapped children and young people* (The Warnock Report). London, England: Department for Education and Science.

West, T. G. (1997). *In the mind's eye: Visual thinkers, gifted people with dyslexia and other learning difficulties, computer images, and the ironies of creativity*. Amherst, NY: Prometheus Books.

2 Documenting the Role of UK Agricultural Colleges in Propagating the Farming-Dyslexia-Entrepreneurship Nexus

Robert Smith, Gillian Conley and Louise Manning

Introduction

It is acknowledged that the incidence of dyslexia in the farming industry is significantly higher than in the average population (Conley, Smith, Smith, & McElwee, 2015). Whilst it is prevalent in farming, we argue that it is also so in other land-based industries such as in equine and forestry. The research of Conley et al. (2015) examined the incidence of dyslexia in the UK farming community; its common symptoms and manifestations and how these affect everyday and longer-term farming practices and strategies; the coping mechanisms and skillsets that farmers who experience dyslexia develop to overcome the condition; the effect upon the individual farmer, their family and on the farm business and finally what lessons can be learned on how to alleviate the negative aspects of dyslexia. To do this, they focussed on the 'Farming with Dyslexia Project' and the inspirational stories of Sandy

McCreath, a farmer from the Dumfriesshire area, and Sandy Murray, a crofter from the Highlands, who were instrumental in highlighting the effect dyslexia had on their farming practice. The project came about when in responding to the concerns of farmers with dyslexia, the National Farmers Union of Scotland (NFUS) provided support and encouragement to all parties involved. This resulted in the setting up of a project committee to inform the work.

In this exploratory chapter, we focus on what we refer to as the Farming-Dyslexia-Entrepreneurship nexus, which is predicated upon three linked notions—namely:

- the growing recognition and importance of farm, or agricultural, entrepreneurship (see Carter, 1996, 1999, 2003; Carter & Rosa, 1998; Iaquinto & Spinelli, 2006; Sharma, Tiwari, & Sharma, 2010; Alsos, Carter, & Ljunggren, 2011; Fitz-Koch, Nordqvist, Carter, & Hunter, 2018),
- the appreciation of the role dyslexia plays in shaping entrepreneurial propensity (Logan, 2001; Smith, 2008; Logan, 2009; Logan & Martin, 2012; Franks & Frederick, 2013; Farrell, Styles, & Petersen, 2016),
- the growing awareness of the incidence and impact of dyslexia in farming (see the works of Smith, Conley, McElwee, & Smith, 2015, Conley et al., 2015, Smith, Conley, Smith, & McElwee, 2016; collectively, the aforesaid studies highlight the incidence and potential effect of the condition within the industry.

The first notion is based on the growing appreciation of the role of entrepreneurship in agriculture, the farming industry and the idea of the farmer as 'entrepreneur' (McElwee, 2006, 2008) and the rapidly expanding literature on the subject. The second notion is becoming an established facet of the entrepreneurship and business literatures, whilst the third is, as yet, a protean and under-theorised literature.

Much of what we know about this fascinating nexus comes to us from farmers and practitioners self-reporting their own tendencies associated with dyslexia, and from documentary sources such as journalistic articles, particularly in the farming press. Nevertheless, it is difficult to obtain empirical evidence of the incidence of dyslexia in land-based industries, making reliance on the anecdotal important.

Another vital source of knowledge comes from industry practitioners (such as the authors) who work in the Further Education (FE) and Higher Education (HE) sectors which educate and upskill those working in the agricultural industry. In the UK, this role is performed by rural colleges and universities. Such institutions cater to the equine, farming and forestry industries. Indeed, it is whilst attending vocational or educational courses at such educational institutions that many engaged in the farming industry are first formerly diagnosed with dyslexia, or with symptoms of dyslexia. Another source of information is the increasing body of pedagogic literature being produced that focuses on agricultural and land-based academic institutions and the higher incidence of dyslexia in the student body. It has been suggested that students in Greece who experience dyslexia gravitate towards agricultural subjects because they perceive the industry as relying less on written language (Stampoltzis & Polychronopoulou, 2008). The proportion of students with dyslexia in food and agriculture courses extends to 10%–20% in the UK (Richardson, 2009; Webster, 2016), 23% of students in the US (Pense, 2009; Pense, Watson, & Wakefield, 2010) and 27.6% in the United Arab Emirates (Aboudan, Eapen, Bayshak, Al-Mansouri, & Al-Shamsi, 2011).

This link between formal education and the discovery of dyslexia and other learning difficulties is of vital importance. Indeed, Gasson (1998) stresses the value to the industry of 'better-educated farmers' in being more entrepreneurially proactive but bemoans the fact that there is no single authoritative source of information on the educational attainment levels of UK farmers. Nevertheless, Gasson suggests that at least one-third and possibly half of all UK farmers today have pursued FE and HE courses leading to qualifications, largely in agriculture or related subjects. Of these, about 4%–6% have degrees, a similar number have Higher National Diploma (HNDs) and between a quarter and a third have FE qualifications from full-time or part-time study.

Methodology

The primary methodology used in the compilation of this chapter is that of 'Documentary Research' (Scott, 2014) from media and press sources, as well as netnography (Kozinets, 2015). Indeed, much of the material which inspired this research stream comes from press articles and stories written by UK-based journalists on the topic documenting the problems faced by the farmers in their everyday work. In Conley et al. (2015), use was made of learning stories to capture the context of the learning environment that enables and constrains learning and progress over time. Such learning stories (Lave, 1997) relate to aspects of learning in relation to the condition of dyslexia. Learning stories are distinctly social and are set in particular, situated communities of practice (Lave & Wenger, 1991). A questionnaire (Smith et al., 2015) was used to collect the learning stories, which were analysed using the framework shown in Table 2.1. The questionnaire was updated in 2018 for the purpose of this chapter (Table 2.1).

Establishing an Appropriate Literature Base

We commenced with a literature review of extant research to synthesise and establish an appropriate literature base and theoretical underpinning to inform the empirical research. As scholars and practitioners of the rural, we were aware that dyslexia had a vocational element in that higher incidences of it can be found in certain occupations such as farmers, engineers, artists or amongst criminal fraternity (Taylor, 2003; Kirk &Reid, 2001). Our focus is on:

- the growing recognition and importance of farm or agricultural entrepreneurship,
- the appreciation of the role dyslexia plays in shaping entrepreneurial propensity,
- the growing awareness of the incidence and impact of dyslexia in farming and the equine industry.

It is of note that whilst there are established academic journals on the topic of dyslexia such as 1) *Dyslexia: An International Journal of Research & Practice*, and 2) *the Annals of Dyslexia*, very little has been published in relation to dyslexia in land-based industries.

The Growing Recognition and Importance of Agricultural Entrepreneurship

Traditionally, farmers were regarded as being conservative in nature, anti-entrepreneurial and risk-averse in their practices (McElwee, 2006). Indeed, farming is very much an occupation that one 'learns

Table 2.1 Dyslexia–Sample Screening Questionnaire

Question No.	Dylexia – Sample screening questionnaire, applied in relation to the inquiry: Does dyslexia influence the entrepreneurial propensity of farmers and their ability to conduct business? Questions:	Testing which function?
1.	Are you a slow writer, for example does it take you more than ten minutes to write or copy a paragraph of text for farm paperwork?	Memory Processing Speed
2.	Do you get anxious when trying to write your ideas down on paper or complete paperwork, such as cattle passports?	Anxiety
3.	Do you make persistent spelling mistakes with common words such as writing the months of the year or days of the week? Or do you frequently mix up letters in words such as the letter 'b' and 'd'?	Spelling difficulties Letter reversal directional confusion/visual difficulties
4.	Do you have difficulty clearly distinguishing maths notation like x for multiplication and – for minus or do you often mix up numbers such as 6 and 9?	Coding & Decoding
5.	Do you have difficulty planning and organising paperwork or business ideas on paper?	Organisation
6.	Do you often mix up dates and times and sometimes miss work/personal appointments?	Organisation
7.	Do you have directional confusion, for instance can you tell your left-hand side from your right-hand side of your body?	Directionality
8.	Do you find it difficult to remember mathematical formulae such as the 8 times table or mathematical instructions, for example how to multiply numeric fractions such as ½ X ¾?	Memory
9.	Do you often write letters of words in the incorrect order, for example the letter 'E' before the letter 'I' in words such as 'piece'?	Sequencing
10.	Do you get anxious over how you are going to complete set practical tasks or written tasks by deadlines?	Lack of confidence
11.	Do you have difficulty following oral instructions? Either given by a person or noted from a telephone conversation in your own hand writing.	Memory & Concentration
12.	Can you effectively contribute to a verbal discussion? For example in a group situation at a farmers meeting or on a one-to-one basis.	Speech & Comprehension
13.	Would you be able to get your bearings in a large building, such as a college or a hospital?	Visuo-motor skills

(Continued)

Table 2.1 (Continued)

Question No.	Dylexia – Sample screening questionnaire, applied in relation to the inquiry: Does dyslexia influence the entrepreneurial propensity of farmers and their ability to conduct business? Questions:	Testing which function?
14.	What was your favourite subject to study at school? Did you require any additional academic support at school either during your primary or secondary school years?	Comprehension Long-term memory
15.	Is your writing difficult to comprehend?	Visuo-motor skills
16.	Do you find form filling difficult and time consuming?	Concentration
17.	Which way do you best understand information given to you? Visual (e.g. using diagrams, drawings and/or symbols) Auditory (e.g. listening to discussions, recording information and playing it back) Reading/writing?	Concentration Speech & Comprehension
18.	Has dyslexia prevented you from taking up a farming opportunity you would otherwise have liked to undertake?	Lack of confidence
19.	Has dyslexia influenced your everyday farming practices in any way(s)? Give examples.	Concentration
20.	Does dyslexia influence how you conduct your business with the outside world/farming community? Give examples.	Concentration Speech & Comprehension
21.	Have you developed any individual coping strategies to cope with or mask the problem?	Personal skills
22.	If you did not have dyslexia, do you think you would be farming differently?	Adaptability Sequencing

An early version of the dyslexia questionnaire (copyrighted © by G. Conley in 2015) was published in 2015 in the Royal Agricultural Society of England (RASE) Members' Agri-bulletin 1704 (Smith et al., 2015). This table is an updated version of the questionnaire (copyrighted © by G. Conley in 2018).

by doing' (Foster & Rosenzweig, 1995) through a process of 'situated learning' (Lave & Wenger, 1991). Indeed, one is often socialised into its practices as 'farm-reared children' educated on farms by generations of farmers and farming communities (Gasson, 1998). Nevertheless, there is a growing recognition and importance of farm or agricultural entrepreneurship in the academic literature (see–Carter, 2003; Alsos, Carter, & Ljunggren, 2011; Fitz-Koch, Nordqvist, Carter, & Hunter, 2018). This growing interest in studies and textbooks on the topic runs parallel to the notion of the farmer as 'entrepreneur,' as advocated by McElwee, (2006, 2008). This surge in the literature is a testament to the fact that increasingly farmers are becoming more entrepreneurial in their approach. As McElwee (2006, 2008) argues, farmers increasingly have no option but to become more entrepreneurial in both their core and diversified business interests. Nevertheless, the expanding literature has yet to seriously impact the curriculum of the majority of agricultural colleges and universities.

Agricultural colleges and universities play a major part in educating farmers and the future employees of such businesses into farming ways and practices. There are currently 24 such institutions spread across the UK. These act as independent businesses providing practical industry-wide education and training. Most are autonomous, traditional establishments which operate with an independent skills-based curriculum. A few, such as The Royal Agricultural College at Cirencester, now the Royal Agricultural University (RAU); Harper Adams University and the Scottish Rural Universities and Colleges (SRUC) are progressive in their outlook and entrepreneurial ethos. Indeed, at the RAU there is now a specific business school concentrating on entrepreneurship, and a few other progressive institutions have entrepreneurship or enterprise mentioned in their curriculum. Nevertheless, there are few specific modules taught on the subject of agricultural or farm-based entrepreneurship.

This patchwork educational system emerged from the need for the provision of local agricultural colleges within most counties in the UK. The number of such institutions has slowly dwindled over the years due to increasing competition, and most provide a wide variety of certificated, skills-focussed, short courses on practical aspects of agriculture and agri-business, offering a wide variety of qualifications. Many colleges have formed alliances with existing universities or, as with the RAU, Harper Adams University and SRUC, gained university status. Some universities have a longstanding tradition of agricultural science provision, such as the Universities of Nottingham, Reading and Cambridge.

This consolidation of educational delivery combined with a greater focus on agri-business education is in line with the findings of Biere (1998) who reported on the increasing trend for agriculture courses to move towards a more business-orientated curriculum. Moreover, Mulder and Kupper (2006) highlighted a need for management involved in agriculture education to be more entrepreneurial and display courage, ambition and innovation ability. They called for the amalgamation of smaller agriculture colleges into larger units, and for the need to increase the curriculum to include programmes in non-agricultural domains (such as entrepreneurship).

In a similar vein, Etling and Barbuto (2002) made a call for the globalisation of colleges of agriculture in terms of entrepreneurship development programs, because agricultural education has been an essential factor in the success of agricultural development in the Netherlands and elsewhere. Indeed the educational content of such courses needs to reflect the needs of the work environment and job market (Yaghoubi, 2010). Specialist agricultural universities need to demonstrate that they consistently meet or exceed government, research community, employers' and societies' expectations in terms of developing economic and social entrepreneurial skills in their student body (Manning, 2018). There are influences that the agricultural university needs to address including gender influences where females perceive themselves as less entrepreneurial, but a work placement can overcome such social learning and subjective norms (Manning & Parrott, 2018).

The Appreciation of the Role Dyslexia Plays in Shaping Entrepreneurial Propensity

Dyslexia is a real, but often hidden, issue among the farming community which influences the entrepreneurial propensity of farmers and other rural occupations. A propensity is an inclination or natural tendency to behave in a particular way, and an entrepreneurial propensity is an inclination to behave entrepreneurially (Conley et al., 2015).

Statistical work carried out by Dyslexia Scotland indicates that one out of every five rural residents may experience dyslexia, finding it expressed in reading, spelling and arithmetical problems.

Most people with dyslexia cope well with the 'hands-on', practical side of farming but experience problems in recording information on official forms or when engaging in formal learning (Conley et al., 2015). The British Dyslexia Association states that 10% of the U.K. population experiences dyslexia (Webster, 2016). In a study at Harper Adams University, Webster (2016) suggested that 20% of the student population reported experiencing a specific learning difficulty. Webster provides evidence of the problems encountered and the support provided by such institutions to students with dyslexia.

Dyslexia is a hereditary condition and the brains of people with dyslexia are said to be wired differently than the brains of people without dyslexia, resulting in some big positives as well as some big challenges. Dyslexia is a spectrum learning difficulty recognised under the Disability Scotland Act, 2010 and equivalent. Common, generic signs are:

- Slowness in learning to read, write and spell
- A need to read something several times before it is understood
- Continuing to make visual errors in reading, e.g. saying 'was' for 'saw' or 'bad' for 'dad'
- Making bizarre spelling errors that seem unrelated by sound to the intended word
- Difficulties working out sums, problems remembering instructions and confusing or forgetting telephone numbers
- Problems saying long, complicated words or using the wrong name for something, or appearing forgetful or disorganised

As reported in Conley et al. (2015), dyslexia has well-documented advantages and disadvantages; people with dyslexia are often highly intelligent and articulate and, despite having difficulty in learning to read or interpret words, letters and other symbols, they generally possess excellent long-term recall. This is often combined with poor short-term memory but is compensated by creative, three-dimensional (3D) thinking and an ability to think in images. They often confuse left and right; hide difficulties from co-workers, friends and family and seek employment in jobs that mask difficulties. They excel at problem-solving but become frustrated with long forms or sequential processes, and they think outside-the-box. Their symptoms increase dramatically with stress and they require vastly more concentration to read and interpret words than people without dyslexia. They possess a strong sense of justice and thrive in careers (such as farming and the equine industry) where visual-spatial, hands-on-skills can be realised. There is an enduring stigma associated with the condition and many do not report it, including students in agricultural education. This may be through fear of the consequences or through a misplaced sense of shame. Notwithstanding this, Marazzi (2011) argues that far from being a traumatic stigma, dyslexia is a gift and should be regarded as an entrepreneurial skill.

Farming is becoming less of a vocation and more of a business (McElwee & Annibal, 2010) and there is a growing appreciation of learning difficulties such as dyslexia in business per se. In particular, it is now widely accepted that entrepreneurial propensity is affected by learning difficulties or conditions such as dyslexia, dyspraxia, Attention-Deficit/Hyperactivity Disorder (ADHD), Attention Deficit Disorder (ADD), Obsessive Compulsive Disorder (OCD) and some conditions on the Autistic spectrum (see Morris, 2002; Logan, 2001; Smith, 2008; Logan, 2009 for relevant studies). Entrepreneurial propensity influences how one does business and is shaped by one's upbringing, socialisation and exposure to business practices. This is also true in a student body where there can be a marked influence of entrepreneurial legacy from parents and grandparents who participate in family businesses such as agriculture (Manning & Parrott, 2018).

Farrell et al. (2016) examined support services for farmers who experienced dyslexia and investigated how trainees with dyslexia can be supported in workplaces and classrooms and how they can be assisted strategically with the transition between these two environments. They developed a guide for trainees, tutors, training advisers and employers, outlining strategies to improve learning outcomes for trainees with dyslexia and proposed a wraparound support model to guide decision-making about good practice interventions which effectively support trainees with dyslexia. They recommended a targeted learning approach augmented by teaching resources and the provision of more professional development workshops for practitioners.

The study of Conley et al. (2015) articulated the communicational strategies adopted by entrepreneurs to overcome dyslexia. Table 2.2 draws together a typology of generic communicational strategies adopted by entrepreneurs to cope with dyslexia and other learning difficulties with four elements: Pictorial (P), orality (O), behavioural (B) and cognitive (C). Readers with dyslexia may find that some of these strategies resonate

Table 2.2 Specific Communicational Strategies Adopted by Entrepreneurs

Pictorial [P]	*Orality [O]*
Write important details on hand to overcome bad memory.	Learn by listening/Socratic dialogues.
Think in 3D technicolor pictures instead of words. Treat dyslexia as having computer-aided design (CAD) in their brain.	Prefer voicemail to e-mail as it is so much easier to understand and visualize by hearing.
Learn plots and characters in books from pictures. Look at the big picture as a story and envisage how it will end.	Do not keep paper records.
	Surround themselves with verbal people who like to talk.
Prefer summaries in three pages or less with major points highlighted in yellow.	Utilise homespun advertisement campaigns.

Behavioural [B]	*Cognitive [C]*
Avoid using computers.	Shortcut rigorous step-by-step process beloved of sequential thinkers.
Use filo-fax.	Contextualise elements of the story where they fit best.
Bluff way through problems.	Perform mental warm-up exercise each morning.
Avoid maths.	Practice trigger words that confuse.
Use teaching/learning tools.	Fast-forward past the smaller, logical steps of sequential thinkers.
Are highly selective about information input and revise points of importance.	Synthesize things differently and quicker than other people.
Memorise key points.	Wander around themes.
Concentrate on the end results.	Rely on conceptual thinking.
Hire translators to turn intuitive concepts and ideas into reality and interpret ideas to linear thinkers.	Grab abstract information from the environment, often being unaware of its origin.
Minimise reading/writing to conserve energy.	Grasp maximum meaning from minimum content/context.
Commit everything to memory, thus negating working from a script, to avoid mistakes and be dramatic, flexible and able to improvise.	Scan reads, pulling out meaning.
Hire details people, linear thinkers and analysts.	Alternate between apparent disinterest and maniacal focus.
Build a team to shore up weaknesses.	
Alternate between apparent disinterest and maniacal focus.	
Rely on others for telephone numbers.	
Use Global Positioning System to avoid getting lost easily.	
Hide lack of reading ability from others and refuse to show anyone their handwriting.	
Cultivate a casual, can't-be-bothered-with-it management style that avoids the written word.	

(Continued)

Table 2.2 (Continued)

Behavioural [B]	Cognitive [C]
Delegate tasks requiring reading. Avoid the corporate office and travel from place to place observing, talking to customers, making changes. Organize old information into different patterns easily to hide inability to write.	

(Source: Adapted from Morris, 2002; Smith, 2008)

with them. The work of Conley et al. (2015) considered issues of dyslexia from the perspective of local economic development and regeneration at a time of changing government policies and procedures that can affect all types of businesses, causing increasing pressure on industries with a range of salaries and positions such as farming and equine to become more entrepreneurial, whilst employees at all levels still have to navigate the effects of dyslexia in everyday life and work.

The Equine Industry

Equine businesses are heterogeneous, usually situated in a rural environment often resulting from the creation of a stand-alone business or via farm diversification, agri-tourism and leisure and a drive for pluriactivity to improve overall business economic performance (Nickerson, Black, & McCool, 2001; Rantamaki-Lahtinen & Vihinen, 2004; Lobley & Butler, 2010).

Listening to the Anecdotal Evidence

We document anecdotal evidence from websites and blogs which have yet to be incorporated into the academic literature, but use it as grey literature that adds to the more general discourse on the issues of dyslexia in the rural context.

Documenting the 'Farming With Dyslexia Project'

The project came about due to the combined efforts of farmers Sandy McCreath and Sandy Murray, Scotland's Rural College

(SRUC) and Scottish National Farming Union (SNFU), who experienced dyslexia. The formation of a working group posited the following objectives:

- Raise awareness of dyslexia, to reduce the stigma and promote the abilities of individuals experiencing dyslexia which are of great benefit to the agricultural industry.
- Engage with the Scottish government and other stakeholders to ensure measures to recognise dyslexia among the farming community are appropriate.
- Ensure systems of communication with regulatory bodies are more accessible for farmers and crofters with dyslexia, with a choice of delivery options.

Importantly, the group was set up for all persons associated with agriculture, not just farmers. The group's inaugural meeting was held on 3 September 2014 and included representatives from National Farming Union Scotland (NFUS), the Scottish Government's Rural Payments Inspection Directorate, Forestry Commission Scotland, Dyslexia Scotland and Scotland's Rural College along with four farming and crofting members of National Farming Union (NFU) Scotland who have dyslexia. A dedicated telephone number was set up for members. Since its inception, it has helped and supported several hundred students and farmers with issues relating to dyslexia. In March 2015, the Member of the Scottish Parliament (MSP), Claudia Beamish, hosted a Parliamentary reception in support of NFUS's dyslexia campaign and the campaign has attracted considerable press. In May 2015, NFUS launched its Best Practice in Communications Guide to address the challenges faced by farmers and crofters with dyslexia in accessing information.

There have been several success stories including the inspirational story of Kirstie Baird, a student at the SRUC Ayr campus who was diagnosed whilst studying and became a project ambassador (see Hanning, 2016). Kirstie coped with the practical aspects of her degree by a dint of perseverance and determination but found the academic aspects challenging. She had issues with concentration, spelling and reading and overcame this with the use of coloured pens and paper to help her focus on and remember the information taught. She received learning support from college staff to help her with her tendency to skip ahead when writing answers.

Kirstie graduated with a 2.1 and is now pursuing a career in farming. The initiative is a classic example of what combined support can achieve, and acts as a potential template for other countries to adopt. The instances of dyslexia highlighted by the initiative in the farming industry are important but more work is required to replicate the studies in the equine and land-based industries.

Table 2.3 Getting Help

Dyslexia affects every sufferer differently, but support is available to ensure that its effect on you and your farming business is minimised. Whether you're looking to grow your confidence or seeking ongoing professional assistance for an employee or relative, there are many options available to you:

FAQs	*Solutions/Answers*
'I struggle with the farm's form-filling.'	Ask a relative or trusted friend to proofread your submission. You retain your independence but have an extra pair of eyes to pick up on any errors. If you're uncomfortable approaching someone you know, charities such as Dyslexia Action and the British Dyslexia Association can advise on finding additional support.
'I'm leaving agricultural college, but want continued support for my dyslexia.'	Specialist teachers and assessors will exist locally, so speak to your disability co-ordinator and adviser at your college or university or a dyslexia charity to help you find someone suitable.
'I want to help one of the farm's dyslexic employees.'	The government's Access to Work initiative is a free specialist disability service that gives practical employment-related advice and support for those working, self-employed or looking for employment.
'Is there any technology available to help my dyslexia?'	Assistive technology exists such as voice recognition software, text-to-speech communication aids and organisational aids such as mind-mapping software and electronic calendars.

FAQs	Solutions/Answers
'As a parent, what support is available for my dyslexic child?'	Independent Parental Special Education Advice offers free and independent legal information, advice and support to help get the right education and support for children and young people. Dyslexia Action has also produced a guide for parents on what support you should expect from your school.

Documenting the Incidence of Dyslexia in the Equine Industry

To date, there are no known articles in academic journals relating to dyslexia in the equine industry. Consequentially, our knowledge comes to us from newspaper accounts, magazine articles, personal anecdotes and blogs. For example, in an equine industry blog written on Dyslexia Day, 2017 Anne Clarke came out as being a person who experienced dyslexia because she 'wanted to celebrate my own dyslexia in this blog and help remove any shame associated with it' (Clarke, 2017).

Indeed, Clarke did not find out she was someone with dyslexia until she went to university and was diagnosed with the condition. She also revealed that her daughter also experienced dyslexia. Clarke highlighted our studies into dyslexia (see Smith et al., 2015; Conley et al., 2015; Smith et al., 2016), arguing that the same 'issues could be mirrored in the equestrian industry too,' suggesting that as great communicators riding school employees with dyslexia build up a great rapport with clients.

Another anecdote collected relates to the jockey and horse trainer with dyslexia—James Ewart of Craig Farm, Langholm and Dumfriesshire. James grew up on the farm and later attended the RAU at Cirencester before riding out with the legendary John Jo O'Neill. From there, he joined up with Ferdy Murphy, winning his first race. James spent four years in France with the legendary trainer Guillaume Macaire where he won more races, becoming Champion Amateur circa 2000–2001. James has trained over 100 winners and over 300 placed horses. James openly acknowledges that his success was driven by his dyslexia, and the hands-on nature of his operational philosophy.

Whilst it is acknowledged that most farmers and rural employees will be diagnosed whilst at agricultural college, there is still a pressing need for help. See Table 2.3 for details of how to get help (Conley et al., 2015).

Although the previous statements highlight the increasing awareness of dyslexia in land-based industries, there is a pressing need to expand the academic and practical awareness to include the incidence of other learning difficulties such as dyspraxia, ADHD, ADD, OCD and some conditions on the Autistic spectrum, in the farming, equine and other land-based industries.

Concluding the Discussion and Joining the Anecdotes

This chapter has been instrumental in highlighting the importance of the Farming-Dyslexia-Entrepreneurship nexus and the important role played by the UK's agricultural colleges and universities in diagnosing dyslexia and providing support to students who experience dyslexia. Furthermore, it highlights the importance of the link between dyslexia and entrepreneurship and provides some examples of how such institutions are helping propagate an entrepreneurial ethos amongst farmers and agricultural students. There is an evident need for both dyslexia and entrepreneurship to feature more fully in the curriculum.

Moreover, the academic literature and the stories narrated previously, when taken into consideration alongside the work of the 'Farming With Dyslexia' group and the anecdotes of James Ewart and Anne Clarke, provide evidence from the equine industry to demonstrate the prevalence of dyslexia in the land-based industries. Although the 'Farming With Dyslexia' group continues until this day, one of its founding members, Sandy McCreath, no longer engages and has publicly accused the Scottish government of continuing to neglect farmers who experience dyslexia by failing to support them. He highlights the fact that not enough is being done. McCreath has stated that although 'the NFUS thinks the dyslexia campaign has been a great success . . . nothing has changed.' He is of the opinion that although the initiative creates the perception that something is being done, the NFUS and various partners are doing nothing. This chapter gives voice to the Farming-Dyslexia-Entrepreneurship nexus and illustrates what the government, the authorities and, in particular, what the FE and HE sectors are doing to support those within rural communities to cope with and benefit from the gift of dyslexia.

References

Aboudan, R., Eapen, V., Bayshak, M., Al-Mansouri, M., & Al-Shamsi, M. (2011). Dyslexia in the United Arab Emirates University-A study of prevalence in English and Arabic. *International Journal of English Linguistics, 1*(2), 64–72. https://doi.org/10.5539/ijel.v1n2p64

Alsos, G. A., Carter, S., & Ljunggren, E. (2011). *The handbook of research on entrepreneurship in agriculture and rural development.* Cheltenham, UK: Edward Elgar.

Biere, A. W. (1998). Involvement of agricultural economics in graduate agribusiness programs: An uncomfortable linkage. *Western Journal of Agricultural Economics, 13*(1), 128–133. Retrieved from https://core.ac.uk

Carter, S. (1996). The indigenous rural enterprise: Characteristics and change in the British farm section. *Entrepreneurship and Regional Development, 8*(4), 345–358. https://doi.org/10.1080/08985629600000019

Carter, S. (1999). Multiple business ownership in the farm sector: assessing the enterprise and employment contributions of farmers in Cambridgeshire. *Journal of Rural Studies, 15*(4), 417–429. https://doi.org/10.1016/S0743-0167(99)00004-2

Carter, S. (2003, May). Entrepreneurship in the farm sector: Indigenous growth for rural areas. In O. J. Borch & L. Rønning (Eds.), *Entrepreneurship in regional food production* (pp. 22–47, Proceedings of 2nd Nordic Workshop on Entrepreneurship in Regional Food Production). Bodø, Norway: Nordland Research Institute. Retrieved from www.researchgate.net/

Carter, S., & Rosa, P. (1998), Indigenous rural firms: Farm enterprises in the UK. *International Small Business Journal, 16*(4), 15–27. https://doi.org/10.1177/0266242698164001

Clarke, A. (2017). *Dyslexia in the equestrian sector.* Handcross, UK: Connected Thinking Equestrian Consultancy. Retrieved from https://connectedthinkingpr.co.uk/

Conley, G., Smith, R., Smith, A., & McElwee, G. (2015). *Researching the influence of dyslexia on entrepreneurial propensity in the farming community: A preliminary study.* Glasgow, UK: Crichton Institute, University of Strathclyde and Strategic Partners.

Etling, A. W., & Barbuto, J. E. (2002). Globalizing colleges of agriculture. In *Proceedings of the 18th annual conference of the Association for International Agricultural and Extension Education (AIAEE)* (pp. 104–111). Durban, South Africa: AIAEE. Retrieved from www.researchgate.net/

Farrell, M., Styles, M., & Petersen, L. K. (2016). *Supporting dyslexic trainees in classroom and workplace environments.* Adelaide, Australia: VOCED Plus, National Centre for Vocational Education Research (NCVER). Retrieved from http://hdl.voced.edu.au/10707/420299

Fitz-Koch, S., Nordqvist, M., Carter, S., & Hunter, E. (2018). Entrepreneurship in the agricultural sector: A literature review and future research opportunities. *Entrepreneurship Theory and Practice, 42*(1), 129–166. https://doi.org/10.1177/1042258717732958

Foster, A. D., & Rosenzweig, M. R. (1995). Learning by doing and learning from others: Human capital and technical change in agriculture. *Journal of Political Economy, 103*(6), 1176–1209. https://doi.org/10.1177/1042258717732958

Franks, K., & Frederick, H. (2013). Dyslexic and entrepreneur: Typologies, commonalities and differences. *Journal of Asia Entrepreneurship and Sustainability, 11*(1), 95–115. Retrieved from www.researchgate.net/

Gasson, P. H. (1998). Educational qualifications of UK farmers: A review. *Journal of Rural Studies, 14*(4), 487–498. https://doi.org/10.1016/S0743-0167(98)00028-X

Hanning, J. (2016). *Farming with dyslexia: One woman's story.* Jackson, CA: Learning Success. Retrieved from www.learningsuccessblog.com/

Iaquinto, A., & Spinelli, S., Jr. (2006). *Never bet the farm: How entrepreneurs take risks, make decisions—And how you can, too.* San Francisco, CA: Jossey-Bass.

Kirk, J., & Reid, G. (2001). An examination of the relationship between dyslexia and offending in young people and the implications for the training system. *Dyslexia, 7*(2), 77–84. https://doi.org/10.1002/dys.184

Kozinets, R. V. (2015). *Netnography: Redefined.* London, England: SAGE.

Lave, J. (1997). The culture of acquisition and the practice of understanding. In D. Kirshner & J. A. Whitson (Eds.), *Situated cognition: Social, semiotic and psychological perspectives* (pp. 17–36). Mahwah, NJ: Lawrence Erlbaum.

Lave, J., & Wenger, E. (1991). *Situated learning: Legitimate peripheral participation.* Cambridge, UK: Cambridge University Press.

Lobley, M., & Butler, A. (2010). The impact of CAP reform on farmers' plans for the future: Some evidence from South West England. *Food Policy, 35*(4), 341–348. https://doi.org/10.1016/j.foodpol.2010.04.001

Logan, J. (2001). *Entrepreneurial success: A study of the incidence of dyslexia in the entrepreneurial population and the influence of dyslexia upon the entrepreneur* (Unpublished doctoral thesis), University of Bristol, UK.

Logan, J. (2009). Dyslexic entrepreneurs: The incidence; their coping strategies and their business skills. *Dyslexia, 15*, 328–334. https://doi.org/10.1002/dys.388

Logan, J., & Martin, N. (2012). Unusual talent: A study of successful leadership and delegation in entrepreneurs who have dyslexia. *Journal of Inclusive Practice in Further and Higher Education, 4*(1), 57–76. Retrieved from www.brainhe.com/

Manning, L. (2018). Enabling entrepreneurial behaviour in a land-based university. *Education and Training, 60*(7/8), 735–748. https://doi.org/10.1108/ET-03-2017-0036

Manning, L., & Parrott, P. (2018). The impact of workplace placement on students' entrepreneurial attitude. *Higher Education, Skills and Work-based Learning, 8*(1), 56–69. https://doi.org/10.1108/HESWBL-05-2017-0030

Marazzi, C. (2011). Dyslexia and the economy. *Angelaki: Journal of the Theoretical Humanities, 16*(3), 19–32. https://doi.org/10.1080/0969725X.2011.621216

McElwee, G. (2006). Farmers as entrepreneurs: Developing competitive skills. *Journal of Developmental Entrepreneurship, 11*(3), 187–206. https://doi.org/10.1142/S1084946706000398

McElwee, G. (2008). A taxonomy of entrepreneurial farmers. *International Journal of Entrepreneurship and Small Business, 6*(3), 465–478. Retrieved from www.researchgate.net/

McElwee, G., & Annibal, I. (2010). Business support for farmers: An evaluation of the Farm Cornwall project. *Journal of Small Business and Enterprise Development, 17*(3), 475–491. https://doi.org/10.1108/14626001011068743

Morris, B. (2002, May 13). Overcoming dyslexia. *Fortune Magazine.* Retrieved from https://archive.fortune.com/

Mulder, M., & Kupper, H. (2006). The future of agricultural education: The case of the Netherlands. *The Journal of Agricultural Education and Extension, 12*(2), 127–139. https://doi.org/10.1080/13892240600861658

Nickerson, N. P., Black, R. J., & McCool, S. F. (2001). Agritourism: Motivations behind farm/ranch business diversification. *Journal of Travel Research, 40*(1), 19–26. https://doi.org/10.1177/004728750104000104

Pense, S. L. (2009). Curricular needs of students with specific learning disabilities in Illinois secondary agricultural education programs. *Journal of Agricultural Education, 50*(2), 89–101. Retrieved from https://files.eric.ed.gov/

Pense, S. L., Watson, D. G., & Wakefield, D. B. (2010). Learning disabled student needs met through curriculum redesign of the Illinois agricultural education core curriculum. *Journal of Agricultural Education, 51*(2), 117–127. Retrieved from https://opensiuc.lib.siu.edu/

Rantamaki-Lahtinen, L., & Vihinen, H. (2004, October). The role of equine industries in Finnish rural development—Rural entrepreneurship and policy perspectives (pp. 1–10). Preliminary draft of a paper presented at *Horse management—Premises and landscape* (Seminar 367). Alnarp, Sweden: Nordic Association of Agricultural Scientists (NJR). Svala, C. (Seminar Secretariat) Lantbrukets byggnadsteknik (LBT). Retrieved from www.researchgate.net/

Richardson, J. T. (2009). The academic attainment of students with disabilities in UK higher education. *Studies in Higher Education, 34*(2), 123–137. https://doi.org/10.1080/03075070802596996

Scott, J. (2014). *A matter of record: Documentary sources in social research.* London, England: John Wiley.

Sharma, M. C., Tiwari, R., & Sharma, J. P. (2010). *Entrepreneurship in livestock and agriculture.* New Delhi, India: Vedams Books Pvt Ltd/CBS Publishers & Distributors Pvt Ltd India.

Smith, R. (2008). Being differently abled: Learning lessons from dyslexic entrepreneurs. In R. T. Harrison & C. M. Leitch (Eds.), *Entrepreneurial learning: Conceptual frameworks and applications* (pp. 291–312). Abingdon, UK: Routledge.

Smith, R., Conley, G., McElwee, G., & Smith, A. M. J. (2015). *Articulating the farming with dyslexia conversation* [Paper 1704, Members Agri-bulletin]. Royal Agricultural Society of England. Retrieved from www.researchgate.net

Smith, R., Conley, G., Smith, A. M. J., & McElwee, G. (2016). Assessing the impact of "Farming with dyslexia" on local economies. *Local Economy, 31*(4), 529–538. https://doi.org/10.1177/0269094216655404

Stampoltzis, A., & Polychronopoulou, S. (2008). Dyslexia in Greek higher education: A study of incidence, policy and provision. *Journal of Research in Special Educational Needs (JORSEN), 8*(1), 37–46. https://doi.org/10.1111/j.1471-3802.2008.00100.x

Taylor, K. (2003). Occupation choices of adults with and without symptoms of dyslexia. *Dyslexia, 9*(3), 177–185. https://doi.org/pdf/10.1002/dys.239

Yaghoubi, J. (2010). Study barriers to entrepreneurship promotion in agriculture higher education. *Procedia-Social and Behavioral Sciences, 2*(2), 1901–1905. https://doi.org/10.1016/j.sbspro.2010.03.1006

Webster, D. M. (2016). Listening to the voice of dyslexic students at a small, vocational Higher Education Institution to promote successful inclusive practice in the 21st century. *International Journal of Learning and Teaching, 2*(1), 78–86. https://doi.org/10.18178/ijlt.2.1.78-86

3 Dyslexia, Entrepreneurship, and Education in Singapore

Deborah Hewes and
Geetha Shantha Ram

Introduction

Singapore takes great pride in its academic outcomes for its students and, in a 2018 Organisation for Economic Co-Operation and Development (OECD) report, (Mahmud, 2018) Singapore was found to be one of the most academically resilient nations. As the people of Singapore are its only natural resource, academic progress is something that the country takes very seriously. Therefore, when students struggle to attain grades necessary for higher education, there is the potential for such students to be looked upon negatively and, consequently, it causes great concern for parents who watch their children struggle and fail. There is a culture and belief in Singapore that to be able to contribute to the progress of Singapore you need to be academically successful, achieve a tertiary education and then find a good paying job.

In response to the Singaporean preoccupation with academic excellence, the Ministry of Education, Singapore, has recently announced certain critical and strategic changes such as removing examinations for students in the primary one and two levels, targeting instead for a more holistic approach to evaluating student learning and achievements. Similarly, 'secondary one' students will not be required to take mid-year examinations and report books for students will no longer include positional ranks, comparing the individual with their peers in class (Ministry of Education, 2018). Additionally, there has been a continued effort to encourage Singaporean parents to see the value in a polytechnic and vocational education, where traditionally a university degree was always seen as a guarantee for success. All change requires time, and, despite these efforts, the majority of Singaporeans still equate academic success with success in life.

Therefore, implicit in this culture of the pursuit of academic excellence is the inevitable stigma when students face difficulties in learning. The stigmatisation of a learning difference is, therefore, a major concern for the Dyslexia Association of Singapore (DAS) and the students that it supports. A Singaporean study by the Lien Foundation in 2016 revealed that 30% of those surveyed found Singapore to be inclusive when it involved children with special needs, in contrast to the 25% who found Singapore to be an inclusive society. While that suggests that Singapore was more inclusive in the area of special needs, only 32% believed that typically developing children are comfortable interacting with children with special needs and only one in ten Singaporeans were sure about how to interact with children with special needs. Not surprisingly, 65% were concerned that children with special needs were at risk of being bullied (Lien Foundation, 2016). Although attitudes are clearly evolving in Singapore towards inclusiveness and acceptance of children with special needs, further growth is needed for societal acceptance of diverse student strengths as well as acceptance of the weaknesses of dyslexia.

Embrace Dyslexia

In a concerted effort to change the conversation about learning differences in Singapore and to make a conscious move to highlight the strengths and talents of individuals with learning differences, the DAS launched the Embrace Dyslexia campaign (DAS, 2020). The 'Embrace Dyslexia' campaign was launched in 2014 with a seminar featuring Thomas West as a guest speaker who helped to deliver the positive dyslexia message. The campaign gathered personal stories of those with dyslexia and found a strong unified voice and a platform. The sharing by everyone was truly enlightening and inspirational. Many had the determination, passion and willpower to make a significant and meaningful contribution to Singapore. Arguably they were not defeated by dyslexia, far from it; many were, in fact, empowered by it.

Many of these personal stories were published in the book, *Embrace a Different Kind of Mind, Personal Stories of Dyslexia* (Hewes, 2015). The first story in the book was that of the late Mr Lee Kuan Yew, Singapore's first Prime Minister and recognised as Singapore's founding father. Mr Lee revealed he had dyslexia in 1996 and his announcement helped remove some of the stigma of having a learning difference and paved the way to better public awareness and acceptance of dyslexia.

The late DAS President, Jimmy Daruwalla, commented about Mr Lee, '[the] greatest thing he did for us was to remove the stigma' (Wan, 2017, p. 6). Daruwalla was the presiding President of DAS from 1992 until his untimely death in July 2016. He was a true crusader for the dyslexia cause and his work was recognised and rewarded by Singapore. Daruwalla saw dyslexia as an asset. He often said, 'the only natural resource available to us in Singapore is human capital. We cannot afford to let even one single child fall by the wayside' (Hewes, 2015, p. xvi).

Daruwalla was a true believer, and he often quoted the London Cass Business School research study by Julie Logan, which found that 35% of successful entrepreneurs in the US identified themselves as experiencing dyslexia (Logan, 2009). He believed that there were more entrepreneurs with dyslexia because of their ability to see the big picture, that they had the drive and determination to succeed because of the failure they had experienced frequently in their earlier years and they had developed creative solutions to deal with their failures (Hewes, 2015, p. xvi). Daruwalla hoped a similar study would be completed in Singapore and mentioned this on many occasions in his speeches on behalf of DAS. He hoped that a study would reflect favourably on Singapore and that individuals with dyslexia would be looked upon as being able to contribute to Singapore despite their struggles with learning.

Entrepreneurs With Dyslexia

When we think of successful people who experience dyslexia, we immediately visualize the likes of the Formula One (F1) racer Sir Jackie Stewart, chef and entrepreneur Jamie Oliver, paleontologist Jack Horner, actress Keira Knightly and the highly successful entrepreneur Richard Branson. Not surprisingly, a 2003 study conducted by the British Broadcasting Corporation found that 40% of about 300 millionaires were either people with dyslexia or had related difficulties (Malpas, 2017). Additionally, a US study found that 35% of US entrepreneurs were individuals with dyslexia, which follows a UK study revealing that, in comparison to the average citizen, a UK entrepreneur is five times more likely to experience dyslexia (American Management Association, 2019). Although the sample size of the study was small and therefore the results must be interpreted with caution, there appears to be clear links made between success, entrepreneurs and dyslexia. Malpas (2017) investigated what people with dyslexia attributed their success to. Highly successful individuals who experience dyslexia are therefore determined, out-of-box thinkers and problem solvers, creative, pause and think before acting, have found the right purpose and place that amplifies their strengths, confident, empathetic, personable and sociable with good conversational skills and are strategic with awareness in using appropriate coping strategies. While we have read about these successful individuals with dyslexia and can recognise these traits in them, how do we enable all our learners with dyslexia to find their successes?

Three successful entrepreneurs with dyslexia are featured later in this chapter, and their stories reflect the similar challenges and successes faced by people with dyslexia all over the world. The first story is about a talented designer, inventor and creator of educational toys, Gary Seow. Diagnosed with dyslexia in his late 40's, he is very grateful for the diagnosis which provided the key to understanding why he struggled so much with learning and in his working life. The second story is about Patrick Siah, a talented interior designer with a master's degree in architecture. Patrick was diagnosed early with dyslexia and his story reflects how successful someone with dyslexia can be, when supported early in education, and how individuals with dyslexia and with superior visual talents can be successful. The final story is about Edward Yee, Singapore's first Rhodes Scholar in 14 years. Edward is very vocal about his dyslexia and how it has made a significant difference in his education journey and in his words, 'I am successful because of my dyslexia, not in spite of it' (Yee, 2018).

Gary Seow–Inventor and Creator of Educational Toys*

Gary's story was originally published in the book Embrace a Different Kind of Mind, Personal Stories of Dyslexia.

(Hewes, 2015)

Like many individuals with dyslexia at Gary's age (late fifties), diagnosis and understanding of why they have struggled with learning have come late in life. Gary was only diagnosed in his late 40's with dyslexia, and his diagnosis gave him a lot of relief. Gary remarked,

> *Suddenly I understood all my frustrations and confusions in my earlier years—the last piece of the puzzle to the great mystery after my diagnosis.*
>
> (Hewes, 2015, p. 172)

Gary went through many jobs at all different levels and he realised that he could not work at the same pace as his colleagues especially using spreadsheets, interpreting charts and graphs and remembering numbers and figures. He was once publicly accused of falsifying accounts in front of his work colleagues which was embarrassing and humiliating. Gary had not keyed in his sales figures and targets correctly, which, whilst he didn't do so deliberately, was a big mistake he admits.

So, when his wife, Carrie Chan, said she would partner with him in their own business, he was delighted to have control over his own destiny. Their two young children at the time were the inspiration for their company. They were looking for teaching resources for their children and found that there was not a one-stop shop that stocked unique educational toys and resources, and so KYDZ International was founded, a distributor and maker of educational toys for young children (Broc Consulting, 2017). In his own business, Gary is now able to focus on his strengths and he delegates to his wife and staff the things that he is not good at. He turned his disability into a strength driven by a passion to better empower those like him.

Gary believes that dyslexia is his gift and this allows him to design his new toys faster than reading. He explains that he would prefer to listen to someone describing a problem to him than read a document describing the issue. Technology has liberated him; he now listens to audio books and watches YouTube videos, he uses spell checker apps but still uses his wife to help him communicate with others.

Gary is a big picture thinker and does not like the detailed decisions that come with business, especially the accounts. Gary says that he is also a picture thinker; he visualises things in pictures and everything that he designs he can see in three-dimensional (3D) manner. He has a clear understanding in his mind of his designs and how they come together. He also has a strong pattern awareness and can make connections that others do not see. He has the ability to turn things inside out and see them shifting perspective, and this gives him the creativity to design his unique toys.

The toys that Gary creates are beautiful and unique. He finds peace when he is making things with his hands, playing with the toys and being able to take them to other countries and see how they are adopted by children in other cultures. He can visualise his projects and where his next project will take the business. He loves to combine new materials with his ideas in trying to fill a gap that he sees in the market. He designs toys with the child in mind and you can see the child within Gary when he demonstrates how to use the toys he creates. Gary believes that dyslexia is positively correlated with creativity. Because learning is hard for him, it forces him to think harder and creatively out of the box to find solutions. Combined with this hard-working ethic and this tenacity, he feels blessed to be able to devote his talents into his own business.

For Gary, design is part of his DNA. Gary says that it is his greatest joy to have control over his own environment and run his own business, so he can do what he is truly good at and bring in people to do the things he doesn't like; 'I shine better when I can control my own destiny' (Hewes, 2015, p. 174).

Patrick Siah–Interior Designer*

> *Patrick's story was originally published in the book* Embrace a Different Kind of Mind, Personal Stories of Dyslexia.
>
> (Hewes, 2015)

Mr Patrick Siah, the owner of an interior design firm, W5A LLP, was diagnosed with dyslexia when he was ten years old. Learning was a real struggle for Patrick, and he said of his learning when in primary school, 'Everyone around me was trying their best to help me, and I was trying hard, really hard. No results. I felt like the tortoise in 'The Tortoise and the Hare' except that this tortoise would never win the race' (Hewes, 2015, p. 181). Despite his struggles in learning, Patrick worked hard, and with the support of DAS, was able to pass his Primary School leaving exam and move onto secondary school.

Patrick's aspirations to become an architect were due to two factors. Firstly, Patrick grew up watching Pierre Png's character, architect Phua Chu Beng, on the local sitcom, Phua Chu Kang. His quirky portrayal of an architect holding rolled up pieces of paper, together with his white helmet, made him want to be like him. (Dyslexia Association of Singapore, 2012). Secondly, he excelled in Design and Technology (D&T) in secondary school. People with dyslexia can be talented in three dimensional (3D) visual concepts, and Patrick capitalized on these skills to perform well in this subject. Patrick recalls,

> *I found myself learning very well in classes involving 3D elements and that reaffirmed my calling for the architecture industry.*
>
> (Hewes, 2015, p. 182)

Patrick was able to achieve the 'Tan Kah Kee Young Inventors Award' in secondary school, which for him was a life-changing event and added to his dream of becoming an architect.

Patrick chose to go to the University of Melbourne where he graduated with a bachelor of environment degree, majoring in architecture and a Master of Architecture degree, with high distinction. Patrick's master's thesis was titled 'An Architectural Exploration into Dyslexia.' The thesis project, a 'School for Dyslexics' as well as the 'Headquarters for the Australian Dyslexia Association' explored the social paradigms of youths who experience dyslexia, the educational and political issues that have arisen as well as an alternate relationship of space and pedagogy supporting dyslexia.

On graduation, Patrick returned to Singapore and was employed by a large architectural firm. While there he took the opportunity to learn from the experts around him, he learned to listen and take notice about what they were doing. He was privileged to be surrounded by experts, and using them as mentors and asking the right questions helped Patrick to develop further as an architect. At the firm he worked at, he was completing more large-scale international work but Patrick wanted to focus on smaller, more intimate projects in Singapore. So, when the time was right, at 27 years old, Patrick decided to open his own business, W5A. W5A was named after the Singapore Polytechnic Architecture Block, a learning space that brought back many fond memories for Patrick. He remembers the long nights he would sometimes spend trying to finish assignments and projects. So W5A represented the foundation of the working spirit he felt here in Singapore at Singapore Polytechnic where he started to embrace his dyslexia (Singapore Polytechnic, 2014).

Patrick's vision of his company is to,

> *[d]eliver the amazing. [With a] vision to deliver unparalleled design solutions and service, which is distinctive, distinguished and exceptional. At W5A we are dedicated to creating awesomeness.*
>
> (W5A Design, 2018)

On reflection, Patrick says,

> *I would not have been where I am today without the support from my family, the Dyslexia Association of Singapore, and a goal. That goal was to be an architect someday. For students like me, and especially my two nephews who also have dyslexia, the most important thing is to never give up even if you feel like you're the worst at a lot. Embrace this wonderful gift and you will never regret it!*
>
> (Hewes, 2015, p. 183)

Edward Yee–Rhodes Scholar and Change Maker Who Experiences Dyslexia*

> **Edward's story was originally published in* Embrace a Different Kind of Mind, Personal Stories of Dyslexia.
>
> (Hewes, 2015)

Edward Yee is the co-founder of GivFunds, who lends extremely low-cost loans to social enterprises across South Asia. Taking an ecosystem-level approach, Givfunds partners with some of the largest social enterprise aggregators in the region to lend at scale to existing pools of social enterprises (GivFunds, 2018). Edward explains that his dyslexia has helped him as he journeyed from a struggling student to a Rhodes Scholar and now has big plans for the world.

Like any person who experiences dyslexia, Edward Yee struggled in his early education. Fortunately, his mother was quick to see the signs and responded immediately. She read about dyslexia and sent her son for an assessment at the DAS. He was nine. Of course, at that time, Edward was not aware of the situation. It was only after his parents received the assessment report that they sat down with him and explained that he had dyslexia.

Fast forward to secondary school, Edward was accepted into the Integrated Programme in Secondary 3, where he skipped O Level examinations and went straight to the National Junior College. There he was able to utilise his dyslexia better due to the versatile teaching methods and subjects that he studied. He began seeing things much clearer.

> *The multidisciplinary education and opportunities to learn beyond the textbooks helped me develop an inkling of, in the words of Charlie Munger, Worldly Wisdom. This education also encouraged me to embrace how I think differently. The relative freedom from major examinations allowed me to take on various extra-curricular activities, attend Model United Nation (MUN) Conferences and organise events. My experiences have helped me appreciate thinking differently.*
>
> (Hewes, 2015, p. 249)

During National Service, his interest in investments and fund management sparked, and he even decided then that he was going to be a value investor in the future. Then, his passion shifted to entrepreneurship. While his initial motivation was monetary gain, eventually Edward realised that this was not what his goal in life was. It took a few failures and advice from his mentor to give him the wakeup call he needed.

> *My mentor asked me, is this something that I wanted to do in the next 6 or 7 years in my life? Is this something that I see myself doing long term? And the answer really was, no.*
>
> (Yee, 2018, p. 69)

With that, Edward packed his bags and he began a journey of self-discovery. He spent about a month at Bangladesh with Muhammad Yunus at Yunus Centre where he learnt about social enterprises and social businesses. He extended his break to find his purpose; and for about three and a half months, Edward went backpacking across Southeast Asia.

> *I met the most amazing people. People who taught me the meaning of empathy and what it means to be a humble human being. When I talked to people who appeared to be the outcast of society, I realised that they were not just made up of unfortunate tales. They were people who have stories like us. They were people with dreams and problems. They are more multifaceted than we think. Meeting these people was incredibly inspiring and I learned a lot from them along the way. That journey helped me find my purpose.*
>
> (Yee, 2018, p. 69)

Travelling across India on an 8,000 km train journey with over 500 people for 16 days from Mumbai and back on Jagriti Yatra, Edward crossed paths with social entrepreneurs, change makers and Non-Governmental Organisation founders. He met a girl who had never stepped her foot out of her province, but she and four others have taught over 4,000 women how to use the internet – and they learnt it all by themselves. 'That is when you really bonded with people and where the magic really happens. It was on that train journey that I found my co-founder and key advisor for GivFunds.'

Since then, GivFunds has won many awards such as the Epilogue Social Entrepreneurship Competition and the Ideasinc Accelerator Award for 2017. GivFunds is a social organisation that lends low-cost loans at scale to South Asian social enterprises. Through an ecosystem-level approach and tech-enabled processes, Edward and his team unlock sustainable capital for social enterprises to create greater impact and change lives.

The Rhodes Trust prides itself in its mission to identify and develop leaders to achieve public good. Each year, a class of 100 scholars, selected from over 60 countries. The trust prepares their scholars to make a positive impact on the world by providing a combination of a collaborative and dynamic environment, intensive and challenging education and a focus on character, service and leadership. As the nature of the scholarship aligns with his ambitions to make a difference using the world's funds, Edward applied for it. Edward is looking forward to studying at Oxford University, undertaking a master's programme in Social Data Science and Evidence-Based Social Intervention and Policy

Evaluation. He believes these degrees would help him better design a social intervention programme and measure its impact, as well as utilise data to create outcomes and allocate resources better (Lim, 2018).

> *I never really saw dyslexia as something to overcome but a strength/ tool to make use of. Throughout my schooling years, I was able to solve problems differently from others and was never wholly able to solve them the conventional way taught by teachers. Dyslexia also helped me understand that it is okay to fail, but to embrace and learn from mine and others' failures, hence my favourite quote by Sir Isaac Newton, 'If I have seen further, it is by standing on the shoulders of giants.' There is an African proverb that says, 'If you want to go fast, go alone. If you want to go far, go together.'*
>
> (Dyslexia Association of Singapore, 2018)

Reflecting on his dyslexia, Edward states that it has helped him to think differently. He is a believer that people with dyslexia have a different way of looking at the world. Unfortunately, he knows that many individuals who experience dyslexia do not reach the point of being able to see that.

> *If you ask around, who do you think are iconic people who are very different in the world today? They will bring up names like Henry Ford, Richard Branson, Albert Einstein, Steve Jobs and all of them are dyslexic. I think it's the advantage of seeing the world in a very different lens, both by nature and nurture. Nature because of dyslexia, nurture because of the way you overcome your challenges in the earlier days. My dyslexia helped me see in a different light and to some extent I see a greater duty to give back. If I pick a different route today and choose not to go down the path of helping social entrepreneurs, I do not think I can forgive myself 10 to 20 years on when I look back at this moment. That, to me, is how dyslexia shaped them. That is why I said I am here because of dyslexia and not despite it.*
>
> (Yee, 2018, p. 69)

Edward sees himself working to help change makers through providing capital and finance that they and he can make a greater impact in the world.

Education in Singapore

In Singapore, a great deal is known about the experiences of children with dyslexia; however, while dyslexia is commonly understood as a learning difficulty, it is still largely seen from the context of young children and the support and understanding provided for children in preschool, primary and secondary levels. Too few people understand the contribution to the economy made by individuals with dyslexia and we are still learning about the experiences of young adults in tertiary education and those in the workforce. Therefore, it is crucial that we remind ourselves that dyslexia is a lifelong learning difficulty and its challenges evolve with the expectations of the different levels of education, in careers and in society.

Some common challenges at the tertiary level include grappling with cross-faculty modules, multitasking, project management and a greater expectation to manage note taking and independent studies. As recounted by a student support officer, one such student, Reuben, was enrolled in university and despite his best efforts, found the challenges and the fear of stigmatisation overwhelming. He eventually dropped out of university, believing that he had overreached in pursuing a college degree. Based on our experiences in supporting young adults who have dyslexia, many students, like Reuben, choose not to disclose their dyslexia or pursue support due to a poor appreciation of needs. For fear of ostracisation and/ or stigmatisation, many young adult students prefer to keep their dyslexia a secret from their schoolmates and teachers, choosing instead to struggle in silence.

Teachers too are often unable to support them at that level due to inadequate training and resources and may have the perspective that students who have made it that far in their educational journey must know how to deal with it. Not surprisingly, the preference not to reveal their dyslexia is not peculiar to students and is, in fact, common among working adults too. Kindersley (2016) observes that working adults may not want to reveal their dyslexia as a lack of clarity on what it is among colleagues and employers may result in their weaknesses being highlighted or amplified. Their dyslexia may also impact their career progression, where they may be overlooked for promotions. Incidentally, even their employment may be affected.

In spite of the challenges, which incidentally are global concerns, there have been some positive developments and the post-secondary and tertiary educational landscape in Singapore has evolved over the past decade. Increasingly, there is an acknowledgement of the presence of learners with dyslexia and other specific learning differences in Institutes of Higher Learning (IHL) and some attention is being paid to them. However, existing policies and funding largely cover students with more visible disabilities, but tend to miss out on students with hidden handicaps like dyslexia. Following consultations with various IHLs, it quickly became clear that to best support post-secondary learners with dyslexia, a holistic support model must be employed that combines raising of awareness, a formal investigation of needs and training for teachers to identify and support learners in school.

Thus, was born a vision—the 360° Pact (Samsudin & Shantha Ram, 2018). This pact is based on a framework that effective intervention begins with internal awareness raising, which includes a cognisance of both staff and peers, a formalised and systematic screening and identification effort whereby the students themselves, teachers and classmates might be able to recognise signs of need and teacher readiness. The 360° Pact is simplified by these three words prompting action–KNOW, FIND AND LEARN:

KNOW—we hope to work through three different levels:

1. The students and peers: Students and peers will be engaged via library talks, exhibitions and encouraged to participate in Community Service projects that involve a developing understanding of what dyslexia and learning disabilities are.
2. Staff: Staff too will be exposed to dyslexia through talks, exhibitions and access to experts and platforms for forums to dialogue with specialists will be created for them.
3. School: At the school level, the administration is encouraged to initiate and normalise the conversation about dyslexia and learning disabilities through posters and visuals, and highlighting voices of students with dyslexia through their publications, etc.

FIND—as dyslexia is a hidden disability, the next step in the pact requires an active effort to find these learners. Using screeners and checklists to first identify at-risk learners (before encouraging and supporting these learners to be assessed so as to fully appreciate their learning profiles, needs and strengths). Find is also an important step for us to better appreciate the extent of the prevalence of dyslexia in IHLs.

LEARN—This is seen through two groups: Teachers/staff and students.

1. Teachers/Staff: Teachers and staff are then encouraged to receive training to better support these learners in their classrooms. Professional exchanges with the schools Special Education Needs unit and case management discussions promote further refinement of the knowledge and skills required to support learners in their classroom.

2. Students: By working with the schools, provision of intervention programmes targeting areas such as study skills, digital literacy, executive functioning and metacognition are made available for learners with dyslexia in this final step. Further, compulsory modules or workshops on supporting peers with needs are recommended to build a group of student mentors who can support their fellow students with needs.

A similar effort by the British Dyslexia Association, to improve workplace environments and encourage a Dyslexia-Friendly workplace, comprises the acronym CAPPUCCINO. Beetham (2016) describes the training that is conducted to promote environmental changes in the workplace where the following is considered:

- Culture of the organisation—are they prepared and embracing or simply performing a policy-related change?
- Awareness raising—to increase their understanding of dyslexia and associated difficulties.
- Practical and reasonable adjustments are suggested to fully embrace diverse co-worker(s).
- Peer support systems are then encouraged for the continued support.
- Unlawful practices avoided—to educate human resources and leaders of the organisation on policies against discrimination.
- Communication, which needs to be Dyslexia-Friendly, is emphasised both internally as well as externally.
- Computers and assistive technology can level the playing field but should be accompanied by the awareness that different tools will benefit different users and that not all tools will be suitable for all.
- Individual assessment and support—this involves a meeting with a Workplace Needs Assessor, who then makes recommendations for the necessary accommodations.

- NO to failure, where with the right support and accommodations an employee who has dyslexia will be able to achieve.

These are frameworks that can holistically improve the circumstances for current and future young adults with dyslexia, but the conviction to begin the process of change is key to any stage of success.

Conclusion

Through the case studies of these three successful entrepreneurs who have dyslexia, we can begin to appreciate and understand both the challenges and strengths of people with dyslexia. Inspired by these true stories, we hope the conversation at the tertiary institution levels continue by raising awareness of dyslexia within the educational institutions and by assisting teachers to identify students with needs in classes.

Interestingly, while inherent characteristics of successful people who experience dyslexia are important, Scott, Scherman and Phillips (1992), found that a significant difference between people with dyslexia who were successful or not, was the existence of a strong champion—someone who believed in them and found ways for them to highlight their strengths, as we've seen in Gary's case study in the shape of his wife. Through the joint efforts by the ministry and organisations like DAS, we as a community can champion the cause for our individuals who experience dyslexia and perhaps hope to recruit many believers in our efforts.

And yet there is more work that needs to be done, and our tertiary learners and those in the workforce must join in as we affirm and empower everyone living with dyslexia. Alumni groups made up of individuals who have dyslexia can then formalise mentoring of others like them, which is a critical piece of this puzzle to empowerment efforts. Mentors, as witnessed by Edward's experiences, are instrumental in shaping the dreams and aspirations of young people with dyslexia.

Continued research and studies are important to elucidate the way forward. Investigations into the incidence rates of dyslexia in IHLs and the continued review of support structures and their effectiveness are necessary. Additionally, DAS, as a Singapore organisation that is looked upon as an expert in the field of dyslexia and learning differences, it still has a long way to go in its development to support adults with dyslexia and it looks towards partners in the industry for guidance on how to do this. Further studies into Singaporean entrepreneurs who experience dyslexia are currently being conducted by the author, Deborah Hewes, and results of this research were released in 2020 (Hewes, 2020). As with the research conducted by Logan (2009), from the London Cass Business School, this Singaporean research study will explore the incidence and attributes of entrepreneurs in Singapore who are dyslexic, with the addition of controls who are not themselves dyslexic to inform the results. Combining the power of research to establish prevalence with continued advocacy and the appropriate support, DAS looks to a future for all that embrace dyslexia completely.

References

American Management Association (AMA). (2019). *AMA self study*. Retrieved from www.amanet.org/

Beetham, J. (2016). Dyslexia friendly workplace. In V. van Daal & P. Tomalin (Eds.), *The dyslexia handbook* (pp. 163–166). Bracknell, UK: British Dyslexia Association.

Broc Consulting. (2017). *Brand spotlight -KYDZ international*. Retrieved from http://webcache.googleusercontent.com/

Dyslexia Association of Singapore (DAS). (2012, October 4 to December 30). Patrick Siah, aspiring architect. *FACETS*. Retrieved from www.das.org.sg/

Dyslexia Association of Singapore (DAS). (2018). *Edward Yee. DAS blog, DAS student alumni stories*. Retrieved from https://das.org.sg/

Dyslexia Association of Singapore (DAS). (2020). *About embrace dyslexia*. Retrieved from https://das.org.sg/

GivFunds. (2018). *About us*. Retrieved from http://givfunds.com

Hewes, D. (2015). *Embrace a different kind of mind–Personal stories of dyslexia*. Singapore: Dyslexia Association of Singapore.

Hewes, D. (2020). Entrepreneurs with dyslexia in Singapore: The incidence, their educational experiences, and their unique attributes. *Asia Pacific Journal of Developmental Differences, 7*(2), 157–198. DOI:10.3850/S2345734120000103

Kindersley, K. (2016). Dyslexia in the workplace: Awareness and adjustments are essential. In V. van Daal & P. Tomalin (Eds.), *The dyslexia handbook* (pp. 167–174). London, England: British Dyslexia Association.

Lien Foundation. (2016). *Inclusive attitudes survey part 1. Views of the general public*. Singapore: Lien Foundation. Retrieved from www.lienfoundation.org/

Lim, J. (2018, October 19). Dyslexia helped him become who he is today, says first Singapore Rhodes Scholar in 14 years. *Today*. Retrieved from www.todayonline.com

Logan, J. (2009). Dyslexic entrepreneurs: The incidence; their coping strategies and their business skills. *Dyslexia, 15*, 328–334. https://doi.org/10.1002/dys.388

Mahmud, A. H. (2018). *Singapore ranks high on educational mobility: OECD report*. Singapore: Channel News Asia. Retrieved from www.channelnewsasia.com/

Malpas, M. (2017). The characteristics of successful dyslexic adults. In P. Tomalin & K. Saunders (Eds.), *The dyslexia handbook* (pp. 231–236). London, England: British Dyslexia Association.

Ministry of Education (Singapore). (2018). *Learn for life—Preparing our students to excel beyond exam results*. Singapore: Ministry of Education. Retrieved from www.moe.gov.sg/

Samsudin, N. A., & Shantha Ram, G. (2018, June). *A 360° post-sec pact* [Conference presentation in Uniting Ideas in Teaching Excellence: Specific Learning Differences (UnITE SpLD) Conference]. Singapore: Dyslexia Association of Singapore (DAS). Retrieved from www.youtube.com/

Scott, M., Scherman, A., & Phillips, H. (1992). Helping individuals with dyslexia succeed in adulthood: Emerging keys for effective parenting, education and development of positive self-concept. *Journal of Instructional Psychology, 19*(3), 197–204. Retrieved from https://search.proquest.com/openview/

Singapore Polytechnic. (2014). At 27 he has his own company. *Spirit, 3*, 31. Retrieved from sp.edu.sg/docs/

W5A. (2018). *Profile*. Retrieved from http://www.w5a.com.sg/profile.html

Wan, W. (2017). *Clearly different: Dyscovering the differences*. Singapore: World Scientific.

Yee, E. (2018). Edward Yee, dyslexic Rhodes scholar and change maker from Singapore. *FACETS, 3*, 68–70. Retrieved from das.org.sg/

4 Entrepreneurship, Dyslexia, and the Modern World

A Positive Psychology Approach

Poliana Sepulveda and
Roderick Nicolson

Introduction

Theories and definitions about entrepreneurship have taken a number of different approaches. According to Gartner (1988), entrepreneurship has been categorised as a behaviour description; Gartner, Bird, and Starr (1992) discuss entrepreneurship as a type of organising exploring its relationship to organisation behaviour theory, at the same time describing entrepreneurship theory as emergent. Others, such as Shane and Venkataraman (2000), explain entrepreneurship as focusing upon the exploitation of opportunities. Entrepreneurship theory has continued to develop. Definitions of entrepreneurship may focus on such broader personal characteristics as owning a business, being active in management, or even expressing the intention of pursuing these actions; other definitions may take a stricter view.

It is useful to look at definitions of entrepreneurship, but, regardless of theory or definition, more people than ever seek to be entrepreneurs. Some individuals want to pursue entrepreneurship because of the freedom to work with flexibility. Others want to escape from a pre-decided, standardized structure, and there are even those who have an inner wish to achieve something unique and specific in their lives. For all these purposes, people who experience dyslexia seem more likely to be the ones who seek entrepreneurship opportunities throughout life; attuned to this approach as responses to their early challenges to learning. Gartner (1985) argues that entrepreneurs are composed of a very diverse group but they all have something in common, in their personality traits.

Although dyslexia has been broadly studied, specific issues concerning the relationship of people who experience dyslexia with entrepreneurship have had few publications. Two such publications are by Smith (2008) and Franks and Frederick (2013). Both of these used secondary sources to examine the overlap of entrepreneurial and traits associated with dyslexia in order to arrive at an understanding of the characteristics of entrepreneurs who experience dyslexia. The best-known study in this area is Logan (2009), which is the subject of this chapter and its underpinning empirical research (Sepulveda, 2013, 2014).

Entrepreneurs, Entrepreneurship and Entrepreneurial Traits

Rauch and Frese (2007) support the view that personality traits are responsible for making someone an entrepreneur. A meta-analysis by Zhao and Seibert (2006) also confirms that entrepreneurship can be predicted by personality traits.

Rauch and Frese describe entrepreneurs as having essential, defining parameters; this differentiates them from others. The authors consider that an entrepreneur needs to be someone who is ready to find and exploit new opportunities; they also need to act rapidly when taking decisions under stressful and uncertain contexts. The authors also state that entrepreneurs have to work more, and harder, than non-entrepreneurs do, since they have to be the ones with the vision. These demands require entrepreneurs to have a great diversity of abilities, knowledge and specific and general skills (Shane & Venkataraman, 2000; Venkataraman & Sarasvathy, 2001).

Furthermore, Rauch and Frese (2007) consider that in order to accomplish all the tasks previously stated, entrepreneurs have to have traits such as: the need for achievement, autonomy, internal locus of control, innovativeness, proactivity, generalized self-efficacy, resilience and also risk-taking. They take the view that the need for achievement belongs in the entrepreneur's list of traits because, along with their tasks, entrepreneurs also need to be aware of their performances and what has been done well. This trait creates a sense of challenge for entrepreneurs and makes them responsible for their results.

Innovativeness is another trait that has been seen as essential for entrepreneurs, since they have to look for new ideas and new solutions; it also helps them in problem solving. According to Rosenbusch and Bausch (2005), innovation is related to a company's success. This confirms that people can be entrepreneurs even when not owning their own business, because the innovation can take place in any business, their own or others'.

Generalised self-efficacy is considered to be a personality trait of importance for entrepreneurs (Baum & Locke, 2004) because people who perform highly in this characteristic tend to persevere when uncertain situations and problems arise, in order to win the challenge and also to find opportunities within the difficulties.

Another trait that is very common to see in entrepreneurs is the need for autonomy. They would rather have control over a situation, being people who prefer to set goals, develop their work and control it by themselves. Entrepreneurs prefer to avoid any restrictions and rules, and so people who have entrepreneurial behaviours often choose to start their own business rather than work for a company (Cromie, 2000).

The last trait that Rauch and Frese find to be fundamental for entrepreneurs is internal locus of control. People who have this characteristic strongly believe that outcomes depend on their own actions. In a business context, this means that the profits they generate are the consequence of their hard work. People with high internal locus of control strive to achieve their goals and persist more to achieve their outcomes. This is essential for starting and maintaining a successful business (Rauch & Frese, 2007).

Positive Psychology and Dyslexia

Medical theory and psychological discourse explain dyslexia in terms of deficit, focusing on its identity as a learning disorder. However, another perspective within psychology, known as positive psychology, discusses the advantages and good qualities that people with dyslexia may have, compared to people without dyslexia. According to Sheldon and King (2001), positive psychology is the science that studies the strengths, qualities and virtues of human beings. They state, '*Positive Psychology revisits the average person, with the interest in finding out what works, what is right, and what is improving'* (Sheldon & King, 2001, p. 216).

Positive psychology focuses on the motives, capacities and potential of individuals. Sheldon and King argue that positive psychology can be surprisingly difficult to accept by many scholars and psychologists because they have been trained to view positivity in a cynical manner, to ask questions and to generate a sense of doubt in relation to it. However, excess dubiousness can naturally lead to a negativity bias that may just see one perspective and not have a clear or coherent understanding of the reality of a scenario.

Positive psychology has three main areas. The first is that of positive experiences, which includes optimism, well-being, happiness and self-determination. However, these could be dependent on a specific moment of happiness; that is why the second thread is positive personality. Out of all positive psychology studies, the underlying common finding is that individuals are self-directed, self-organising and flexible beings. The approaches for the second thread take into consideration an explicit developmental aspect, which is the view that a human being has an endlessly-feeding supply of strengths which unfold throughout their entire life.

The third thread in positive psychology is that individuals belong to a social context and are in a state of constant experience with other individuals. Thus, positive psychology recognizes positive institutions such as family, schools, companies and society as characteristic of the final thread (Seligman & Csikszentmihalyi, 2014).

According to Peterson, Maier, and Seligman (1993), another key theory influencing positive psychology is that of learned helplessness. This suggests that individuals who have experienced traumatic events in life may feel unworthy and disempowered, and reluctant to take actions, believing that outcomes from past experiences could be reproduced in the present. It is clear at this point that positive psychology is trying to change the old purpose of psychology. In the past, the common aim was to cure the negatives, but positive psychology has argued that such a process does not necessarily produce positives.

Nowadays, with positive psychology's approach, practitioners have sufficient knowledge to work on prevention, and the amplification of a client's strengths. Drawing on this new approach may enable society to have much stronger individuals—mentally and emotionally—by taking into consideration the effects of mental well-being. Moreover, a fundamental goal for positive psychology is the re-orientation of traditional pyschology, with a focus on stronger, fulfilled and more productive people (Seligman & Csikszentmihalyi, 2014).

Some scholars do not endorse the movement of positive psychology, claiming that it places too much pressure on the individual and that it sends a separate message to society (Held, 2004). Nonetheless, as Peterson states:

> Nowhere does this definition say or imply that psychology should ignore or dismiss the very real problems that people experience. Nowhere does it say or imply that the rest of psychology needs to be discarded or replaced. The value of Positive Psychology is to complement and extend the problem-focused psychology that has been dominant for many decades.
>
> (Peterson, 2009, p. XXIII)

The highest aim of positive psychology is to re-direct the efforts of psychology away from a more remedial, reformative preoccupation with the worst scenarios in life and towards developing and evolving the highest qualities in a person. Its purpose is to focus on the building of society's strengths, leading to the prevention rather than the remediation of mental illness (Seligman, 2002; Simonton & Baumeister, 2005). This perspective illuminates the phenomenon of entrepreneurship when manifested in conjunction with dyslexia, allowing for examination and positive discussion of traits identified as characteristic of entrepreneurs who experience dyslexia.

A positive psychology perspective provides a useful context for Logan's (2009) research, since this can be seen as supporting a positive view regarding dyslexia. Logan considers that, compared to others, people who experience dyslexia tend to be more entrepreneurial, since they seek new standards and new structures. This happens because very often they struggle to feel comfortable or happy in their employment, and they may feel pressure to catch up with other employees. This is likely to be a reason why they choose to open their own businesses. The qualities they present, according to Logan (2009), are valuable when it comes to starting their own venture; these are strongly related to entrepreneurial behaviours, as described by Rauch and Frese (2007). In addition, Eide and Eide (2012) identify qualities such as creativity, resilience, empathy and communication skills as providing advantages enabling individuals with dyslexia to succeed in work and in life generally.

When Entrepreneurs Experience Dyslexia: Entrepreneurial Traits and Strategies

Julie Logan's research (2009) explores the intersection of entrepreneurship and dyslexia, comparing dyslexia in entrepreneurs, in corporate managers and in the population generally; her research also compares characteristics in the UK and the USA. Using a business-focussed definition of entrepreneurship (Bolton & Thompson, 2000), Logan conducted a study with 139 adults, in which 102 were entrepreneurs and the other 37 were corporate managers. Out of the sample, 39 adults were people who experienced dyslexia and 100 were people without dyslexia.

Logan's study indicates that there is a high incidence of entrepreneurs experiencing dyslexia (92.3% of all respondents with dyslexia, 26% of total respondents). There is a smaller percentage of people with dyslexia who are corporate managers. Logan herself states that '[t]here is a significantly higher incidence of dyslexia in entrepreneurs than in the corporate management and general US and UK populations' (Logan, 2009, p. 328). Morgan and Klein report research comparing the incidence of entrepreneurs in an American sample of people with dyslexia (15%) with the reported incidence of being a corporate manager, which was found to be less than 1% (Morgan & Klein, 2000). Taken together, these studies show how much greater the incidence of people with dyslexia being entrepreneurs is compared with corporate managers.

Logan (2009) states that people with dyslexia learn coping strategies from an early age, due to their educational struggle, until they reach self-awareness of their strengths and weaknesses and can find their own equilibrium. She considers that these strategies can provide a good competitive advantage for the entrepreneurial world. Logan identified three main groups of variables, relating to: Business characteristics, personal qualities and experience in childhood and youth.

Although people who experience dyslexia may show interesting and valuable qualities when working in a company, they may suffer a lack of support and recognition within the establishment. Starting a business of their own may allow people with dyslexia to concentrate their qualities on a purpose which seems more useful to them, with entrepreneurship being an area where they can use their strengths for their own benefit. They may employ their creativity by using coping strategies which help them to overcome their weaknesses, for example by delegating a task in which they themselves would struggle and lose too much time (Logan, 2009).

In Logan's study, it is notable that entrepreneurs with dyslexia were found to have the same level of personal confidence as entrepreneurs without dyslexia, suggesting that they did not feel undermined by the experience of having dyslexia. A further finding identified through Logan's sub-group study showed that both entrepreneurs and corporate managers with dyslexia considered that their communication skills were strong. No specific findings were evident for: "[s]elf-confidence, public speaking, artistic ability and sport ability" (Logan, 2009, p. 335).

In addition to coping strategies, entrepreneurs who experience dyslexia may also have other significant traits that help them to succeed in the entrepreneurial world, such as creativity, empathy and entrepreneurial orientation (Reid & Kirk, 2001). The characteristics found by Logan among entrepreneurs with dyslexia included delegation, risk-taking and good communication skills. Confirmation of these is found in the qualitative empirical research described next.

A Further Examination of Traits Among Entrepreneurs Who Experience Dyslexia

In an empirical study using qualitative methods (Sepulveda, 2013), ten entrepreneurs with dyslexia were interviewed in order to discuss the themes that clustered around entrepreneurial traits and those which clustered around traits associated with dyslexia, with the intention of establishing whether people who experience dyslexia are more likely to have entrepreneurial behaviours. The interviewees included four from the University of Sheffield, selected from a previous data set, and six from Brazil, contacted through the Brazilian Dyslexia Association. A total of 11 trait and behaviour themes were identified:

- Communication skills
- Resilience
- Delegation/team work/shared tasks
- Vision
- Proactivity
- Risks with precautions
- Empathy

- Freedom
- Entrepreneur family
- Ask for help/modesty
- Control

Some of these themes confirmed Logan's analysis, but some traits were newly identified by the study.

Communication Skills

This trait, according to Logan's (2009) study, was found to be strong in entrepreneurs with, as opposed to those without, dyslexia. The latter ranked themselves as average to good in this trait, while the majority of entrepreneurs with dyslexia considered themselves to be 'very good.' Nicolson, Fawcett, Berry, Jenkins, and Dean (1999) argue that good communication skills are part of the coping strategies of people who experience dyslexia, compensating for their disadvantage in writing skills. Both Smith (2008) and Franks and Frederick (2013) also note the importance of good communication skills for entrepreneurs who experience dyslexia.

Sepulveda's study confirms this; the most important trait found, in among around 80% of the participants, was good communication skills. Entrepreneurs in this qualitative study who experienced dyslexia showed this trait consistently. The trait is fundamental because possessing this characteristic means that a person is likely to have a persuasive personality. This can increase the performance level of leadership tasks and tasks associated with sales, as suggested by Clarke (2007). Clarke considers that this relationship between persuasion and entrepreneurship is not only about communication, dialogue and a linguistic process but rather is an entire relational perspective, which, '[a]llows us to examine how entrepreneurs use a variety of means to create meanings and convince others of the validity of the venture' (Clarke, 2007, p. 91).

Communication is a crucial skill for being successful in the business world and this helps entrepreneurs with dyslexia to inspire others by having, or achieving, a vision (Logan, 2009). Logan states that entrepreneurs who experience dyslexia understand this skill to be a great advantage, since it facilitates networking, clarity when setting goals, the establishment of trust and also the motivation of those who work with them. It can influence other characteristics, such as networking and persuasiveness. These in turn can transform a company's vision in concrete ways, having a positive effect on the company's overall performance.

Delegation

Logan's (2009) study found that entrepreneurs with dyslexia were more likely to have the delegation quality in their personality than entrepreneurs without dyslexia. In her study, Logan found that the majority of her respondents delegated tasks in which they felt weak, such as writing a memo. She points out the importance of delegating while growing a business, because the right person would be fitted into the right task, saving money and time when those tasks are executed. According to Mazzarol (2003) and Timmons (1999), delegation is an important factor for entrepreneurs because it is a good predictor for business growth. However, they also state that it is a difficult trait to have and maintain since it requires good relationships and also trust in partners and co-workers. These authors consider that entrepreneurs who have this trait are more likely to have a faster growth in their businesses.

In Sepulveda's study, this trait of delegation appeared strongly among the participants. This confirms Logan's findings and supports the conclusion that entrepreneurs with dyslexia have this trait as an entrepreneurial advantage, making for a positive influence upon the speed of a company's growth. This strategy gives rise to two points of interest. The first of these is that entrepreneurs who experience dyslexia must have good awareness in order to delegate the right tasks; the second is that good relationships and trust are needed in order to perform well when delegating those tasks. A reason for this may be that entrepreneurs who experience dyslexia learn since early childhood about their weaknesses; consequently, they are aware about when it would be advantageous for another person from the business team to execute a specific task.

Delegation and team-working skills in the personalities of entrepreneurs with dyslexia may be linked to the fact that they are likely to be very self-aware, due to previous personal experiences. Delegation could be a trait that advantages entrepreneurs with dyslexia over entrepreneurs without it, since they may benefit when it comes to working in teams and apportioning work.

Risk With Precautions

Logan's (2009) study identified a relationship between people with dyslexia and risk-taking. In her study, entrepreneurs without dyslexia ranked themselves as having a high level of risk-taking, while entrepreneurs with dyslexia perceived themselves as less risk-averse, having a 'very high' level of risk-taking. However, as previously mentioned, one of the participants was also diagnosed with Attention-Deficit/Hyperactivity Disorder (ADHD), so this finding cannot exclude the possibility of another relationship between ADHD and risk-taking.

In Sepulveda's study, risk-taking was an important characteristic found in the majority of the participants, supporting Logan's finding. However, Sepulveda's research found this to be mitigated by precaution-taking. The characteristic was strongly evidenced in the qualitative research, with all of the participants saying that they would take risks but with some precautions. These precautions included:

- having the proper knowledge,
- having a specific background,
- knowing the environment in which they were planning to operate,
- being financially careful.

Risk-taking and working under pressure were two results that appeared in different answers in this study, however in the analysis they were found to be related. This is because once entrepreneurs who experience dyslexia do not feel afraid of taking diverse risks, they are consequently not scared to work in uncertain situations. According to Rauch and Frese (2007), entrepreneurs have a very high internal locus of control, which means that they feel they can control their outcomes at uncertain situations. Their business risk-taking is high, since entrepreneurs believe that they can prevent issues by predicting them. Since they believe they can control their outcomes in this way, if the solution to a business task or problem suggests itself to them, they are not afraid to face uncertain situations and are ready to work under pressure.

Resilience

Resilience is one of the traits newly identified by Sepulveda. It appears to be a fundamental entrepreneurial characteristic which can provide advantages to entrepreneurs, for example when they are working in unusual situations.

Masten (2001) and Ungar, Dumond and McDonald (2005) argue that a person who has lived through a traumatic experience without giving up and has been able to maintain their normal psyche can be considered as resilient. Individuals with dyslexia may have suffered considerable bullying and prejudice in their lives, and the majority of participants in the qualitative research may have had to overcome situations of this kind. With this in mind, it could be said that people who experience dyslexia are resilient beings.

Vision

Vision, as a characteristic, appeared strongly among the respondents in Sepulveda's (2013) qualitative research. The majority of the participants in the study saw themselves as visionaries. Vision was a trait much mentioned by academics, for example Rauch and Frese (2007); these authors see its importance for entrepreneurs in providing the first step in setting goals, seeing new opportunities and tackling challenges. However, this trait was not discussed in the literature about dyslexia. This indicates that it is a newly-identified trait for entrepreneurs who experience dyslexia, as shown by the qualitative research.

Proactivity

In the qualitative study, the characteristic of having a proactive personality was a newly-identified trait for respondents, being found strongly among the entrepreneur participants who experienced dyslexia. The majority of respondents considered themselves to be proactive.

Frese and Fay (2001) state that a proactive personality is something intrinsic and individual for each person. According to them, proactivity is a fundamental trait needed by entrepreneurs because it is related to the necessary ability to influence environments when setting up their own business. An entrepreneur has to be the role model for their whole organization, and if they do not provide the first step then their employees may not follow their lead (Crant, 1996). Proactivity may be one of the most important traits that an entrepreneur should have.

Empathy

Empathy was found as a new trait present in potential entrepreneurs with dyslexia as a result of the qualitative research. This can be explained through the understanding that since entrepreneurs with dyslexia have strong communication skills, this can lead them to be more outspoken and responsive people, which in turn can have an effect on how empathetic they are.

Johnson (2003) points out that empathy is a characteristic that can be a personality trait predictor for entrepreneurs. He states that entrepreneurs are often more inclined to be person-oriented rather than task-oriented. This can be a valuable trait, since once an individual is leading an entire company they have to ensure that colleagues and employees are working in teams. To do otherwise can cause the company to have a poor performance and a poor result at the end of the month. Empathy, then, appears to be another quality demonstrated by entrepreneurs who experience dyslexia, giving them an advantage in communication and understanding that has an impact upon their business competitiveness.

Freedom

A further new trait identified by the qualitative research was freedom. The majority of participants said that they preferred to work under pressure and also performed better in these circumstances. They claimed that stressful and pressured situations made them feel more focussed and provided them with more challenges, suggesting that the characteristics of freedom (autonomy), control and resilience can be set against such stresses.

Interestingly, there is a possible connection between control and the need for autonomy (freedom) shown in in relation to entrepreneur behaviour; these are traits which entrepreneurs with dyslexia demonstrate strongly, according to the findings of this study. Connecting these with the risk-taking finding, the conditions required in order for entrepreneurs to take business risks are that they have to be in uncertain situations and perform well in such situations. In addition, they have to be very resilient. The desire for freedom and control of the situation, together with resilience, override the uncertainty of the business situation.

Furthermore, Poon, Ainuddin, and Junit (2006) consider that stress tolerance is important for a good performance when a person is running their own business, because entrepreneurs have to take personal and financial risks constantly, and are also likely to be overworking, which itself can be very stressful. The authors define stress tolerance as the equilibrium state for successful entrepreneurs.

Family

An interesting result found in the qualitative study was the influence of the family upon the career choices of entrepreneurs who experienced dyslexia. All the participants in the sample stated that they had a family member who was an entrepreneur. In the majority of the cases they mentioned parents rather than more distant relatives.

This confirms Logan's (2009) finding, which showed a positive influence from the families of entrepreneurs with dyslexia on their decisions to open their own businesses. Logan noted that parents' influence is also related to the fact that dyslexia is often hereditary; parents with dyslexia could be role models for their entrepreneurial children through their running of a successful family company at the same time as coping with dyslexia.

However, in the qualitative research, one participant stated that her sister also experienced dyslexia, indicating that while entrepreneur family members may be important for the career choices of people with dyslexia the fact of those family members being parents with dyslexia may not. While, in this variable, it is possible to identify the importance of the family in the matter of entrepreneurial career choices, further research would be needed to clarify these findings.

Ask for Help/Modesty

The trait identified as ask for help/modesty was also found among respondents in the qualitative research; this trait has not been discussed in previous studies concerning either entrepreneurship or dyslexia. There may be a relationship between this characteristic and dyslexia because, from an early age, learners who experience dyslexia become self-aware of weaknesses and have to develop coping strategies. The trait is also relevant for entrepreneurship, with its relationship to growth and its importance in asking for help from network contacts such as partners, co-workers and experts.

Control

According to previous literature and to the findings of the qualitative research (Sepulveda, 2013), it was possible to create a link with the trait of control, based upon analysis identifying internal locus of control and risk-taking. Participants in the research stated that whenever they feel they have control of the situation, they feel that they are performing at their best and it is the most comfortable situation for them. This was an important finding in the qualitative study, the result corroborating Logan's (2009) and Rauch and Frese's (2007) views about entrepreneur behaviours; specifically, that if they think they can control the outcomes, entrepreneurs will take a business risk and feel more comfortable. Rauch and Frese explained how control is related to the need for autonomy, stating,

> Need for control is also associated with entrepreneurs' avoidance of restrictive environments; they prefer to make decisions independent of supervisors, to set their own goals and develop their own plans and actions, and to control goal achievement themselves. People with high need of autonomy want to be in control.
>
> (Rauch & Frese, 2007, p. 359)

Expanding the awareness and understanding of traits found among entrepreneurs who experience dyslexia helps to create a more nuanced appreciation of how they go about doing business. Fitzgibbon and O'Connor (2002) consider that people with dyslexia develop fundamental coping strategies to overcome their weaknesses, and state that these strategies make their entrepreneurial characteristics much stronger. Smith goes further, stating that, 'Entrepreneurs turn dyslexia deficits into advantages' (Smith, 2008, p. 24). The wider discussion of traits evidenced by respondent entrepreneurs who experience dyslexia, as described in this chapter, offers some indications as to the ways in which this might occur.

Conclusion

The qualitative research described in this chapter confirmed findings from the previous literature. People who experience dyslexia were found to be resilient beings, possibly because of traumas they had suffered in their early age but which they were able to overcome, and, in doing so, were able, later, to develop strengths. Entrepreneurs who experienced dyslexia preferred the freedom of autonomy, giving them control over a business situation, but were also found to be strong in delegation skills, which contributed highly to effective team-working and sharing of tasks. Such traits are crucial for entrepreneurs, supporting their awareness of their own strengths and weaknesses and helping them to develop the skill of delegating the right tasks to the right people.

The findings of the qualitative research present a usefully expanded insight into the traits of entrepreneurs with dyslexia, many of which were predicted by Logan (2009) and by others and some of which are new. However, the traits of family entrepreneurship and vision were not broadly commented upon in the literature before, and the trait of ask for help/modesty was not mentioned at all. It may be the case that this trait is in some way linked with confidence, or its lack, and further investigation of this characteristic may be useful.

The most important traits for entrepreneurs with dyslexia, as confirmed by this study, were:

- family influence in choosing an entrepreneurial career,
- freedom, since entrepreneurs with dyslexia do not enjoy having rules, standards and structures imposed by their workplace,
- empathy, relating to how person-oriented the entrepreneur is in the workplace, and its importance when an entrepreneur aims to develop team-working at their company,
- risk, with protective precautions, linked to the characteristic of entrepreneurs' high level of internal locus control,
- proactivity, identified by theory and by the study participants as being a characteristic of entrepreneurial behaviour that is presented in entrepreneurs who experience dyslexia, since they are likely to be self-starters and to seek for opportunities,
- communication skills, which was highly predicted by authors in both dyslexia and entrepreneurship.

A profile emerges of people with good communication skills which do not depend on information exchange through literacy. The literature indicates that people with dyslexia find it difficult and stressful to work in companies that have their own hard rules and standards. They would rather have situations where they can command their own days, determining their daily choices and controlling the outcomes. The traits and behaviours identified in the literature, and in the qualitative research described in this chapter, are characteristics which lend themselves to this kind of entrepreneurial action. Whether such traits include genetic influences beyond that of a genetic component for dyslexia remains a question for further research.

For individuals who experience dyslexia, good communication skills can be a way to compensate for literacy skills compromised by dyslexia. Being good at communication is crucial for an entrepreneur since this ability is related to persuasion. For entrepreneurs, and particularly for entrepreneurs with dyslexia, it is a necessary, and fundamental, trait. Since entrepreneurs who experience dyslexia are less likely to rely on information conveyed through the medium of literacy, it may be a key characteristic, and, as such, worthy of further research.

The qualitative research described in this chapter follows the perspective of positive psychology, focusing on the positive characteristics developed by entrepreneurs with dyslexia. In doing so, it sheds further light upon the tendencies and preferences of entrepreneurs who experience dyslexia, as individuals and as a group. These characteristics, combining non-genetic traits and acquired behaviours developed through their own personal propensities, can be turned to advantage as strategies. These may enable individuals with dyslexia to become effective entrepreneurs, should their interests and drives lead them in that direction.

References

Baum, J. R., & Locke, E. A. (2004). The relationship of entrepreneurial traits, skill, and motivation to subsequent venture growth. *Journal of Applied Psychology, 89*(4), 587–598. Retrieved from https://citeseerx.ist.psu.edu/

Bolton, B., & Thompson, J. (2000). *Entrepreneurs: Talent, temperament, technique.* Oxford, UK: Butterworth-Heinemann.

Clarke, J. S. (2007). *Seeing entrepreneurship: Visual ethnographies of embodied entrepreneurs* (Doctoral thesis). University of Leeds, UK. Retrieved from http://etheses.whiterose.ac.uk/

Crant, J. M. (1996). The proactive personality scale as a predictor of entrepreneurial intentions. *Journal of Small Business Management, 34*(3), 42–49. Retrieved from www.researchgate.net/

Cromie, S. (2000). Assessing entrepreneurial inclinations: Some approaches and empirical evidence. *European Journal of Work and Organizational Psychology,* 9(1), 7–30. https://doi.org/10.1080/135943200398030

Eide, B., & Eide, F. (2012). *The dyslexic advantage: Unlocking the hidden potential of the dyslexic brain.* New York, NY: Hudson Street Press/Penguin.

Fitzgibbon, G., & O'Connor, B. (2002). *Adult dyslexia: A guide for the workplace.* New York, NY: John Wiley and Sons Inc.

Franks, K., & Frederick, H. (2013). Dyslexic and entrepreneur: Typologies, commonalities and differences. *Journal of Asian Entrepreneurship and Sustainability,* IX(1), 95–115. Retrieved from www.researchgate.net/

Frese, M., & Fay, D. (2001). Personal Initiative (PI): An active performance concept for work in the 21st century. *Research in Organizational Behavior, 23,* 133–187. https://doi.org/10.1016/S0191-3085(01)23005-6

Gartner, W. B. (1985). A conceptual framework for describing the phenomenon of new venture creation. *Academy of Management Review, 10*(4), 696–706. https://doi.org/10.5465/amr.1985.4279094

Gartner, W. B. (1988). "Who is an entrepreneur?" Is the wrong question. *American Journal of Small Business, 12*(4), 11–32. https://doi.org/10.1177/104225878801200401

Gartner, W. B., Bird, B. J., & Starr, J. A. (1992). Acting as if: Differentiating entrepreneurial from organizational behavior. *Entrepreneurship Theory and Practice, 16*(3), 13–32. https://doi.org/10.1177/104225879201600302

Held, B. S. (2004). The negative side of positive psychology. *Journal of Humanistic Psychology, 44*(1), 9–46. https://doi.org/10.1177/0022167803259645

Johnson, S. (2003). Social entrepreneurship literature review. *New Academy Review, 2,* 42–56.

Logan, J. (2009). Dyslexic entrepreneurs: The incidence; their coping strategies and their business skills. *Dyslexia, 15,* 328–334. https://doi.org/10.1002/dys.388

Masten, A. S. (2001). Ordinary magic: Resilience processes in development. *American Psychologist, 56*(3), 227–238. Retrieved from www.ocfcpacourts.us/

Mazzarol, T. (2003). A model of small business HR growth management. *International Journal of Entrepreneurial Behavior and Research, 9*(1), 27–49. https://doi.org/10.1108/13552550310461036

Morgan, E., & Klein, C. (2000). *The dyslexic adult in a non-dyslexic world.* London, England: Whurr.

Nicolson, R., Fawcett, A. J., Berry, E. L, Jenkins, I. H., Dean, P., & Brooks, D. J. (1999). Association of abnormal cerebellar activation with motor learning difficulties in dyslexic adults. *The Lancet, 353*(9165), 1662–1667. https://doi.org/10.1016/S0140-736(98)09165-X

Peterson, C. (2009). Foreword. In C. R. Snyder & S. J. Lopez (Eds.), *Oxford handbook of positive psychology* (p. XXIII). Oxford, UK: Oxford University Press.

Peterson, C., Maier, S. F., & Seligman, M. E. P. (1993). *Learned helplessness: A theory for the age of personal control.* New York, NY: Oxford University Press.

Poon, J. M. L., Ainuddin, R. A., & Junit, S. H. (2006). Effects of self-concept traits and entrepreneurial orientation of firm performance. *International Small Business Journal, 24*(1), 61–82. https://doi.org/10.1177/0266242606059779

Rauch, A., & Frese, M. (2007). Let's put the person back into entrepreneurship research: A meta-analysis on the relationship between business owners' personality traits, business creation, and success. *European Journal of Work and Organizational Psychology, 16*(4), 353–385. https://doi.org/10.1080/13594320701595438

Reid, G., & Kirk, J. (2001). *Dyslexia in adults, education and employment.* Chichester, UK: Wiley.

Rosenbusch, N., & Bausch, A. (2005, January). *Does innovation really matter? A meta-analysis on the relationship between innovation and business performance* [Presentation at Babson College Kauffman Foundation Entrepreneurship Research Conference], Babson College, Babson Park, MA.

Seligman, M. E. P. (2002). Positive psychology, positive prevention, and positive therapy. In C. Snyder & S. Lopex (Eds.), *Handbook of positive psychology* (pp. 3–9). Oxford, UK: Oxford University Press. Retrieved from www.positiveculture.org/

Seligman, M. E. P., & Csikszentmihalyi, M. (2014). Positive psychology: An introduction. In M. Csikszentmihalyi (Ed.), *Flow and the foundations of positive psychology* (pp. 279–298). Dordrecht, The Netherlands: Springer.

Sepulveda, P. (2013). *Entrepreneurial tendencies in dyslexic adults: Quantitative and qualitative analyses* (Unpublished master's thesis). University of Sheffield, UK.

Sepulveda, P. (2014, September). Dyslexics and their entrepreneur behaviours. In R. Dautov, P. Gkasis, A. Karamanos, T. Lagkas, A. Prodromidou, & A. Ypsilanti (Eds.), *Proceedings of the ninth annual south-east European doctoral student conference* (pp. 671–690). Sheffield, UK: South East European Research Centre, University of Sheffield. Retrieved from www.researchgate.net/

Shane, S., & Venkataraman, S. (2000). The promise of entrepreneurship as a field of research. *Academy of Management Review, 25*(1), 217–226. https://doi.org/10.5465/amr.2000.2791611

Sheldon, K. M., & King, L. (2001). Why positive psychology is necessary. *American Psychologist, 56*(3), 216–217. http://dx.doi.org/10.1037/0003-066X.56.3.216

Simonton, D. K., & Baumeister, R. F. (2005). Positive psychology at the summit. *Review of General Psychology, 9*(2), 99–102. https://doi.org/10.1037/1089-2680.9.2.99

Smith, R. (2008). Being differently abled: Learning lessons from dyslexic entrepreneurs. In R. Harrison & C. M. Leitch (Eds.), *Entrepreneurial learning: Conceptual frameworks and applications* (pp. 291–312). Abingdon, UK: Routledge.

Timmons, J. A. (1999). *New venture creation: Entrepreneurship for the 21st century* (5th ed.). Singapore: McGraw-Hill.

Ungar, M., Dumond, C., & McDonald, W. (2005). Risk, resilience and outdoor programmes for at risk children. *Journal of Social Work, 5*(3), 319–338. https://doi.org/10.1177/1468017305058938

Venkataraman, S., & Sarasvathy, S. D. (2001). Strategy and entrepreneurship: Outlines of an untold story. In M. A. Hitt, R. E. Freeman, & J. S. Harrison (Eds.), *Blackwell handbook of strategic management* (pp. 650–668). Oxford, UK: Blackwell Publishers Ltd.

Zhao, H., & Seibert, S. E. (2006). The big five personality dimensions and entrepreneurial status: A meta-analytical review. *Journal of Applied Psychology, 91*(2), 259–271. Retrieved from http://pdfs.semanticscholar.org/

5   Dyslexia, Entrepreneurship, and Transition to Decent Work

Maximus Monaheng Sefotho

Introduction

This chapter explores dyslexia, entrepreneurship and transition to
decent work with a focus on youth with dyslexia. After the exclusionary
development agenda of the millennium development goals, world leaders
heeded the plight of people with disabilities for inclusive economic
growth through decent work for all. The 2030 Agenda for Sustainable
Development has goal 8 dedicated to decent work for inclusive economic
growth for all; 'Fostering humane and productive work in conditions
of freedom, equity, security and dignity' (Sengenberger, 2001, p. 39).
Ghai (2003) describes decent work as encapsulating 'employment, social
protection, workers' rights and social dialogue' (p. 113).

Employment in the context of inclusion encompasses both formal and
informal inclusionary and dignified employment. All workers deserve to
be protected from work that may be harmful to their well-being, therefore
must enjoy healthy working conditions. Human rights are central to
issues of inclusion and sustainable development. Workers' rights must
be protected at all times for there to be social justice. Social dialogue
is critical to bring about social cohesion between the excluded and the
excluding. Social dialogue could promote epistemological empowerment,
creating space for the silenced voices of the excluded to express
themselves without fear or favour. Paremiography is the well-spring

that provides 'the evaluative force of a proverb' to give deep meaning to language and culture for social connectedness and eventual participation in entrepreneurship and decent work (Aciobăniţei, 2012, p. 277). Paremiography is the collection of proverbs, while paremiology pertains to the study of proverbs 'for their linguistic, didactic or ethnolinguistic value, since antiquity' (Sevilla-Muñoz, 2016, p. 667). Both aim at curating meaning hidden in proverbs for educational purposes.

The chapter establishes an understanding of dyslexia and then reviews dyslexia in the workplace, and how young people with dyslexia face a dilemma transitioning into the world of work. The chapter equally reviews dyslexia and entrepreneurship as an alternative to decent work. The Basotho ontology of disability provides a theoretical framework that serves as an instrument of empowerment for youth with dyslexia. Wadlington and Wadlington (2005) established that there are misconceptions about dyslexia among educators that warrant deliberate efforts to try to understand it. The next section is about understanding dyslexia.

Dyslexia is a neuro-developmental disorder (Wajuihian & Naidoo, 2011) specifically affecting reading and spelling of words (Hultquist, 2006). It is generally agreed that dyslexia evades definition (Petretto & Masala, 2017) but that it encompasses 'difficulties in word recognition, spelling, and phonological recoding' (Tunmer & Greaney, 2010, p. 231). The Greek etymology of dyslexia derived from two words: δυσ—dys (meaning hard or difficult) and λέξις—lexis (meaning word or words) (Tunmer & Greaney, 2010), while lexia derived from alexia (inability to understand writing) denotes an impairment in regards to word recognition, spelling and phonology. Dyslexia, therefore, can be perceived as the most common type of language learning disorder affecting approximately 80% of persons with learning disabilities (Handler & Fierson, 2011).

Despite its ubiquity, dyslexia is a complex-to-understand type of neuro-developmental learning disability, especially in less resourced contexts. However, it is imperative that teachers understand this complex learning disability to empower them to handle learners with dyslexia effectively. Dyslexia is a complex phenomenon; nevertheless, an inclusionary definition by Lyon (1995) illuminates our understanding thus:

> Dyslexia is one of several distinct learning disabilities. It is a specific language-based disorder of constitutional origin characterized by difficulties in single word decoding, usually reflecting insufficient

phonological processing. These difficulties in single word decoding are often unexpected in relation to age and other cognitive and academic abilities; they are not the result of generalized developmental disability or sensory impairment. Dyslexia is manifest by variable difficulty with different forms of language, often including, in addition to problems with reading, a conspicuous problem with acquiring proficiency in writing and spelling.

(Lyon, 1995, p. 9)

Three important aspects from this quotation focus on problems of reading, writing and spelling. Generally, all learners require these fundamental skills for transition from education to the world of work (Bell, 2010). Owing to the complexity of dyslexia, theories tend to focus on certain aspects but fail to provide an all-encompassing definition (Tunmer & Greaney, 2010). This in essence makes it difficult for teachers to understand how to identify and help learners with dyslexia early (Snowling, 2013). Teachers from less-resourced contexts may not access complex diagnostic ways of identifying dyslexia, but they can tell when a child experiences problems of reading, writing or even spelling words. This chapter identifies Response to Intervention (RTI) as a model to facilitate effective inclusion of learners with dyslexia among others (Fox, Carta, Strain, Dunlap, & Hemmeter, 2009). The RTI interventions de-emphasize a wait and see approach, and takes a more decisive and preventative style where children are supported to reach their learning goals based on 'timely screening, ongoing progress monitoring, and data-based decisions' (Fox et al., 2009, p. 2). The goals of interventions are to enhance the confidence of learners with dyslexia so that they can become functional and sufficiently independent to enter the world of work.

Dyslexia and the Workplace

It is generally difficult for most people with a disability to enter the world of work. It is particularly challenging for people with dyslexia to find sustainable employment, as they could require support to communicate effectively where written language is a factor (Kirby & Gibbon, 2018) as well as to organise activities around work and manage time (de Beer, Engels, Heerkens, & van der Klink, 2014). Locke, Scallan, Mann and Alexander (2015) identify phonological awareness, short-term memory,

processing speed, visuospatial skills and sequencing skills as some of
the characteristics of people with dyslexia that can have an impact on
the workplace. People with dyslexia also tend to suffer from 'increased
anxiety and susceptibility to burnout and depression' (Locke et al., 2015,
p. 395). These are likely to negatively affect relationships and efficiency
in the workplace and therefore propel negative attitudes from some
employers who poorly understand dyslexia (Burns & Bell, 2010).

Dyslexia and workplace experiences vary greatly in different contexts.
Skinner and MacGill (2015) studied women with dyslexia who combined
motherhood and work and found that highly educated women were
encouraged to develop their careers, however, running the risk of exposing
their dyslexia at work. Nalavany, Logan and Carawan (2018), highlight
the importance of self-efficacy and emotional experience with dyslexia
in the workplace, that they sometimes yield unpleasant feelings. It is
therefore important that within inclusive working spaces (Bell, 2010),
workers with dyslexia are provided with support in order to encourage
them to participate in work (de Beer et al., 2014). Personal narratives of
resilience by teacher trainees with dyslexia revealed that despite negative
attitudes, these teachers developed a positive self-concept and self-esteem
by virtue of participating in the workplace (Glazzard & Dale, 2013).
A study of Finnish and English teachers with dyslexia emphasises the
importance of empathy and understanding in order to expand inclusion
and social equality (Burns & Bell, 2010).

Exponentially high unemployment of youth around the world
poses challenges to many developing nations, as they are unable to
absorb multitudes of young people in the labour market. Sub-Saharan
Africa is also home to 42 countries where youth unemployment rates
never seen before pose an employment drought threat (Ackah-Baidoo,
2016). Youth with dyslexia are no exception to the twenty-first century
dilemma of ever-rising youth unemployment. Even though some youth
with disabilities manage to enter the world of work, they continue to
experience discrimination and limited career guidance opportunities,
necessitating consideration of transition programmes to support them
(Lindsay, Stinson, Stergiou-Kita, & Leck, 2017). Despite policies
emphasising inclusion of workers with disabilities in the workplace,
they continuously experience their needs being less understood (Shier,
Graham, & Jones, 2009).

Transition to Decent Work

Inclusive economic growth and attainment of the 2030 sustainable development goals depend on the provision of decent work for all. Pioneered by the International Labour Organisation (ILO) in 1999, decent work represents 'opportunities for women and men to obtain decent and productive work in conditions of freedom, equity, security and human dignity' (International Labour Organisation, 1999, p. 3).

Decent work is further explained to mean 'acceptable' or 'adequate' work and working conditions for the poorest and most vulnerable (Anker, Chernyshev, Egger, Mehran, & Ritter, 2003, p. 152). Youth with dyslexia could be classified as poor and most vulnerable in the workplace, especially in less developed countries. Recently, decent work occupied an important space among the 17 sustainable development goals as a goal perceived to support the drive towards global economic growth.

Transition to decent work therefore becomes fundamental for youth with dyslexia, especially in emerging countries. Emerging economies are confronted with slow global economic growth, unchanging and elevated unemployment rates and rising vulnerable employment among others. Transition emerged as a policy imperative in the United States of America under the Individuals with Disabilities Education Act (IDEA), which set a mandate for schools to provide transition services for young people with disabilities (McMahan & Baer, 2001). Transition programmes continue to be relevant as youth with disability in general and those with dyslexia in particular still experience 'high dropout rates,' discrimination at school and 'lag far behind their peers without disabilities' with fewer prospects of employment (Stodden, Conway, & Chang, 2003, p. 30). Transition is, however, less well-researched in emerging countries.

Central to the aim of transition is support towards sustainable employment. However, the labour market landscape might not be ready for workers with disabilities, thus indicating the need for systematised support for youth with dyslexia among others. Engelbrecht, Van Niekerk, Coetzee and Hajwani (2017) suggest supported employment, as participation in work can have a therapeutic effect (van Niekerk, 2009). The alternative to employment by youth with dyslexia could be participating in entrepreneurship. This chapter encourages participation in entrepreneurship as a way to accommodate the needs of youth with dyslexia and a specialised approach to transition to decent work.

Dyslexia and Entrepreneurship

Entrepreneurial potential could be a central ingredient of survival in the absence of formal employment, especially for people with disabilities. Renko, Parker Harris, and Caldwell (2016) note that 'people with disabilities are more likely to be self-employed than the general population . . . even though they face many challenges' (p. 555). This chapter focuses on nascent entrepreneurship as a type that could be considered inclusive of people with disabilities. Kessler and Frank (2009) describe a nascent entrepreneur as:

> [a] person who is (alone or with others) now trying to start a new business; who expects to be the owner or part owner of the new firm, who has been active in trying to start the new and independent firm in the past 12 months.
>
> (Kessler & Frank, 2009, p. 722)

The implications of this definition indicate the willingness to develop a business venture and, indeed, the time suggested may be longer in the case of people with disabilities, especially youth with dyslexia.

In this chapter, the nascent entrepreneur is perceived as a person with a disability (dyslexia) who over a period of time has been trying different business ideas in order to create decent work mainly for his or her own livelihood. The nascent entrepreneur is not necessarily a novice but is resilient in order for the venture to survive (Davidsson, 2006). Within the South African context, nascent entrepreneurship could be equated to informal home-based township entrepreneurship within the informal business landscape (Ntema, 2016). Many people in townships survive through home-based ventures. People with disabilities also participate as encouraged by wisdom gleaned from paremiology found in diverse languages within the South African cultural tapestry. In this chapter, Basotho paremiology serves as theoretical lens to illuminate meaning in relation to dyslexia and entrepreneurship.

The Basotho Ontology of Disability–Dyslexia

Basotho are the people of the kingdom of Lesotho, an independent and small enclave within South Africa (Chitereka, 2010; Pitikoe, 2017). Basotho also form a greater part of the people of South Africa who mainly reside in the Free State province, one of the nine of the Republic of South Africa. The language of Basotho is Sesotho, whose richness is generally stored in the proverbs used to guide the people. This chapter subscribes to the philosophy of existentialism, whose concern in about making meaning of people's existence and the freedom to be who they were created to be. A paradigm that subsumes existentialism as used in this chapter is social constructivism, where meaning is conjointly constructed. Ontology (reality) under this paradigm is socially constructed. Therefore, the Basotho, as a collective, have regarded children with disabilities as equally as precious as any other human being. Although this inclination is presented through a mother in a patriarchal society, the Basotho regard a mother as the face and representation of a home.

Basotho ontology of disability provides a positive approach towards people with disabilities. Emerging from the proverb Sehole ho 'm'a-sona ha se lahloe, loosely translated to mean 'a mother would never abandon her child with disability,' this descriptive ontology presents an attitude enshrined in existentialism and Ubuntu as philosophies aimed at the well-being of human beings. The word sehole signifies a maimed (synonyms—disabled, impaired, disfigured and put out of action) person (Guma, 1971). The descriptions mainly refer to physical disability. Semumu (a dumb person), according to the language of the day, would today be referred to as a person with speech problems. This may be seen as closer to phonological dyslexia, although the true sense of Semumu refers to one with no speech at all.

A descriptive ontology is described as a cognitive-level representation, which assists in the formation of a particular worldview (Peuquet, 2002). Basotho's worldview of not abandoning a child with a disability appears to be counter-balancing the negativity generally promoted by other worldviews such as the medical model of disability. Literature is very scarce on disability in Lesotho (Chitereka, 2010). However, Leshota (2011) observes that, historically, Basotho had classifications and specific terms that described different forms of disabilities. Based on a related proverb, Sehole se setle ho 'm'a sona, (Sekese, 2011, p. 207) describing parents of a child with disabilities as having great love for him or her, and Basotho positively affirm persons with disabilities. Traditionally, people with disabilities in Lesotho were afforded special protection not only by the family but also by the chief, who gave them chores and fed and clothed them as part of the chieftains' overall responsibility of ensuring the well-being of the community members. People with disabilities were considered as one of the vulnerable groups who deserve community care.

This chapter is informed by a qualitative study that was conducted on a purposive sample of ten parents of youth with intellectual disabilities who were narratively interviewed in Maseru–Lesotho. The parents were members of the Intellectual Disability Association of Lesotho (IDAL); an association founded by parents of children with intellectual disabilities in 1992. The key question parents answered was: What does the proverb Sehole ho 'm'a-sona ha se lahloe mean to you? The participants indicated that the proverb strengthens their love and dedication to their children and gives them more power to protect them. The majority of the parents who were interviewed shared experiences of great challenges they faced due to the disabilities of their children but, despite that, they felt the need to protect their children, nurture and give them opportunities like others. In today's societies, people with disabilities are expected to become contributing members of their communities and nations. The drive to develop entrepreneurial spaces that accommodate them if transition to decent work fails is expected to enhance opportunities for meaningful participation in building societies in which they live. It is then important to empower youth with dyslexia to be ready to transition into the world of work.

Empowerment of Youth With Dyslexia

Youth empowerment has gained popularity in recent years, yet little has been done in the area of empowering youth with dyslexia in emerging countries (Jennings, Parra-Medina, Hilfinger-Messias, & McLoughlin, 2006). Empowerment is a multifocal phenomenon whose aim is the optimisation of individual and collective potentials for social change. In this chapter, empowerment of youth with dyslexia is approached from the metaphor of the African three-legged pot of the empowerment theory (Perkins & Zimmerman, 1995), a critical social theory of youth empowerment (Jennings et al., 2006) and the theory of change perspectives (Morton & Montgomery, 2011). The empowerment theory promotes individual well-being, mutual assistance and a responsive community (Perkins & Zimmerman, 1995). This theory is ideal in as far as it can address self-efficacy and self-esteem challenges of youth with dyslexia for their well-being while encouraging communities to be positively responsive to the needs of these youth. The empowerment theory could also benefit from the principles of Ubuntu, such as a moral theory and the ethics of care in promoting the well-being and inclusion of youth with dyslexia in decent work (Metz, 2011).

The critical social theory of youth empowerment was developed by Jurgen Habermas, guided by the social philosophy and an empirical sociology (Scott, 1978). A social philosophy is concerned with social issues (Bunge, 1989), such as dyslexia, entrepreneurship and transition to decent work, according to the focus of this chapter. Empirical sociology focuses on the social interactions between people in order to influence policy-making for resolving social problems (de Boise, 2012). Critical social theory promotes three central principles that are technical, practical and emancipatory (Scott, 1978, p. 2). These may be considered in assisting youth with dyslexia in relation to engaging the technical understanding of what dyslexia entails and what challenges are faced by people with dyslexia, and they could be empowered to overcome these challenges. At the practical level, the critical social theory could guide educators and practitioners to devise practical interventions that address individual needs of youth with dyslexia as a diverse group. Central to the empowerment of youth with dyslexia is creating opportunities for them to play a central role in how to address their needs for entrepreneurship and transition to decent work. The epistemological assumption made in this chapter is that youth with dyslexia could use the theory of change as an instrument to address the challenges of participating in entrepreneurship for the transition to decent work.

The theory of change could be another strategy that could empower youth with dyslexia to transition into decent work. In this chapter, a theory of change is perceived as a theory and practice approach that prompts youth with dyslexia to engage in entrepreneurial activities for transition into decent work. De Silva et al. (2014) regard a theory of change as 'a pragmatic framework which describes how the intervention affects change' (p. 2). Stein and Valters (2012) suggest that a theory of change must serve three important purposes: 'as a precise planning tool, way of thinking and a way of developing a politically informed and reflexive approach to development' (p. 5). The diagram in Figure 5.1 is suggested as a route which youth with dyslexia could follow to participate in entrepreneurship and transit to decent work.

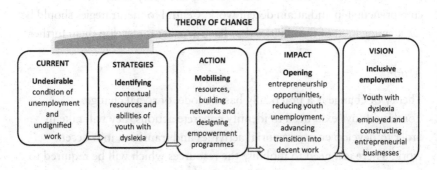

Figure 5.1 Theory of Change for Decent Work

Current

In order to change their current situation of an undesirable condition of unemployment and undignified work, youth with dyslexia need to renounce such conditions and decide for a change towards inclusive employment and decent work. This part of the theory of change requires them to describe in detail what the problem is that needs their attention in order to change it. In light of this chapter, unemployment and undignified work are the current conditions facing youth with dyslexia as examples of many other problems for which theories of change can be developed. In order to achieve this, contextual resources could be mobilised through networking with diverse stakeholders as well as the Dyslexia International cost-free training supported by the United Nations Educational, Scientific and Cultural Organization (UNESCO). The Open Educational Resource should form a strong literature support for youth with dyslexia to be more empowered regarding an in-depth understanding of dyslexia.

Strategies

Strategies specific to each theory developed need to be identified. The theory of change suggests that in order to make a difference, it is necessary to develop strategies to address the current undesirable situation. The strategies are pathways that explain how the problem identified is going to be addressed, how what would need to happen would happen and by whom would it be executed. In this section, youth with dyslexia ought to identify the resources they need to act on unemployment, enter into entrepreneurship and attain decent work. Central to the strategies should be the identification of the abilities they have in order to develop them further.

Action

Theory of change is a practically based model of social change. Youth with dyslexia need to identify concrete actions they will take in order to develop entrepreneurial activities and transition into decent work. There is a need to mobilise the resources which will be required to implement the strategies. Networking is also central to the actions to be taken. Youth with dyslexia need to establish networks of practitioners working in dyslexia and networks such as support groups for themselves with peers with similar experiences. At this stage, it is imperative to develop models of empowerment programmes which will address their needs. If required, the youth might have to mobilise support for specialists in the youth empowerment project who would guide them.

Impact

A theory of change developed would have to reflect the envisaged impact expected. This would have to be described in measurable terms in order to allow for an evaluation to determine whether there is a realisable impact or not. Impact ought to provide for both reflexive action and tangible results (Stein & Valters, 2012). In light of this chapter, impact must be measured in terms of a number of entrepreneurship opportunities accessed by youth with dyslexia and a certain percentage of reduction in unemployment and transition into decent work. It should be obvious how many young people with dyslexia participate in decent work as a result of the programme they developed.

Vision

The vision is equal to the end goal of the theory of change. In this chapter, the end goal is inclusive employment for youth with dyslexia. The theory of change developed would have achieved its goal if youth with dyslexia are employed and participating in decent work and many access opportunities to construct entrepreneurial businesses. The vision expressed in this chapter for youth with dyslexia aligns with the transformative aim driven by the Sustainable Development Goals (SDGs) (Adams, 2017).

The SDG in particular strengthens the vision through target 8.b, with the aims that by 2020 there will be a developed and operational global strategy for youth employment, and the ILO Global Jobs Pact will be implemented (Pisano, Lange, Berger, & Hametner, 2015).

Social Dialogue as a Platform for Youth With Dyslexia in Education

Social dialogue as a platform for youth with dyslexia could be an agent of pedagogical transformation in education and transition into the world of work. Generally, social dialogue is perceived to refer to discussions, consultations, negotiations and joint actions (Hyman, 2010), as well as 'a historical institution' (Stevis & Creation, 2010, p. 6). Social dialogue is an international framework adopted at national levels within several countries of the world under the National Economic Development and Labour Council (NEDLAC) as a negotiation forum and platform for social dialogue (Dentlinger, 2017). Rightfully promoted through ILO, social dialogue is well placed to promote interests of youth with dyslexia through education and entrepreneurship for transition into the world of work.

Youth with dyslexia are mostly misunderstood, overlooked and generally experience adversity educationally and socially (Alexander-Passe, 2018). On the contrary, Alexander-Passe (2016) argues that promotion and emphasis of success could leverage positive results in the overall life experiences of people with dyslexia. Education could be a powerful policy instrument to use the positive experiences of success as an effective conduit for social dialogue. Promoting the voices of learners with dyslexia through debates, improved writing as well as other forms of communication could extend social dialogue towards access to decent work. Recognition of the often-hidden intelligence possessed by learners with dyslexia should be central to the business of teaching and learning and could be used to address career aspirations of youth with dyslexia. Stories of success as investigated by Alexander-Passe (2017) and from other parts of the world could be used as best practices in promoting a positive attitude towards people with dyslexia.

Basotho indigenous education (Letseka, 2013) imparted through systems such as thakaneng (van Jaarsveld, Vermaak, & van Rooyen, 2011) and khotla (Matšela, 1979) in the Sesotho culture used to be foundational among children who grew up together in helping those with bohole (disability) to find their voices. Matšela (1979, p. 116) categorises thakaneng as a place where girls slept together under the watch of an old widowed woman, and khotla was for boys. Thakaneng and khotla were places of nurturing and cultural training designated for young people and were an equivalent of the peer education system in English. These were places where young people lived together and learned important lessons in preparation for adulthood. Thakaneng and khotla were out of bounds for adults (except the guardian), as they were respected for young people to take responsibility for their lives. It was here where many lessons were learned and much peer support practised. The Basotho indigenous education promoted equitable informal education based on Ubuntu/botho values in promotion of indigenous epistemologies (Letseka, 2013).

Conclusion

During the interviews and data analysis of ten parents of youth with intellectual disabilities in Maseru–Lesotho, it became evident that regardless of the type and level of disability, parents have hope for their children to access decent work at some point in their lives. Dyslexia in particular ought not to be an impediment to access decent work by youth with dyslexia as long as they are provided with support. In the absence of employment, entrepreneurship provides a noble alternative where youth with dyslexia could be supported to develop nascent entrepreneurship projects guided by the positive Basotho ontology of disability. Empowerment programmes are believed to play a pivotal role in encouraging youth with dyslexia to take control of their lives, and this they can do being guided by the theory of change as a strategy. This chapter suggests the Basotho ontology of disability and the theory of change for use in similar contexts to empower youth to consider entrepreneurship as an alternative to unemployment.

References

Aciobăniţei, M. (2012). Paremiological aspects in the construction of national identity. *Procedia-Social and Behavioral Sciences, 63*, 276–282. https://doi.org/10.1016/j.sbspro.2012.10.039

Ackah-Baidoo, P. (2016). Youth unemployment in resource-rich Sub-Saharan Africa: A critical review. *The Extractive Industries and Society, 3*(1), 249–261. https://doi.org/10.1016/j.exis.2015.11.010

Adams, C. A. (2017). *The sustainable development goals, integrated thinking and the integrated report*. Edinburgh, UK: Institute of Chartered Accountants of Scotland (ICAS). Retrieved from https://pdfs.semanticscholar.org

Alexander-Passe, N. (2016). Dyslexia, success and post-traumatic growth. *Asia Pacific Journal of Developmental Differences, 3*(1), 87–130. https://doi.org/10.3850/S2345734114000232

Alexander-Passe, N. (2017). *The successful dyslexic: Identify the keys for success to achieve your potential.* Rotterdam, The Netherlands: Sense Publishers.

Alexander-Passe, N. (2018). *Dyslexia, traumatic schooling and career success: Investigating the motivations of why many individuals with developmental dyslexia are successful despite experiencing traumatic schooling* (Doctoral dissertation), University of Sunderland, UK.

Anker, R., Chernyshev, I., Egger, P., Mehran, F., & Ritter, J. A. (2003). Measuring decent work with statistical indicators. *International Labour Review, 142*(2), pp. 147–178. https://dx.doi.org/10.2139/ssrn.907034

Bell, S. (2010). Inclusion for adults with dyslexia: Examining the transition periods of a group of adults in England: "Clever is when you come to a brick wall and you have got to get over it without a ladder." *Journal of Research in Special Educational Needs (JORSEN), 10*(3), 216–226. https://doi.org/10.1111/j.1471-3802.2010.01167.x

Bunge, M. (1989). Social philosophy. In M. Bunge (Ed.), *Treatise on basic philosophy* (pp. 354–389, Vol. 8). Dordrecht, The Netherlands: Springer. https://doi.org/10.1007/978-94-009-2601-1_12

Burns, E., & Bell, S. (2010). Voices of teachers with dyslexia in Finnish and English further and higher educational settings. *Teachers and Teaching: Theory and Practice, 16*(5), 529–543. https://doi.org/10.1080/13540602.2010.507964

Chitereka, C. (2010). People with disabilities and the role of social workers in Lesotho. *Social Work & Society, 8*(1), 82–93. Retrieved from https://socwork.net/

Davidsson, P. (2006). Nascent entrepreneurship: Empirical studies and developments. *Foundations and Trends in Entrepreneurship, 2*(1), 1–76. Retrieved from http://eprints.qut.edu.au/

de Beer, J., Engels, J., Heerkens, Y., & van der Klink, J. (2014). Factors influencing work participation of adults with developmental dyslexia: A systematic review. *BMC Public Health, 14*(1), 77. https://doi.org/10.1186/1471-2458-14-77

de Boise, S. (2012). The coming crisis?: Some questions for the future of empirical sociology in the UK. *Graduate Journal of Social Science, 9*(2), 40–64. Retrieved from http://gjss.org/

Dentlinger, L. (2017). *The relevance and effectiveness of Nedlac as a social dialogue forum: The Marikana crisis* (Doctoral dissertation), University of Pretoria, South Africa. http://doi.org/10.1186/1745-6215-15-267

De Silva, M. J., Breuer, E., Lee, L., Asher, L., Chowdhary, N., Lund, C., & Patel, V. (2014). Theory of change: A theory-driven approach to enhance the Medical Research Council's framework for complex interventions. *Trials, 15*, 267.

Engelbrecht, M., Van Niekerk, L., Coetzee, Z., & Hajwani, Z. (2017). Supported employment for people with mental disabilities in South Africa: Cost calculation of service utilisation. *South African Journal of Occupational Therapy, 47*(2), 11–16. http://dx.doi.org/10.17159/231-3833/1017/v47n2a3

Fox, L., Carta, J., Strain, P., Dunlap, G., & Hemmeter, M. L. (2009). *Response to intervention and the pyramid model.* Tampa, FL: Technical Assistance Center on Social Emotional Intervention for Young Children, University of South Florida.

Ghai, D. (2003). Decent work: Concept and indicators. *International Labour Review, 142*(2), 113–145. https://doi.org/10.1111/j.1564-913X.2003.tb00256.x

Glazzard, J., & Dale, K. (2013). Trainee teachers with dyslexia: Personal narratives of resilience. *Journal of Research in Special Educational Needs (JORSEN), 13*(1), 26–37. https://doi.org/10.1111/j.1471-3802.2012.01254.x

Guma, S. M. (1971). *An outline structure of Southern Sotho*. Pietermaritzburg, South Africa: Shuter & Shooter.

Handler, S. M., & Fierson, W. M. (2011). Joint technical report-learning disabilities, dyslexia, and vision. *Pediatrics, 127*(3), e818–e856. https://doi.org/10.1542/peds.2010-3670

Hultquist, A. M. (2006). *An introduction to dyslexia for parents and professionals*. London, England: Jessica Kingsley Publishers.

Hyman, R. (2010). *Social dialogue and industrial relations during the economic crisis: Innovative practices or business as usual?* Geneva, Switzerland: International Labour Organisation (ILO). Retrieved from www.ilo.org/

International Labour Organisation (ILO). (1999, June). Report of the director-general: Decent work. In *Presentation at 87th International Labour Conference*. Geneva, Switzerland: https://www.ilo.org/public/english/standards/relm/ilc/ilc87/rep-i.htm. Retrieved from www.ilo.org/

Jennings, L. B., Parra-Medina, D. M., Hilfinger-Messias, D. K., & McLoughlin, K. (2006). Toward a critical social theory of youth empowerment. *Journal of Community Practice, 14*(1–2), 31–55. https://doi.org/10.1300/J125v14n01_03

Kessler, A., & Frank, H. (2009). Nascent entrepreneurship in a longitudinal perspective: The impact of person, environment, resources and the founding process on the decision to start business activities. *International Small Business Journal, 27*(6), 720–742. https://doi.org/10.1177/0266242609344363

Kirby, A., & Gibbon, H. (2018). Dyslexia and employment. *Perspectives on Language and Literacy, 44*(1), 27–31. Retrieved from https://pure.southwales.ac.uk/

Leshota, P. L. (2011). *A deconstruction of disability discourse amongst Christians in Lesotho* (Doctoral dissertation), University of South Africa, Pretoria.

Letseka, M. (2013). Educating for Ubuntu/botho: Lessons from Basotho indigenous education. *Open Journal of Philosophy, 3*(2), 337. http://dx.doi.org/10.4236/ojpp.2013.32051

Lindsay, S., Stinson, J., Stergiou-Kita, M., & Leck, J. (2017). Improving transition to employment for youth with physical disabilities: Protocol for a peer electronic mentoring intervention. *JMIR Research Protocols, 6*(11), e215. http://doi.org/10.2196/resprot.8034

Locke, R., Scallan, S., Mann, R., & Alexander, G. (2015). Clinicians with dyslexia: A systematic review of effects and strategies. *The Clinical Teacher, 12*(6), 394–398. https://doi.org/10.1111/tct.12331

Reid Lyon, G. R. (1995). Toward a definition of dyslexia. *Annals of Dyslexia, 45*(1), 1–27. https://doi.org/10.1007/BF02648210

Matšela, Z. A. (1979). *The indigenous education of the Basotho and its implications for educational development in Lesotho* (Unpublished doctoral thesis), University of Massachusetts, Boston.

McMahan, R., & Baer, R. (2001). IDEA transition policy compliance and best practice: Perceptions of transition stakeholders. *Career Development for Exceptional Individuals, 24*(2), 169–184. https://doi.org/10.1177/088572880102400206

Metz, T. (2011). Ubuntu as a moral theory and human rights in South Africa. *African Human Rights Law Journal, 11*(2), 532–559. Retrieved from www. scielo.org.za/

Morton, M., & Montgomery, P. (2011). *Youth empowerment programs for improving self-efficacy and self-esteem of adolescents* (Campbell Systematic Reviews: 5). Oslo, Norway: The Campbell Collaboration. Retrieved from https://core.ac.uk/

Nalavany, B. A., Logan, J. M., & Carawan, L. W. (2018). The relationship between emotional experience with dyslexia and work self-efficacy among adults with dyslexia. *Dyslexia, 24*(1), 17–32. https://doi.org/10.1002/dys.1575

Ntema, J. (2016). Informal home-based entrepreneurs in South Africa: "How non-South Africans outcompete South Africans." *Africa Insight, 46*(2), 44–59. Retrieved from www.ingentaconnect.com/

Perkins, D. D., & Zimmerman, M. A. (1995). Empowerment theory, research, and application. *American Journal of Community Psychology, 23*(5), 569–579. https://doi.org/10.1007/BF02506982

Petretto, D. R., & Masala, C. (2017). Dyslexia and specific learning disorders: New international diagnostic criteria. *Journal of Child Development Disorders, 3*(4), 19. Retrieved from https://iris.unica.it/

Peuquet, D. J. (2002). *Representations of space and time.* New York, NY: Guilford Press.

Pisano, U., Lange, L., Berger, G., & Hametner, M. (2015). *The sustainable development goals (SDGs) and their impact on the European SD governance framework* (European Sustainable Development Network (ESDN) Quarterly Report, no. 35). Vienna, Austria: European Sustainable Development Network. Retrieved from www.sd-network.eu/

Pitikoe, S. (2017). Basotho herders learn through culture and social interaction. *Learning, Culture and Social Interaction, 13*, 104–112. https://doi.org/10.1016/j.lcsi.2017.03.003

Renko, M., Parker Harris, S., & Caldwell, K. (2016). Entrepreneurial entry by people with disabilities. *International Small Business Journal, 34*(5), 555–578. https://doi.org/10.1177/0266242615579112

Scott, J. P. (1978). Critical social theory: An introduction and critique. *British Journal of Sociology, 29*, 1–21.

Sekese, A. (2011). *Mekhoa le maele a Basotho.* Morija, Lesotho: Morija Sesuto Book Depot.

Sengenberger, W. (2001). Decent work: The International Labour Organization agenda. *Dialogue and Cooperation, 2*, 39–54.

Sevilla-Muñoz, J. (2016). Paremiography in Spain since the end of the 19th century: Problems, methods and results. *Open Linguistics, 2*(1), 666–678. https://doi.org/10.1515/opli-2016-0037

Shier, M., Graham, J. R., & Jones, M. E. (2009). Barriers to employment as experienced by disabled people: A qualitative analysis in Calgary and Regina, Canada. *Disability & Society, 24*(1), 63–75. https://doi.org/10.1080/09687590802535485

Skinner, T., & MacGill, F. (2015). Combining dyslexia and mothering: Perceived impacts on work. *Gender, Work & Organization, 22*(4), 421–435. https://doi.org/10.1111/gwao.12102

Snowling, M. J. (2013). Early identification and interventions for dyslexia: A contemporary view. *Journal of Research in Special Educational Needs (JORSEN), 13*(1), 7–14. http://doi.org/10.1111/j.1471-3802.2012.01262.x

Stein, D., & Valters, C. (2012). *Understanding "theory of change" in international development: A review of existing knowledge* (JSRP and TAF collaborative project, JSRP Paper 1, Justice and Security Research Programme). London, England: International Development Department, London School of Economics and Political Science. Retrieved from eprints.lse.ac.uk/

Stevis, D., & Creation, J. (2010). *International framework agreements and global social dialogue: Parameters and prospects* (Employment working paper no. 47). International Labour Organisation, Job Creation and Enterprise Development Department, Geneva, Switzerland. Retrieved from www.ilo.org/

Stodden, R. A., Conway, M. A., & Chang, K. B. (2003). Findings from the study of transition, technology and postsecondary supports for youth with disabilities: Implications for secondary school educators. *Journal of Special Education Technology, 18*(4), 29–44. https://doi.org/10.1177/016264340301800403

Tunmer, W., & Greaney, K. (2010). Defining dyslexia. *Journal of Learning Disabilities, 43*(3), 229–243. https://doi.org/10.1177/0022219409345009

van Jaarsveld, A., Vermaak, M., & van Rooyen, C. (2011). The developmental status of street children in Potchefstroom, South Africa. *South African Journal of Occupational Therapy, 41*(1), 5–8. Retrieved from www.scielo.org.za/

van Niekerk, L. (2009). Participation in work: A source of wellness for people with psychiatric disability. *Work, 32*(4), 455–465. https://doi.org/10.3233/WOR-2009-0856

Wadlington, E. M., & Wadlington, P. L. (2005). What educators really believe about dyslexia. *Reading Improvement, 42*(1), 16–33. Retrieved from www.researchgate.net/

Wajuihian, S. O., & Naidoo, K. S. (2011). Dyslexia: An overview. *African Vision and Eye Health, 70*(2), 89–98. https://doi.org/10.4102/aveh.v70i2.102

6 Towards a Dyslexia Superpower

Reflections on the Year in the Life of a Dyslexic Professor of Entrepreneurship

Nigel Lockett

Introduction

Out of sheer necessity, this chapter is a cut-down version of 52 weekly blogs totalling nearly 30,000 words, posted by me between December 2016 and December 2017, exploring the personal challenges and organisational advantages of dyslexia (Lockett, 2020). At its core, it advocates the seismic shift from portraying dyslexia as a disability through learning difference to advantage or superpower! In an attempt to retain the sense of unfolding self-awareness, I have maintained the current tense and the sequence of the blogs but dramatically reduced their number and length. In essence, this is a story of disclosure, which resulted in liberation and determination. Liberation from the disability label and determination to do something.

The Dyslexic Professor

Yes, I do mean dyslexic professor not professor of dyslexia. By my 19th birthday, I had failed all my A-levels and couldn't see a positive future—school had been a nightmare. Fortunately, I had two things going in my favour. Firstly, I had passed my motorcycling test! And, secondly, after failing my English General Certificate of Secondary Education (GCSE) examination twice with Fs, an experienced out-of-school English tutor recognised I had learning difficulties and recommended I went to one of the few specialist testing centres. After what seemed like a strange set of questions and tests, I was told I had a very high IQ and dyslexia. The former was a pleasant surprise and confirmed I wasn't stupid and the latter, both a new word to me and unspellable to boot!

There then followed 35 years of struggles, achievements and more struggles as I came to realise that dyslexia was not a learning difficulty but a *learning difference*. This learning difference has shaped me into the person I am today . . . The Dyslexic Professor! My 2017 New Year's resolution was to write a weekly blog related to my experiences as a dyslexic academic.

Who Would Ever Have Thought It?

As an undiagnosed dyslexic in school through the 70s, life was pretty tough. No one had even heard of dyslexia let alone developed effective learning strategies for it. For me that meant years of underachievement and ridicule from teachers (*some very well meaning*) and friends who were as ignorant as everyone else. I still don't like to think of that 8-year-old me, starting at boarding school and sitting in Mrs W's English class.

Throughout my schooling I lived in fear of being asked to read aloud in class. I followed the trail of doom as it snaked around my classmates, getting ever nearer. Desperate attempts to read ahead to the most likely sentence to land on me, was no preparation—it just made things worse. As I stood, eyes going out of focus, words dancing on the page, the first sentence hardly uttered before the laughing started!

Even today, I can't read aloud from the printed page. And yet . . . I can deliver top class lectures on entrepreneurship. My last Advanced Entrepreneurship class scored 100% (Strongly agree/Agree) across all measures—even Feedback! Student evaluations included:

> *Nigel was very enthusiastic and it was very refreshing being taught a module by someone with first-hand experience in the field he was teaching. This module, was by far the best module I have ever undertaken in the entirety of my time.*

Has This Anything to Do With Being Dyslexic?

The journey to the top of leading business schools (University of Leeds and Lancaster University) requires a written PhD. I, and probably everyone else around me, could simply never have imagined that 8-year-old, so fearful of the written word, becoming an entrepreneur, community leader and professor.

Time to See Dyslexia as a Superpower?

We are all familiar with the Marvel comic superheroes—each with their own superpower. I wonder if it's time to rethink our view of dyslexia and focus less on what dyslexic people *can't* do and more on what they *can* do. Yes, I am actually suggesting that we consider dyslexia as a superpower!

In my experience, I have noticed dyslexics appear to be able to deal with complexity, and not just complexity but dynamic complexity— where a myriad of events move with abnormal pace. This ability seems to comprise three capabilities particularly prevalent in dyslexics, seeing:

1. Patterns
2. Objects
3. Shapes

Combining these capabilities with empathy and calmness and you have, in my view, a superpower! *And, which organisations wouldn't want to recruit staff with these superpowers?*

Dyslexic Glass Ceiling?

Many of us will be aware of the glass ceiling or the artificial barriers to the advancement of ethnic minority men and women into senior management and decision-making positions. But, *could it also apply to dyslexics?* Not so much a glass ceiling as a word ceiling.

Of course, I can only refer to my own experience as a manager, entrepreneur, community leader and academic. But, in each role there came a moment when my dyslexia did indeed become a barrier. I'm not looking to blame anyone or any organisation and I recognise I have constructed some artificial barriers of my own. However, I am looking to highlight the real challenges faced by dyslexics in everyday life—more particularly, everyday living in environments full of words!

I will illustrate this point with two examples. The first being more painful to recall than the second:

Firstly, I have been involved in many community projects—from fundraising garden parties to chairing a medium-sized charity through a change in Chief Executive, and from helping set-up an organic food social enterprise to chairing the governing body of a primary school and even being President of my professional body. Of course, I am constantly scanning my environment for threats that might expose me as a dyslexic, but occasionally even I drop my guard.

It is good practice to involve parents and caregivers, in appropriate ways, to support young children's learning in primary schools. This can range from after school clubs to individual support. What could be more natural than for a teacher to ask the Chair of Governors to join the rota of one-to-one reading support for 5 to 7 year olds? The day duly came and I chose a suitable book from my own children's collection and read it through several times to myself. Just as I was leaving to walk to the school, my wife kindly offered to hear me read the book aloud. Even I was surprised by the reality. As soon as I started to read out, I made a simple error, which I heard as a whisper in my head and then a roar as it was gently pointed out. In an instant, I was teleported back to standing in a classroom with eyes going out of focus, words dancing on the page! I completely lost my confidence and accepted the offer to be substituted at very short notice.

Secondly, now in my fourth career, as an academic (previously, and concurrently, as manager, entrepreneur and community leader), I am now enjoying being a Professor of Entrepreneurship at a leading business school. I was recently asked by a University Vice-Chancellor–*What are your career ambitions?* In an instant, I knew the answer was not, *the very top of academia or even nearly the very top!* I decided to disclose my dyslexia and listed the things I couldn't do and that would make it difficult to carry out the full range of duties expected of a leader in modern academia.

Reflecting honestly on this conversation, I think there were in fact three specific things—two related to my dyslexia and one completely different:

- **Names:** Names are difficult for me and new names in particular. It just takes me longer to associate a familiar name to a new face and an embarrassingly long time to pronounce it with confidence. Just imagine graduation. . .

- **Speeches:** I have become more comfortable speaking in public but I am specifically referring to written speeches that senior leaders need to deliver as a normal part of their job. For very senior leaders, these will have been drafted by someone else. Just imagine a public address. . .
- **Admiration:** Now, this might be the main reason! I have been fortunate to work in universities with strong and committed leadership teams. I see the long hours and the sacrifices made by these high performing individuals. I just can't imagine doing that!

So, there might, at least for me, be a dyslexia ceiling. Interestingly, Catherine Drennan, a distinguished Professor of Biology and Chemistry at Massachusetts Institute of Technology, doesn't agree: *'There is no dyslexia ceiling, it doesn't exist, unless you create it in your own mind'* (Drennan, 2015).

The Dyslexic Brain: Words, Words, Everywhere

I can't stop smiling as I start this blog on the dyslexic brain. I will return to this important subject in a moment. I'm smiling because I have just remembered a former business bank manager (Brian) saying, in all earnest, *'Nigel, I do appreciate getting your monthly financial updates but please would you stop writing to me as, Dear Brain!'*

Recent research on how the brain's cortex, more especially the structure of mini-columns (dense versus loose) and axons (short versus long), impacts connections suggests that dyslexia is not a dysfunction but a difference. Of course, I rather like this idea and recognise this might just be because it supports my worldview that dyslexia is a *learning difference*. In this blog, I am drawing mainly on Eide and Eide (2012) and Eden (2016).

Why Would Cortex Structure (Short-Dense and Long-Loose) Affect Connections, and Why Is This Relevant to Dyslexia?

One of the key differences for dyslexics is the ability to see patterns or the forest for the trees or the big picture. This big picture thinking is a function of a cortex structure—more precisely, long axons and loose mini-columns (long-loose) which slows down processing. The opposite is short axons and dense mini-columns (short-dense) which speeds up processing and supports fine-detail thinking. This produces a fascinating spectrum from slow (*big picture thinking*) to fast (*fine detail thinking*), which maps onto dyslexia (*big picture thinking*) and autism (*fine detail thinking*).

Importantly, learning to read (*a function of phonological processing and procedural processing in the left brain*) is enhanced by fine-detail thinking. This might also go some way to explain the challenge words cause dyslexics. The implications for dyslexics are firstly, dyslexia is a difference not a dysfunction and secondly, as I know from my own experience, adult dyslexics can improve their word processing power to a mostly adequate level without losing their big picture thinking!

Vacancy: Dyslexics Need Only Apply

Of course, I'm not suggesting there are jobs that only dyslexics can do. But, just imagine if employers valued the enhanced abilities [*superpowers*] that dyslexia can provide. I have applied for a few senior positions in my time and have been faced with completing the anonymous Equal Opportunities Form. Each time, I think, *Do I have a disability? Should I declare it? What would be the consequences? Is it really confidential?* . . .

It's hard to pick up a newspaper and not read about the latest big challenge faced by a big organisation. These are big complex problems with multiple stakeholders and both political and financial implications. Oh, and probably full of big data. So, if you run one of these organisations, *Who you gonna call?* No, not Ghostbusters!

But, perhaps a group of people with specially honed, big picture thinking (*yes, you know where I'm going!*). But, you recruit your top talent from top graduates from top universities; who have in turn recruited top students with top A-levels; most likely achieved by students with an enhanced ability for fine detail thinking. Really you need both big picture thinking and fine-detail thinking to crack these really big problems. Perhaps this is at the heart of the matter. We have designed an educational system that rewards fine detail thinking and labels the very people with enhanced big picture thinking as dysfunctional. A similar point is very eloquently made by Sir Ken Robinson (2006) in his Technology, Entertainment and Design (TED) Conference talk, 'Do schools kill creativity?' *Who will be the first large organisation to include, 'Evidence of overcoming the challenges of dyslexia' under desirable selection criteria?*

Developing a Superpower Institute

It's all very well me suggesting that employers should recruit staff who have dyslexic superpowers and can show evidence of overcoming the challenges of dyslexia, but that's only half the solution. Surely the key to success is developing programmes that support the learning differences experienced by dyslexics and to enable the further development of big picture thinking. In the context of the higher education sector, let's look at each in turn:

- **Supporting:** Universities recognise that some of their students could have learning difficulties, often called students with specific learning difficulties. Indeed, many have invested time and resources in supporting these students. Typically, through their disability services. So, step one to enlightenment must be to focus on dyslexia as a learning difference and reposition support as Continuing Professional Development (CPD) for the enhancement of existing abilities.
- **Enabling:** Having repositioned support as CPD and, hopefully, engaged with dyslexic academic and professional staff, it's time to think about developing the superpower of big picture thinking. I'm sure that once dyslexics have switched from thinking about their dyslexia as a disability to a difference, they will become aware of their enhanced abilities to see patterns, objects and shapes and be ready to rethink their own educational and work experiences. The challenge of this repositioning shouldn't be underestimated. Remember, many dyslexics will have felt labelled and excluded by an educational system that rewards fine detail thinking.

My Dyslexia Valentine

Of course, I couldn't let the 14th of February pass without reflecting on my 'love hate' relationship with my dyslexia. Well, I say 'love hate' but what I increasingly feel is a love relationship with my dyslexia valentine!

Many will know the *'footprints in the sand'* poem (authorship disputed) in which the traveller experiences hardship and on looking back sees particularly hard periods in their life when there is only one pair of footprints in the sand and turns to their companion and says, '*Why did you abandon me during my most difficult times?*' The gentle reply comes, '*Those were the times I carried you*'. And so it is with my dyslexia. I can now look back and freely acknowledge that what I first saw as a disability, I became aware of as a difference and now increasingly see as an advantage or superpower!

Power of Different

Saltz (2017) makes a compelling case for linking 'disorder' (*including dyslexia*) with 'genius.' The first chapter focuses specifically on dyslexia and, through examples drawn from 'brilliantly' successful dyslexics, highlights four categories which together with 'grit and resilience' could account for this 'power'.

Firstly, experiencing significant trauma in school. Secondly, developing 'work-arounds.' Thirdly, creativity and insight linking to brain differences. Finally, 'tremendous' drive and determination. Looking at each in more detail, we can begin to see how dyslexia can indeed be an advantage or superpower. However, the challenge of recognising the positive aspects of dyslexia appears to start in school and probably continues into college and university.

- **Living with learning differences:** Many dyslexics, myself included, can recall the trauma of school.
- **Developing work-arounds:** To overcome these challenges, dyslexics use their learning difference to create work-arounds.
- **Seeing dyslexia as a gift:** If we assume that human evolution accentuates the positive and eliminates the negative, dyslexia could be an important feature of the survival of the human species.
- **Flourishing as a dyslexic:** So, having experienced the trauma of school, developed the work-arounds and having a host of life enhancing gifts, dyslexics can flourish in later life.

And finally, Saltz highlights that whilst dyslexics have many differences, they seem to have a propensity to develop empathy (Saltz, 2017, p. 37).

Dyslexia Is in the Air

Not only is spring in the air this week, but so too is dyslexia. It seems that several things are coming together which make me feel more optimistic about recasting dyslexia not just as a difference, as opposed to a difficulty, but as an advantage and even a superpower.

Firstly, I now have four guest bloggers crafting their pieces and, secondly, I've just signed off the copy of an article for a national Higher Education sector publication and had my photograph taken today! And finally, a new charity was launched this week—Made By Dyslexia (www.madebydyslexia.org) whose goals are to: Ensure dyslexia is properly understood as a different way of thinking and to work with governments, charities, schools and parents to ensure all dyslexic children are identified early and given the support they need. The launch coincided with the publication of 'Connecting the Dots,' a highly informative report (Griggs, 2017). It includes an explanation of dyslexia thinking skills and the advantages it can bring: visualising, imagining, communicating, reasoning, connecting and exploring.

There's Going Public About Dyslexia and There's GOING PUBLIC!

We all know that any post on social media is public—but, *how many people actually read our blogs?* The answer is that it depends on how many followers you have and whether your blogs contain anything offensive, funny or illegal! Understandably, at least so far, my digital impact has been somewhat limited.

This week, the *Times Higher Education* (THE) decided to publish a series of articles about disabilities on campus and first up was: 'I have decided to go public as the Dyslexic Professor' (Lockett, 2017).

Dyslexia Superpower: Seismic Shift

To be honest, I never thought I would reach the half-way point. I think there are three main reasons (why always three?) I have come this far:

- readers' engagement,
- guest bloggers,
- a growing, and a rather worrying tendency, for self-actualisation.

Dyslexia Superpower: The System Entrepreneur

The mission of the Royal Society for the Encouragement of Arts, Manufactures and Commerce (RSA—www.thersa.org), of which I am a member, is to enrich society through ideas and action and their journal often includes suitably thought-provoking articles.

In 2017 Issue 1, Burbidge argues that the way to tackle the challenges faced by our public services is 'to think like a system and act like an entrepreneur' (Burbidge, 2017). This is predicated on the sometimes unexpected consequences of shocks to society—or in system-talk, emergent properties. He gives the example of an increase in community spirit after a disaster and concludes that we need to recognise the inherent complexity of our world and develop an understanding of the bigger picture (*of course, he really means big picture thinking*).

For me, this all points to the value of big picture thinking so evident in dyslexics and it is no surprise to me that entrepreneurial thinking should also be highlighted. Both are matters close to my heart. Firstly, we now know that the brains of dyslexics are different. This big picture thinking is a function of a cortex structure. Secondly, there are a disproportionately high number of entrepreneurs who are dyslexic—35% of US and 19% of UK entrepreneurs are dyslexic (Logan, 2009). In *Dyslexic entrepreneurs— Why they have a competitive edge* (Tickle, 2015), Tickle writes about Lord Sugar, Anita Roddick, Richard Branson, Jamie Oliver and Ingvar Kamprad.

So, whilst agreeing that to solve big societal problems we need to think like a system and act like an entrepreneur, I can't think of a better place to start than by enabling dyslexics to develop their full big picture thinking skills and additionally recognising that there could be a direct link between dyslexia and entrepreneurial thinking. If true, let's have schools, colleges and universities prioritising big picture thinking and workplaces fit for a dyslexic!

Dyslexia Superpower: Is Edtech Missing an Opportunity?

Just how many 'techs' can we cope with? Biotech, Fintech and, the focus of this article, Edtech. Edtech or education technology refers to a wide range of range of platforms and services to digitise education. Apparently, the latter could grow from $75bn in 2014 to $120bn in 2019. This week's economist leader (The Economist, 2017) argues that education technology and teachers could revamp schools and, more specifically, that this will require three things to be successful:

- Edtech must be evidence-based and this needs to acknowledge the role of the teacher.
- Edtech needs to narrow inequalities in the education system.
- Edtech will only have an impact if teachers adopt it.

Perhaps not surprisingly, it cites many examples of learning facts and tutoring—such as Mindspark (India); Geekie (Sao Paulo); DreamBox (US) and Siyavula Practice (South Africa).

Of course, as The Dyslexic Professor, I'm just as interested in how Edtech can support learning of languages and to engage with language. What struck me was the number of education technology entrepreneurs I knew personally. This is even more surprising when you realise I'm not that well networked and haven't been specifically looking for them! I will share four with you: The amazing Twinkl (www.twinkl.co.uk—Jonathan Seaton); the explosive Webanywhere (www.webanywhere.co.uk—Sean Gilligan); the innovative Synap (synap.ac—James Gupta) and the analytical Wmatrix (http://ucrel.lancs.ac.uk/wmatrix/—Paul Rayson).

Now, back to my hobby horse, how Edtech can support engaging with language. There is also the British Dyslexia Association's New Technologies Committee website (https://bdatech.org) that lists a wide range of assistive technologies under: spellcheckers, prediction, text to speech and e-books, speech recognition, organisation aids and mind maps.

Dyslexia Superpower: Building the Ultimate Dyslexia Library

The ultimate book on dyslexia has just arrived through my letterbox! Nicolson's *Positive Dyslexia* (Nicolson, 2015). Nicolson captures, in a mere 150 pages, the issue, the strengths, the what, the how and the why! I will attempt to summarise his main points next.

Positive dyslexia is about recognising the nine strengths of dyslexia that culminate in unconventional thinking and doing so demands the cessation of sinking into a failing to learn, learning to fail cycle and replacement with *positive assessment*. This catapults (*positive acceleration*) dyslexics by inspirations (*positive ambitions, positive career*) to success in school, work and society by building these strengths into a dyslexic superpower [*my words*] needed by successful organisations and achieved by *talent diversity*. It ends with a call to action: *Positive dyslexia will change the world for good. Its time has come. Please help!*

Unconventional thinking =
Cognitive skills: 1. Big picture thinking, 2. Creativity/Innovation, 3. Visualisation/Spatial thinking
Work skills: 4. Determination/Resilience, 5. Proactivity, 6. Flexible Coping

Social skills: 7. Teamwork, 8. Empathy, 9. Communication

Yep, looks like a superpower, sounds like a superpower, so, it must be a superpower!

Dyslexia Awareness Week: Survival of the Species

It is Dyslexia Day on Thursday the 5th of October. Why might this be of interest to non-dyslexics and what has this got to do with survival of the species?

The publication of 'On the Origin of Species by Means of Natural Selection' by Charles Darwin on 24th November 1859 caused consternation. Nearly 158 years on, there is still debate in many parts of the world on whether evolution or creation theories should be taught in schools. In popular culture, the notion of *survival of the fittest* has gained a strong foothold—not least in business.

Just imagine if the survival, up until this point, of the human species was dependent on neural-diversity—that is the collective abilities within communities (from tribes to nations). This may seem a little farfetched, but bear with me a little longer.

Before the first great civilisations, small communities were dependant on their combined abilities, including fine detail thinking and big picture thinking. I imagine it would be difficult to identify any reason why one might be favoured more than the other. With the advent of languages systems, this was all set to change. Initially pictographic- and logographic-based systems probably had no or little impact on big picture thinkers. However, about 3,000 years ago, alphabet-based languages emerged and, with the aid of printing technologies, in wide use in Western Europe by 1500, came to dominate the sharing of knowledge (and power). So, perhaps not surprisingly, over just 500 years we have managed to design education systems which favour the learning of alphabet-based languages and in so doing have selected for negative attention our big picture thinkers.

If only I had realised this in my English class aged just 8! I could have stood up to Mrs W and said, 'Could I remind you that big picture thinkers have ensured the survival of the species to this moment in time and perhaps a little more respect of my superpower is called for at this very moment!'

Dyslexia Superpower Syllabus: Answers on a Postcard

In this blog, I am asking a simple question whilst knowing fully well the answer is complicated—or at least I hope it is! *What should be included in a course designed to help people, both with and without dyslexia, develop their big picture thinking skills?*

Of course, I'm using 'big picture thinking' as shorthand for visual, spatial thinking that enhances problem solving—I'll simply call this **envisioning,** in the sense of imagining possibilities that might arise in the future. So, *does envisioning capture all the positive characteristics so often found in people with dyslexia and also sound like a desirable skill non-dyslexics would like to acquire?*

As a starter for ten, please see the list of some of my suggestions for *'Envisioning 101'* for first year undergraduates that was delivered over ten weeks:

* introduction,
* developing your creativity,
* picture thinking,
* understanding multiple perspectives,
* working with others,
* communicating your ideas,
* system thinking,
* problem solving in practice 1,
* problem solving in practice 2,
* reflecting on your experience.

Dyslexia Superhero or Survivor?

This week, nearly a year from going public or coming out as an academic with dyslexia, I was asked two questions I found difficult to answer:

* What have you achieved, as a person with dyslexia, to this point in your life—being widely acknowledged as a leader in academia, business and the community?
* What would you say to your 8 year-old self struggling to understand why others around him could read and write whilst he was increasingly being labelled stupid and lazy?

My answer to, *What have you achieved?* was, *I have survived–I am a survivor of dyslexia.* This immediate and heartfelt response says much about my journey through education and work—and is so often heard from people with dyslexia—that success is to survive. I went on to explain that as a dyslexic, I live in a hostile world full of words and with the constant fear of exposure. So, to survive each day is a big achievement and far from any notion of public recognition or superhero status.

But, said the questioner, *you have achieved so much—what would you say to your younger self? That mere survival is all he has to look forward to?* Therein lies the critical flaw in my argument. To survive is not enough—we also need to hope. So, that is the message for my younger self—the hope of a better future, to reinvent dyslexia not as a disability or even a difference but an advantage or superpower.

Ask me again, *What would you say to your younger self?*

I would look that boy straight in the eye and say, *You have been born with a great advantage. Nurture it and it will be your true superpower and it will help all around you to have richer lives.*

A Year in the Life of The Dyslexic Professor!

I've made it! 52 blogs over 12 months = *A Year in the Life of The Dyslexic Professor.*

Of course, this is a moment to look both backwards and forwards. Backwards, to the highlights and unintended consequences and forwards to *so what?* and *what next?* What started, 12 months ago, with a single blog, has ended the year as a commitment to start a movement.

I have learnt two things about blogs; they are intensively personal and, at least for me, cathartic and people read them! So, by good foresight or good luck, I feel liberated and empowered and connected to others.

I have moved from seeing my dyslexia as a disability to a learning difference and now a true superpower, which guides my next steps . . . to quite literally turn the perception of dyslexia on its head. The question is not, *How do we support people with dyslexia in schools, colleges, universities, prisons and workplaces?* but rather, *how can organisations attract people with this dyslexia superpower?*

This is, in essence, a call for valuing diversity. Not because of a law or to do the right thing but because it produces results for both parties—*a win-win of* better organisations and happier people. It's time to commit oneself to a course of action, about which one is nervous, or, put simply, to . . . take the plunge!

> Or as, Mary Oliver (1992) expressed it so profoundly in the last line of The Summer Day. . .
> *Tell me, what is it you plan to do with your one wild and precious life?*

Conclusion

Not surprisingly, the story continued beyond the digital blogs to a public lecture, at the University of Cambridge, and creating a vision for a Superpower Institute. Coming out as a dyslexic has been a truly profound experience and meeting other adult dyslexics has been overwhelmingly positive. However, from these brief encounters it would be hard to underestimate the sadness I have observed and the release that acknowledging this can bring. So, any Superpower Institute will need to support dyslexics to enhance their abilities, build their confidence and acknowledge the personal damage and resulting sadness inflicted by inappropriate and outdated educational systems.

For me personally, the journey continues in my work as an academic—including my research, teaching and engagement activities. I do think my dyslexic thinking helps me in all aspects of my work, and disclosing I have dyslexia enables me and others to acknowledge the challenges and promote the advantages. In my experience, the successful modern academic increasingly works in teams, and disclosure provides the opportunity to build neurodiversity into any team from the outset.

There have been two unexpected outcomes from my decision to disclose my dyslexia and continue to blog about being a dyslexic academic every month. Firstly, use of the word superpower. Some non-dyslexics have challenged me because this implies that dyslexia is better and could alienate people who are not dyslexic. I do understand this point but most dyslexics see the joke straight away. Having survived my school days and emerged with a deeply held belief that I am thick, lazy and stupid, I do know I don't actually have a superpower as such but associating this expression with the positive aspects of my dyslexic thinking does help me let go of some of this ingrained negativity. So, I'm still hanging onto the expression 'dyslexia superpower' at the same time as issuing an apology to non-dyslexics. Interestingly, Margaret Rooke's recent book, *Dyslexia Is My Superpower*, explores this very subject from the perspective of young people (Rooke, 2017).

Secondly, supporting university students. This happens in three ways. First, at an individual level with students with dyslexia just contacting me from my own and other universities thanking me for disclosing my dyslexia, as this increases their own confidence. Second, realising that my preferred way of assessing students on my entrepreneurship modules is actually Dyslexia-Friendly! I teach at undergraduate, postgraduate and executive levels and have narrowed down my method of assessment to two types, with the second building on the first. I ask students to work in small groups to create a 5-minute video pitch. To do this, they develop an innovative business idea of their choice and produce a video in any format—animation, filming, slides or any combination—but using a structure (opportunity business models) we have discussed in class. Working in teams on creative projects but with some structure can help all students to perform well and for them to demonstrate the learning outcome of 'developing an entrepreneurial mindset.' The second assignment is to repeat the process individually but this time produce a structured report—much like a bank would ask for when considering lending money. All students benefit from a repeat performance and can concentrate more on their own contribution. For dyslexic students, this, together with the extended time to work on their report, can help them considerably. Finally, I am beginning to work with successful dyslexic leaders and dyslexia specialists to develop an online 'envisioning' or '#dyslexicthinking' module for university science students with dyslexia. Interestingly, this is rapidly moving from supporting learning to empowering employability. Just imagine a workplace which celebrates dyslexia!

References

Burbidge, I. (2017). Altered states. *RSA Journal, 163*(1) (5569), pp. 10–15. Retrieved from www.jstor.org/

Drennan, C. (2015, September). *MIT professor Catherine Drennan on her dyslexia and its advantages.* Talk presented at Dyslexia Advantage Leadership Conference. Edmonds, WA: Dyslexia Advantage. Retrieved from www.youtube.com

Economist. (2017, July 22). Technology is transforming what happens when a child goes to school. *The Economist.* Retrieved from www.economist.com/

Eden, G. (2016). The dyslexic brain. *YouTube*. Retrieved from https://youtube.com/

Eide, B., & Eide, F. (2012). *The dyslexic advantage*. New York, NY: Plume Books, Penguin Group.

Griggs, K. (2017). *Connecting the dots* (Made by Dyslexia Launch Report May 2017). Retrieved from http://madebydyslexia.org/

Lockett, N. (2017, May 15). Disability on campus: I have decided to go public as the dyslexic professor. *Times Higher Education*. Retrieved from www.timeshighereducation.com/

Lockett, N. (2020). *The dyslexic professor*. Retrieved from https://nigellockett.com/blog/

Logan, J. (2009). Dyslexic entrepreneurs: The incidence; Their coping strategies and their business skills. *Dyslexia, 15*, 328–334. https://doi.org/10.1002/dys.388

Nicolson, R. (2015). *Positive dyslexia*. Sheffield, UK: Rodin Books.

Oliver, M. (1992). *New and selected poems*. Boston, MA: Beacon Press.

Robinson, K., Sir. (2006, February). *Do schools kill creativity?* Talk presented at Technology, Entertainment and Design (TED) Conference. New York, NY: TED Foundation. Retrieved from www.ted.com/talks

Rooke, M. (2017). *Dyslexia is my superpower (most of the time)*. London, England: Jessica Kingsley Publishers.

Saltz, G. (2017). *The power of different*. New York, NY: Flatiron Books.

Tickle, L. (2015, January 15). Dyslexic entrepreneurs—Why they have a competitive edge. *The Guardian*. Retrieved from www.theguardian.com/

Part II
Dyslexia

7 Dyslexia and Entrepreneurship
A Theoretical Perspective

Angela Fawcett

Introduction

In this chapter, I shall explore the theoretical basis for the creativity identified in individuals who experience dyslexia which has led to an interest in entrepreneurship and dyslexia. Firstly, let us consider the definition of entrepreneur—this seems to be based on adopting an innovative approach under your own initiative, and being prepared to take risks that may or may not lead to profit. The interest in entrepreneurs and dyslexia stemmed mainly from the work of Julie Logan (2009), who found a higher incidence (19%) of entrepreneurship in individuals who experience dyslexia than the general population (5%–10%). It has long been the holy grail of research for many with an interest in the strengths of dyslexia to identify the potential source of their creativity. So, for example, it is argued that the coping strategies and creativity that students who experience dyslexia develop help them to become entrepreneurs (Everatt, Steffert, & Smythe, 1999). This was demonstrated in this research in tests of visual creativity, where individuals who experience dyslexia produced 30% more examples of uses for a brick and creating pictures from shapes. A range of studies from Gilger and colleagues (see for example Gilger, Talavage, & Olulade, 2013) have also tried to pin down the source of giftedness, but this has proved elusive, although von

Karolyi and colleagues (2001, 2003) have identified spatial strengths in resolving impossible figures (see also Schneps, Brockmole, Sonnert, & Pomplun, 2012). In this chapter, I shall try to provide a theoretically driven causal explanation for this pattern of strengths that may underlie entrepreneurship and dyslexia.

There are many examples of adults who experience dyslexia with exceptional ability, particularly in the arts but also in science, with many anecdotal reports that some of our most famous historical celebrities are individuals who experience dyslexia. It may seem counterintuitive that someone with all the deficits that have been associated with dyslexia should display exceptional talent and persistence in the face of difficulties. However, if we consider first the automaticity deficit (Nicolson & Fawcett, 1990), that I discovered during my PhD, supervised by my colleague Prof Rod Nicolson, then the underlying reasons for these exceptional strengths start to become clearer.

For many years, it has been recognised that children with dyslexia were slow to attain automaticity in reading (LaBerge & Samuels, 1974). This may seem hardly surprising given that dyslexia is often characterised by phonological difficulties, firstly in grasping grapheme/phoneme recognition and then in segmenting and blending (Snowling, 2000) with the overall effect that reading remains slow, inaccurate and effortful. The resultant load on working memory impacts comprehension, and over time it becomes more and more difficult for children who experience dyslexia to access the curriculum.

Our research was the first to demonstrate that this difficulty in learning was not confined to reading or even writing and spelling but applied across the board in all of the skills that we examined. Initially our research focussed on balance, based on the concept that all skills whether cognitive or motor are learnt in the same fashion. Surprisingly we found that adolescents with dyslexia were able to balance when just balancing, but when asked to perform a secondary task, like counting, their performance deteriorated and they wobbled and even fell over (Nicolson & Fawcett, 1990; Fawcett & Nicolson, 1992). We replicated our findings with other age groups of individuals who experience dyslexia, and used other tasks including blindfold balance, and established that a similar profile could be found for the majority of those we worked with.

Naturally, these findings were initially controversial, but since then a number of studies from other research groups have found a similar pattern in individuals who experience dyslexia across the age range, including adults, with at least 50% of individuals who experience dyslexia showing a similar profile (Ramus, Pidgeon, & Frith, 2003; White et al., 2006).

These initial findings of automaticity deficit inspired us to look more closely at a range of skills in children with dyslexia aged 8 to 17 years old, and controls matched for chronological and reading age. The design for our studies, with three age groups, was inspired by Prof Alan Baddeley, who we worked with in studying working memory and dyslexia. Our motivation here was to address all the theories that were prevalent in the 1990s on the causes and symptoms of dyslexia. These included the phonological deficit, the double deficit (Wolf & Bowers, 1999) that identified problems in both speed and phonology, and our own automaticity and cerebellar deficits (Fawcett, Nicolson, & Dean, 1996; Nicolson, Fawcett, & Dean, 2001) that highlighted the importance of motor skills. Interestingly, our data showed that deficits could be found in all of these skills, with children with dyslexia performing worse than the reading age controls in many cases. This confirmed that the problems in dyslexia are much deeper than simply in literacy, although these are the symptoms on which dyslexia is typically diagnosed.

We went on to run a number of comparisons with children with generalised difficulties in order to show that in many areas slow learners made greater progress than children with dyslexia, although both groups showed severe difficulties with phonology (Fawcett, Nicolson, & Maclagan, 2001). This period of research is one of which we are particularly proud, allowing us to draw up a hypothetical causal chain for the development of dyslexia from preschool to age 8.

Working within the framework proposed by Frith (1985), we considered the role of brain cognition and behaviour in dyslexia, focusing on differences at the brain level in cerebellar function and identifying differences in learning at all stages rather than just in the final stage at which performance becomes automatic (Nicolson & Fawcett, 2000). Our research showed that there were problems in getting started, in making more errors and blending skills together. These results showed how difficult it is for even the most committed teachers to make a difference in dyslexia, despite many hours of intervention and support.

The emphasis of our research from this stage onwards was to address learning in dyslexia, in order to understand the pattern of difficulties that we had identified. We concentrated here on the difference between procedural learning (learning how to do things) and declarative learning (learning facts) and identified a procedural learning deficit in dyslexia (Nicolson & Fawcett, 2007). It seemed that even the highest achieving university students with dyslexia showed difficulties in overnight consolidation, a key factor in learning and even in their speed of reading simple words (Nicolson, Fawcett, Brookes, & Needle, 2010).

You may well wonder how all of this theory relates to strengths in individuals who experience dyslexia, and in particular to the role of entrepreneurs. Surely, we are simply identifying further deficits in dyslexia that go well beyond those that other researchers have identified in reading and literacy. So how can we move from this position to arguing that adults with dyslexia have the potential to become world leaders? If we look more closely at the range of theories associated with dyslexia, it is disappointing to note that very few would actually suggest strengths in dyslexia. Even our own cerebellar deficit is more closely associated with deficits than strengths. Indeed, only our automaticity deficit and the procedural learning deficit have anything to contribute on strengths in dyslexia. The procedural learning deficit in fact suggests that weaknesses in procedural learning are compensated by equal or greater strengths in declarative learning, with evidence for this from Hedenius and colleagues (Hedenius, Ullman, Alm, Jennische, & Persson, 2013).

Our most recent theory of Delayed Neural Commitment (DNC; Nicolson & Fawcett, 2018) suggests that dyslexia is associated with minimal brain differences originating during development in the womb, which lead to increased neural noise in visual, auditory and learning networks. This leads to language delays, manifest as phonological difficulties, problems in automatising skills, including articulation and both implicit and explicit skills and difficulty in shedding earlier habits, resulting in greater difficulty in building the networks needed for executive learning and reading.

There is clear evidence for differences in processing sounds from birth (Molfese, 2000), for difficulty based on retaining primitive reflexes (McPhillips, Hepper, & Mulhern, 2000) and for children with dyslexia having difficulty in building the visual word area necessary for fluent reading (Shaywitz et al., 2007) as reflected in the findings of the National Reading panel (National Institute for Child Health and Human Development, 2010). Above all, the DNC allows us to move away from seeing dyslexia as simply a deficit, to consider the possible advantages of processing that might be attributed to dyslexia, as well as consider whether other developmental disabilities could be explained under the same framework, reflecting the co-morbidity so regularly found in dyslexia. The DNC suggests that early learning, executive function and readiness for school are key in ensuring the best outcomes for dyslexia.

Let me explain this further because it is somewhat counterintuitive to see negative aspects of automaticity. Automaticity is truly amazing in most circumstances—once you have learned a skill to the level where it is automatic, you no longer need to think about what you're doing, you can simply go into automatic pilot mode and this frees your higher-level resources for acquiring new skills. This is the basis for all learning—you become competent in one skill, your performance becomes more and more fluid and the skill itself becomes trivial to perform. Unfortunately, individuals who experience dyslexia never fully reach that stage of learning, their performance remains slower, more effortful and more error prone.

Again, in these circumstances how can this possibly lead to strengths in dyslexia? It's necessary here to consider whether automaticity is always a boon—it seems that once you are automatic you lose conscious access to a skill, so in order to describe how you do it to others is almost impossible and your performance becomes fixed into a routine that's impossible to change. This means loss of flexibility in thought, so that you can always produce the right answer but you are limited in the creativity of your thinking. This lack of automaticity could be a major source of strengths as well as weaknesses.

As young infants, we learn from our environment to recognise statistical regularities—this forms the basis of language learning and, in fact, of most academic learning as we grow up. Observing these regularities in the environment allows us to predict and infer correctly, but one major limitation is that this ensures inflexibility. By contrast, because individuals who experience dyslexia have difficulty in acquiring new skills, they typically need to work from first principles in working out their answers rather than immediately knowing the correct response. This frees their thinking to allow greater creativity and originality in their responses. The DNC hypothesis suggests that the mechanism for this is a longer learning period into adolescence and adulthood coupled with the ability to integrate processing across different brain regions

So, does this mean that all individuals who experience dyslexia are exceptional in their thinking and all have the potential to become entrepreneurs? Unfortunately, the experience of school itself can be very destructive for children who experience dyslexia, and many will fall by the wayside and end up unemployed or even in prison. In an environment where there is increasing pressure to achieve high academic results, it is difficult for individuals who experience dyslexia to be successful. A certain resilience is needed to constantly work at the pace necessary to be successful given that, even as a university student who experiences dyslexia, your performance is likely to be slower and more effortful than other students of similar ability (Nicolson et al., 2010). A key to continued success has to be confidence, and this is often lowered, by negative experiences, for individuals who experience dyslexia.

So, does this mean that only the most exceptional individuals who experience dyslexia can become entrepreneurs? My colleague Rod Nicolson introduced the concept of positive dyslexia (Nicolson, 2015), based on our theoretical work, and has argued that society will only become truly successful, once it has recognised the unusual strengths that dyslexia can contribute in the workforce. The basis for positive dyslexia was the recognition by Martin Seligman that, 'Curing the negatives does not produce the positives. . . . The skills of becoming happy turn out to be almost entirely different from the skills of not being sad, not being anxious, or not being angry' (Seligman, 2018, preface); so there is a real need to focus on strengths in order to craft a more fulfilling life for patients.

This seemed to us to apply even more strongly to dyslexia, with the danger that the continuous focus on the areas that a child finds difficult will lower their self-esteem, already damaged by failure, still further. We had begun to identify the ongoing problems in dyslexia as largely attributable to this early experience, which can exacerbate the existing problems into an even more intractable condition. The danger here, of course, is that the skills and strengths which individuals who experience dyslexia can bring to the world are totally overwhelmed by their experiences of failure.

Positive dyslexia identified the effectiveness of pull goals, doing something because you want to, rather than push goals, doing something because you're told to. In a series of interviews with successful adults who experience dyslexia, in Nicolson's research with Sara Agahi, a series of key skills were identified as characteristic of those who went on to achieve success. These included cognitive, social and work skills, capped by unconventional thinking.

A further series of studies into the comparative strengths of students who experience dyslexia and other students at the University of Sheffield identified a decathlon of strengths in dyslexia, including creativity, social skills and big picture thinking. Studies by Poliana Sepulveda highlighted in this book examined the skills of entrepreneurial individuals who experience dyslexia in particular. This research identified key factors in the likelihood of an entrepreneurial career in dyslexia, which included a family background that favoured this development. In effect, adults who experience dyslexia are much more likely to become entrepreneurs if there was a family history of entrepreneurs, particularly when their parents also show aspects of dyslexia. Given that there is around a 50% chance of experiencing dyslexia if you have a parent who experiences dyslexia, this is a strong contributory factor in the heightened incidence of entrepreneurs with dyslexia. Moreover, a family background which encourages the child and adolescent who experiences dyslexia to challenge the over-riding importance of literacy in success is likely to be conducive to the development of entrepreneurs, who can build on recognition from their families of the potential in following unconventional directions.

As researchers, Rod and I have been privileged to work with some outstanding individuals who experience dyslexia across the age range, including the supervision of a number of successful PhD students who experience dyslexia. Our theories on dyslexia have been inspired by this ongoing contact, for me in particular, in a family setting, but also for both Rod and I in the context of both our theoretical and applied research. In the section that follows, I shall describe some of the individuals that I have known who experience dyslexia and what they have contributed to our thinking, starting naturally with my son Matthew, who inspired me to set out on my career in dyslexia research and for me is a living example of positive dyslexia, living his dream. I shall focus particularly on the importance of belief and support within the family, from the early years onwards, as a major factor in success in whatever field the adolescent and adult shows they have the ability to shine in.

Insights From a 30-Year Career in Dyslexia Research

My lifetime interest in dyslexia developed in response to the struggles my son Matt endured within the school system, as has my interest in positive dyslexia. Matthew was identified as experiencing dyslexia at an unusually early age, only 5 and ½ years old, because of his exceptional spoken language skills by contrast with extreme difficulty in grasping the early elements of literacy, such as grapheme/phoneme recognition. This mismatch between his overall ability and his achievement led to great distress for Matthew. As a child who had always been curious and keen to learn in preschool, we had anticipated that he would thoroughly enjoy school life. However, he seemed to have lost all his confidence and zest for life, and regularly woke in the night with pains in his legs.

The psychologist who assessed Matt at the Children's Hospital told him that he would be able to achieve anything that he wanted to in life but he would need to work harder than other children to be successful. At this stage, Matt told us that they used to hold up pieces of paper with words written on them (flashcards) and everyone else knew what it said, so he must be stupid. It was striking to note how much his confidence improved following the diagnosis, when for the first time he could understand why he had such difficulties. However, at primary school, there was little concept amongst his teachers of what dyslexia entailed, and a tendency to dumb down the curriculum for children with difficulties.

This was just the start of a long struggle to learn, where Matthew had extra lessons and several hours of homework to complete while his older sister was able to play, but gradually, over time, Matthew began to acquire literacy. At the age of 7, it was suggested that he should attend a special school in Sheffield that worked with dyslexia, but, in the event, there were other children with greater difficulty and he was allowed to join the local junior school. Matthew at this stage showed exceptional thinking and reasoning skills and in many ways the curriculum for the special skills seemed too immature for him, so it was a relief to us when he was accepted into a mainstream school.

However, this was the beginning of an extraordinarily difficult time for Matthew, where from a high level of spoken language ability he developed a severe stutter which rendered him unable to make himself understood. This was based on misunderstandings within the school system because he was clearly verbally able and yet he was performing so poorly. When the head found that his non-verbal intelligence was at the 99.9th percentile, he told me that Matthew was a naughty little boy who needed his bottom kicked. Fortunately, at this stage a new head arrived with a greater understanding of dyslexia and he helped Matthew to complete his homework by writing down the answers, and so Matthew was able to complete all the work he had not finished in class in a few minutes rather than the hours it had normally taken him to complete by hand.

When Matthew was 8, I started my first degree in psychology as an undergraduate at Sheffield University. Living with dyslexia, particularly with Matthew, inspired my research into automaticity and the theory of conscious compensation that I proposed to account for the extra effort required to achieve normal performance in many skills for children and adults with dyslexia. I had direct experience of the amount of time Matthew was prepared to commit to his work, and his academic turn of thought, as well as the anxiety his difficulties caused him.

It was not easy to combine being a mature student with having two children, but I found it fascinating as a student of psychology, learning about many of the theories involved to try these out on my own family. In particular, Matthew seemed to have an instinctive grasp of ethics, responding as an 8-year old to the Kohlberg dilemma with the recognition that money could never be put above human life, while his 12-year-old sister was concerned about breaking the law. Matthew's thinking is an example of post-conventional morality that only 10%–15% of adolescents attain. This ethical and moral stance characterises Matt as an adult, in both his work and his life-style, refusing to consume like his peers, riding his bicycle and travelling by train rather than by plane in order to sustain the environment.

When I started researching with Rod, his expertise lay in learning while my primary interests lay in dyslexia, and I took the opportunity to interest Rod in the anomalies in performance that might be attributed to dyslexia, introducing him to a range of well-known individuals who experience dyslexia at academic conferences. Over the years, I have also shared with Rod many examples of this mismatch between Matthew's abstract thinking skills and his literacy skills, helping to form Rod's concepts of the enigma of dyslexia.

Over time, it became increasingly clear to me that my husband David had a similar pattern of processing to Matthew. In fact, he'd struggled all his life through schooling, but was able to achieve the full school leaving certificate from his technical school and proceeded to study for a City and Guilds qualification in instrument mechanics. By this stage, David had become a successful technical salesman for Honeywell Controls, and was characterised by his people skills and attention to detail, in order to compensate for his organisational difficulties.

David was eventually diagnosed by my colleague Rod Nicolson, and overwhelmed to discover that many of his skills were superior, despite typical difficulties in speed and memory and characteristic spelling errors that might be attributed to dyslexia. The friendship that developed between our two families, and time spent with David and Matthew, led Rod to develop many of his ideas on positive dyslexia, noting the differences in processing in terms of both unexpected strengths and weaknesses in my family. For me, there is a certain contiguity between the concept of post-conventional thinking and the unconventional thinking which forms the pinnacle of Rod's positive dyslexia triathlon. Moreover, David was the first successful adult who experienced dyslexia to be interviewed for this positive dyslexia study.

Through my research into dyslexia over the years, I have encountered a range of children and adults who experience dyslexia, many exhibiting strengths, including those entrepreneurial skills that have been highlighted in this book. Of course, not all have taken an entrepreneurial route in their careers, but they have been characterised by determination to succeed despite all the odds, another key aspect of positive dyslexia. Moreover, they have been willing to take risks in order to succeed. It is this same determination and risk-taking that I recognise in many of the contributors to this book, who have themselves struggled with dyslexia and overcome it to become successful authors.

In my panel, I think first of Richard, an adult who came into the university for diagnosis for himself and his young daughter, recognising a similar pattern of difficulties in her processing. Having failed a nursing degree because of the difficulties he had experienced in examinations, his diagnosis led him to a new resolution to become a doctor instead. This was entirely based on a recognition of his superior ability, which became fully apparent from his diagnostic assessment and which gave him the confidence to attempt the seemingly impossible. Today, Richard is a highly successful consultant, having benefited from the extra time allowance in his medical examinations to ensure that he could reach his full potential. It is this resilience and risk-taking in the face of failure which to me characterises so many of our entrepreneurs who experience dyslexia. This resonates strongly with the findings that determination and resilience are key factors in positive dyslexia, which both share the characteristics that lie well outside the educational curriculum but are vital for success in life.

I remember one of the members of my panel of adolescents with dyslexia, James, a mature boy with severe difficulties in reading who had taught himself to drive a tractor before he was 12. This enabled him to express his entrepreneurial flair by setting up a potato picking business working for farmers around his home at an age which was clearly well below the official working age. For James, literacy and academic skills were largely irrelevant because he knew that he would always be able to turn his hand to something that would interest him and bring in funds.

For my own brother-in-law, Chris, an intrepid master mariner who lives on his boat and taught adults to sail, before sailing around the world, it seemed the most natural thing in the world in retirement to buy a derelict yacht to renovate and sell. He risked his financial investment, using all the skills to good effect that he had built up in maintaining his own boat, to complete a task that he loved.

Key characteristics here are the confidence that you can be successful and the willingness to risk everything for the opportunity to work under your own initiative. They also highlight the importance of the intuitive empathy which characterises the positive individual with dyslexia, coupled with the ability to negotiate with others to achieve support for their needs. None of these examples are likely to make the headlines but to me they are an excellent illustration of the type of career path that an entrepreneur who experiences dyslexia might take, whether or not they are successful.

Finally, I think of Damien, who I worked with from the age of 8 years old, as part of my panel. He was the one who became so bored by repeating his learning task on the computer that he simply altered the name of the file to prove that his performance had stopped improving. Fortunately, I noticed that the data for this file and the previous file were identical and I was able to successfully thwart his efforts to cheat in order to gain an advantage, in this case relief from boredom. This seemed to me a very entrepreneurial approach, as did his attempts as a 15-year-old boy to set up a date with my PhD student. I recognised that he would go far, based on both cheekiness, effective strategy use and initiative!

My own son Matthew has crafted his own job through his interests as an environmental activist, driven by the need to effect change rather than make money, working first with the Kindling Trust to inspire passion for sustainability and latterly with an international consortium on sustainable climate change, and leading the campaign for the North of England against Trident, our nuclear submarine, for the Campaign for Nuclear Disarmament.

Returning to the wider world of entrepreneurs, in writing this chapter I have been particularly inspired by the story of Adam Neumann, who describes himself as severely dyslexic and an indifferent student, who wanted to create a blueprint for a meaningful life. For him, this involves working for yourself, with a spouse who loves you for your potential and kids whose superpowers it is your mission to unlock. After several failed attempts at setting up a business, including one that focussed on baby grows with removable knees, and another creating women's shoes with collapsible heels (Farley, 2017), Adam had clearly found his niche in his company WeWork. An article in *The Guardian* newspaper showed that Adam has changed the way 210,000 people work. His company was the largest office occupier in London. It was not just office space that Adam was selling but a whole new way of life. His vision is based on the motto 'do what you love' and offers a lifestyle that includes, 'free Artisan coffee, grapefruit infused water and a choice of craft beers' (Neate, 2018). The organisation also arranges parties and events including meditation, boxing and candlelight yoga, in other words, a whole new way of life.

The vision was planned to extend to include a new company, WeLive, which will introduce the concept of dormitory living for adults in Manhattan and Washington, with gyms and spas attached to address the needs of the whole person. Moving into education, they are setting up scholarships for women in technology and are moving into the kindergarten and primary arena with WeGrow. 'If you really want to change the world, change kids when they're two' (Neate, 2018).

They emphasise the use of mentors in education, drawn from their WeWork members, and the potential for basing work spaces around the school itself, to facilitate child-care. Intriguingly, his company rents most of its accommodation from landlords and breaks offices up into really small units that are affordable in the current economic climate. This has meant that the company has grown to over 230 offices in 71 cities over a period of 8 years without the need for Adam himself to invest vast quantities of money, and he is now a multi-billionaire in the process. For me, this was an excellent example of the vision and entrepreneurial skills that characterise successful individuals who experience dyslexia and the positive dyslexia movement.

Conclusions

We have inevitably covered a great deal of ground in this chapter, moving from public understanding of entrepreneurs who experience dyslexia through the literature highlighting their role in society and the positive dyslexia movement that has identified the potential of so many individuals who experience dyslexia to adopt this approach in their life and careers, whether or not they are highly successful. I have taken you through a theoretical explanation for this pattern of processing and established that this can provide a causal explanation for entrepreneurism in individuals who experience dyslexia.

Finally, I have illustrated points in this chapter with accounts of some of the children and adults I have worked with, who have inspired my interest in this field, as well as introducing a phenomenally successful entrepreneur who experiences dyslexia. Let me take you back to Adam Neumann and his approach that was crafted so cleverly towards the burgeoning needs of young people, providing work, culture, home and schools appropriate for this time of austerity. The latest figures suggest that the WeWork approach pioneered by Neumann is struggling, with a drop in the value of the company and the ousting of Neumann for eccentric behaviour.

Despite this, given appropriate support, it seems to me that our entrepreneurs who experience dyslexia have the potential to solve so many of the problems that the younger generation is suffering from in an exciting and innovative fashion. Clearly, my colleague Rod Nicolson (2015) is a visionary in his call for businesses to recognise that the reasons for their success may lie with their entrepreneurs who experience dyslexia, and the key to greater success would be to employ more individuals who experience dyslexia.

References

Everatt, J., Steffert, B., & Smythe, I. (1999). An eye for the unusual: Creative thinking in dyslexics. *Dyslexia, 5*, 28–46. https://doi.org/10.1002/(SICI)1099-0909(199903)5:1 < 28::AID-DYS126 > 3.0.CO;2-K

Farley, T. W. (2017, June 14). *Adam Neumann co-founder and CEO WeWork*. New York, NY: Economic Club of New York. Retrieved from www.econclubny.org/

Fawcett, A. J., & Nicolson, R. I. (1992). Automatisation deficits in balance for dyslexic children. *Perceptual and Motor Skills, 75*, 507–529. https://doi.org/10.2466/pms.1992.75.2.507

Fawcett, A. J., Nicolson, R. I., & Dean, P. (1996). Impaired performance of children with dyslexia on a range of cerebellar tasks. *Annals of Dyslexia, 46*, 259–283. https://doi.org/10.1007/BF02648179

Fawcett, A. J., Nicolson, R. I., & Maclagan, F. (2001). Cerebellar tests differentiate between groups of poor readers with and without IQ discrepancy.

Journal of Learning Disabilities, 24(2), 119–135. https://doi.org/10.1177/002221940103400203

Frith, U. (1985). Beneath the surface of developmental dyslexia. In K. E. Patterson, J. C. Marshall, & M. Coltheart (Eds.), *Surface dyslexia: Neurological and cognitive studies of phonological reading* (pp. 301–330). London, England: Lawrence Erlbaum.

Gilger, J., Talavage, T. M., & Olulade, O. A. (2013). An fMRI study of nonverbally gifted reading disabled adults: Has deficit compensation effected gifted potential? *Frontiers in Neuroscience, 507*, 1–12. https://doi.org/10.3389/fnhum.2013.00507

Hedenius, M., Ullman, M. T., Alm, P., Jennische, M., & Persson, J. (2013). Enhanced recognition memory after incidental encoding in children with developmental dyslexia. *PLoS ONE, 8*(5), e63998. https://doi.org/10.1371/journal.pone.0063998

LaBerge, D., & Samuels, S. J. (1974). Toward a theory of automatic information process in reading. *Cognitive Psychology, 6*, 293–323. https://doi.org/10.1016/0010-0285(74)90015-2

Logan, J. (2009). Dyslexic entrepreneurs: The incidence; Their coping strategies and their business skills. *Dyslexia, 15*, 328–334. https://doi.org/10.1002/dys.388

McPhillips, M., Hepper, P. G., & Mulhern, G. (2000). Effects of replicating primary-reflex movements on specific reading difficulties in children: A randomised, double-blind, controlled trial. *The Lancet, 355*(9203), 537–541. https://doi.org/10.1016/S0140-6736(99)02179-0

Molfese, D. L. (2000). Predicting dyslexia at 8 years of age using neonatal brain responses. *Brain and Language, 72*(3), 238–245. https://doi.org/10.1006/brln.2000.2287

National Institute for Child Health and Human Development (NICHD). (2000). *Report of the National Reading Panel: Teaching children to read.* Washington, DC: National Institute for Child Health and Human Development. Retrieved from www.nichd.nih.gov

Neate, R. (2018, March 23). WeGeneration work, rest and play together in Adam Neumann's empire. *The Guardian.* Retrieved from www.theguardian.com/

Nicolson, R. I. (2015). *Positive dyslexia.* Sheffield, UK: Rodin Books.

Nicolson, R. I., & Fawcett, A. J. (1990). Automaticity: A new framework for dyslexia research? *Cognition, 35*(2), 159–182. https://doi.org/10.1016/0010-0277(90)90013-A

Nicolson, R. I., & Fawcett, A. J. (2000). Long-term learning in dyslexic children. *European Journal of Cognitive Psychology, 12*, 357–393. https://doi.org/10.1080/09541440050114552

Nicolson, R. I., & Fawcett, A. J. (2007). Procedural learning difficulties: Reuniting the developmental disorders? *Trends in Neurosciences, 30*(4), 135–141. https://doi.org/10.1016/j.tins.2007.02.003

Nicolson, R. I., & Fawcett, A. J. (2018). Procedural learning, dyslexia and delayed neural commitment. In T. Lachmann & T. Weis (Eds.), *Reading and dyslexia: From basic functions to higher order cognition* (pp. 236–269). New York, NY: Springer International Publishers.

Nicolson, R. I., Fawcett, A. J., Brookes, R. L., & Needle, J. (2010). Procedural learning and dyslexia. *Dyslexia, 16*(3), 194–212. https://doi.org/10.1002/dys.408

Nicolson, R. I., Fawcett, A. J., & Dean, P. (2001). Developmental dyslexia: The cerebellar deficit hypothesis. *Trends in Neurosciences, 24*(9), 508–511. https://doi.org/10.1016/S0166-2236(00)01896-8

Ramus, F., Pidgeon, E., & Frith, U. (2003). The relationship between motor control and phonology in dyslexic children. *Journal of Child Psychology and Psychiatry and Allied Disciplines, 44*(5), 712–722. Retrieved from www.researchgate.net/

Schneps, M. H., Brockmole, J. R., Sonnert, G., & Pomplun, M. (2012). History of reading struggles linked to enhanced learning in low spatial frequency scenes. *PLoS ONE, 7*(4), e35724. https://doi.org/10.1371/journal.pone.0035724

Seligman, M. E. P. (2018). *Learned optimism: How to change your mind and your life* (2nd ed.). London, England: Nicholas Brealey Publishing

Shaywitz, B. A., Skudlarski, P., Holahan, J. M., Marchione, K. E., Todd Constable, R., Fulbright, R. K., . . . Shaywitz, S. E. (2007). Age-related changes in reading systems of dyslexic children. *Annals of Neurology, 61*(4), 363–370. https://doi.org/10.1002/ana.21093

Snowling, M. J. (2000). *Dyslexia*. Oxford, UK: Blackwell.

von Karolyi, C. (2001). Visual-spatial strength in dyslexia: Rapid discrimination of impossible figures. *Journal of Learning Disabilities, 34*(4), 380–391. https://doi.org/10.1177/002221940103400413

von Karolyi, C., Winner, E., Gray, W., & Sherman, G. (2003). Dyslexia linked to talent: Global visual-spatial ability. *Brain and Language, 85*(3), 427–431. https://doi.org/10.1016/S0093-934X(03)00052-X

White, S., Milne, E., Rosen, S., Hansen, P., Swettenham, J., Frith, U., & Ramus, F. (2006). The role of sensorimotor impairments in dyslexia: A multiple case study of dyslexic children. *Developmental Science, 9*(3), 237–255. https://doi.org/10.1111/j.1467-7687.2006.00483.x

Wolf, M., & Bowers, P. G. (1999). The double-deficit hypothesis for the developmental dyslexias. *Journal of Educational Psychology, 91*(3), 415–438. https://doi.org/10.1037/0022-0663.91.3.415

8   Dyslexia, Trauma, and Traits for Success

Neil Alexander-Passe

Introduction

This chapter researches the experience of learners with dyslexia at school and how these experiences can either positively drive them to success or negatively drive them into helplessness and possibly crime.

The nature vs nurture argument has a long history from John Locke in 1690 (Lowe, 1995) arguing that humans begin in a 'blank state,' being the product of our environment and experiences. Of course Darwin and Beer (1996) and Galton (1895) should not be discounted in this discussion, as argued by Pinker (2003). Locke, Darwin and others have argued that we are the product of our environment, and all human experiences are placed into the mixing pot to create the individuals we are today. Therefore, in the case of those with dyslexia, they are the product of ten or more years of hardship at school, where learning is not generally differentiated to their needs by teachers who do not recognise their different learning needs. Some teachers have been found to perceive children with un-identified dyslexia as lazy and stupid, these teachers demonstrating their:

1. Lack of dyslexia/Special Educational Needs (SEN) awareness
2. Lack of understanding of dyslexia/SEN
3. Lack of training to identify and differentiate to engage all learners in their classrooms, creating a lack of educational opportunity

If success breeds success, then failure may also breed failure; thus it could be argued:

- Successful adults with dyslexia are a product of using failure in a positive way (resilience) and more success reinforces this positivity.
- Unsuccessful adults with dyslexia are a product of using failure in a negative way (learned helplessness) and more failure reinforces this negativity.

Literature Review

Dyslexia

It could be argued that there are two main perspectives concerning dyslexia. One looks at the root causes, be it through heredity or language processing complications in early childhood, with a focus on the deficits that such a condition brings and how they can be overcome through remedial educational interventions. The second perspective looks at the emotional and psychological effects of having a different learning style than that of their friends, family and peers.

This chapter is concerned with the second perspective, looking at both the emotional effects of school and how individuals with dyslexia use such effects in both their childhood and adulthood to bring about positive change.

Defining Success

How each of us defines success is deeply personal. We each have our own definition of success, for some success is about what we accomplish, for others it's who we've become and still to others it's what we own. The central issue is not what your definition of success contains or if it's right or wrong. Instead the central issues should be, 'Have you created your own personal definition of success?'

Success is highly subjective and success to one is not the same to all, as noted by Krakovsky (2014). Success is an extremely hard concept to research. Success is context-based, so it can differ, from when talking about success in engineering to doing a trial for a new pharmaceutical drug (Emens, 2008; Ralph & Kelly, 2014). To summarise the previous definition, one could conclude that success is accomplishing an aim or goal, and in many ways it is aligned with fame, wealth and social status, and this will be the basis of this chapter.

Adults—Successful Adults with Dyslexia

Logan (2001, 2009) investigated the frequency of persons with dyslexia amongst corporate management and entrepreneurs. Her conclusions based on a low response rate (43% in the UK study and 7% in the US study of people with undiagnosed dyslexia) found a higher frequency of self-diagnosed persons with dyslexia as entrepreneurs (from an N=30 US sample). However, due to her small sample size, low response rate, and that no evidence of dyslexia diagnosis was required to participate, such findings should be taken with caution. Logan and others argue that self-employment affords persons with dyslexia the ability to work in their own way, concentrating on their strengths rather than suffering paperwork issues in middle-management. Success also comes through the delegation of paperwork/other tasks so they can concentrate on what they do best, talking to people and coming up with novel/divergent answers to problems. Fitzgibbon and O'Connor (2002) support Logan's conclusions that persons with dyslexia are less likely to thrive in a corporate-structured environment.

Whilst organisations herald well-known businessmen with dyslexia (e.g. Sir Richard Branson and Charles Schwab) as role models, are these realistic? Biographies of such people suggest that they delegate all menial tasks (note-taking, reading and writing emails and checking financial forecasts) that persons with dyslexia are typically less good at. This frees them up to think creatively/divergently, to sell ideas to others and to take risks, which are essential skills for entrepreneurship according to Gatewood, Shaver, and Gartner (1995), Stewart and Roth (2001), and Logan (2001). Branson and Schwab have founded global empires that are built on them acting autonomously—being the brand.

Fink (2002) investigated N=60 successful men and women with dyslexia (e.g. doctors, lawyers, educationalists, filmmakers, computer programmers, writers and administrators), aiming to understand how individuals diagnosed with dyslexia had attained in prestigious careers whilst battling literacy problems. Results indicate:

1. They pursued passionate interests—subjects they were happy to read about and thus improve their reading ability.
2. They developed persistence and empathy—to not give up in the face of struggles/problems and to empathise with others with similar struggles.

3. Mentors were important role models and supporters in struggling times.
4. There was denial of access to chosen careers by others—being discouraged reinforced motivation to overcome barriers.

In Raskind, Goldberg and Higgins (2003), the authors performed a 20 year, longitudinal study of $N=47$ successful and unsuccessful adults with learning disabilities (a similar term for dyslexia that is used in the US, as defined by Elliott & Grigorenko, 2014). Participant success was defined based on six domains (employment, education, independence, family relationships, community relations/interests and crime/substance abuse). The following correlated with success: Perseverance 0.88, Proactivity 0.90, Goal-setting 0.75, Self-awareness 0.69, Emotional stability 0.55, Lack of support systems -0.84, Emotional instability -0.78, Reactivity -0.70, Lack of goal setting -0.70 and Lack of self-awareness -0.58). These would support Logan's (2001, 2009) data.

Dowell (2003), writing for the *Sunday Times*, discussed Tulip Financial Research Ltd's 2003 study of $N=300$ UK millionaires for the British Broadcasting Corporation television programme 'The Mind of a Millionaire.' He noted that the study found that about 40% of respondents had experienced dyslexia. In his article, Dowell went on to report the words of a business psychologist, Adrian Atkinson, who was involved in the research, pinpointing the impact of dyslexia for this group: '*Most people who make a million have difficult childhoods or have been frustrated in a major way . . . Dyslexia is one of the driving forces behind that*' (Dowell, 2003).

Lastly, Scott, Scherman and Phillips (1992) identified a main difference between successful and unsuccessful individuals with dyslexia, with successful individuals having at least one person who believed in them (mostly their mother) and encouraged their talents and hobbies (Morgan & Klein, 2003). Thomson (1990/1996) also noticed that successful people with dyslexia were commonly those who managed by being highly intelligent but who were often under-achievers, failing to attain their potential and sometimes suffering a lifetime of frustration.

Adults—Unsuccessful People With Dyslexia

Morgan and Klein (2003) argue that many undiagnosed children/young people with dyslexia leave school without any formal qualifications resulting in job opportunities being generally limited to unskilled work.

Gaining an interview required many skills which they found extremely challenging: registering for unemployment benefits by completing forms and attending job centres on specific days and at specific times, reading hundreds of job advertisements, requesting and completing application forms, writing personal statements, etc. Disclosure is also a common dilemma for adults with dyslexia.

Whilst UK and US legislation offers technology and other assistance to help people who experience dyslexia in the workplace, many do not take up such facilities due to the perception of reduced promotion prospects (possible discrimination). Morgan and Klein (2003) suggest many with dyslexia would rather turn down career promotion than disclose their reading and writing difficulties, often being given 'well-intentioned but misguided (career) advice' (p. 100) by teachers advising office work for those who have not performed well at school; however, these are 'one of the least suitable options for dyslexic people' (p. 100). This is due to career guidance being incorrectly based on written language skills and academic qualifications, with the 'commonly held assumption that success at school is necessary for success in the workplace' (p. 102). It therefore is no surprise that Kruze (2015) found that 35% of long-term unemployed adults that attended a job centre in Sunderland, UK (*N*=75) were screened with either dyslexia and/or had Attention-Deficit/Hyperactivity Disorder (ADHD). This supports the view made in the UK Parliament (Walmsley, 2012) that 40% of unemployed adults using UK government job centres had dyslexia.

UK research highlights the frequency of dyslexia in UK prisons. Rack's (2005) study in eight Yorkshire and Humberside prisons suggested dyslexia was three to four times more common amongst prisoners than in the general UK population, with an incidence of 14%–31%. He found that 40%–50% of prisoners were at or below the level of literacy and numeracy expected of an 11-year old (Level 1), 40% of whom required specialist support for dyslexia. Rack concluded that dyslexia is three to four times more common amongst offenders than amongst the general population. Herrington, Hunter and Harvey (2005) reported that the Basic Skills Agency Initial Assessment recorded that 60% of prisoners had a reading ability equivalent to or less than that of a 5-year old child. Lastly, the British Dyslexia Association and HM Young Offender Institution Wetherby (2005) indicated that problem behaviour amongst young people with dyslexia was often evident *before they were* identified as having dyslexia, thus it could be argued that their adverse behaviour was the manifestation of undiagnosed learning difficulties. Projects by

Hewitt-Main (2012) suggest that success does not occur for some prison groups with dyslexia due to various unknown causes; however, a lack of early identification and intervention seems evident. Tanner's (2009) study of adults with dyslexia makes use of a 'conundrum of failure' model to explain a typical negative adult experience of dyslexia: system failure, constructed failure, public failure, family failure and personal failure.

The Disability Paradox

Researchers have begun to question why many individuals despite having disabilities become successful, enjoying a good standard of life. Rather than withdrawing and being ashamed of their disabilities, e.g. being in a wheelchair, having depression, suffering from Multiple Sclerosis or a life-threatening illness, they are thriving. Levine, Feldman and Elinson (1983), Lerner and Levine, Malspeis and D'Agostino (1994) argue that the paradox is that many looking at them might imagine a poor life satisfaction, living an undesirable existence; however, current research suggests the contrary.

Albrecht and Devlieger's (1999) qualitative study of $N=153$ individuals with serious and persistent disabilities found that 54.3% reported an excellent or good quality of life, suggesting the paradox. The research found that after the initial shock of disability (e.g. losing limbs in a car crash), their ability to bounce back came from looking at positives, reassessing life's goals and finding religious faith. Those who felt they had a poor quality of life manifested defeatist tendencies and a detachment from life. Albrecht and Devlieger (1999) concluded that those who perceived a high quality of life, whilst having a disability, identified a 'secondary gain' occurring; they 'adapted to their new conditions and made sense of them, finding enriched meaning in their life secondary to their disability'. They 'reinterpret their lives and reconstitute personal meaning in their social roles'; they:

> [u]nderstood their condition, took control, and introduced an order and predictability in their lives. They also learned what is and isn't possible, and developed a value set that helped them make sense of their disability, and harness support and other (support) networks.
>
> (Albrecht & Devlieger, 1999, p. 986)

In essence, they were empowered rather than disempowered by their disabilities, finding the resolve to improve the world and identify a role for themselves in society.

Interestingly any difficulties and scars from their trauma came from their discrepancies: What they would like to do compared to what they could do, what they used to be able to do and what they can now do, etc. This paradox highlights the importance of personal experience with disability in defining: their self, their view of the world, social contexts and social relationships. Lys and Pernice (1995) suggested a negative bias of attitudes and expectations by the public and health care workers towards individuals with disabilities. Connally (1994) also found negative public perceptions of life for individuals with disabilities, understood by the work of Stiker (1999) that disability introduces chaos, ambiguity and unpredictability into the social world of the individual and community. Albrecht and Devlieger (1999) suggest that '*disability shatters preconceived expectations and norms, and calls accepted values and notions of well-being into question*' (p. 980). Antonovsky (1987) and Lundberg (1997) concluded that individuals with disabilities have the capacity to find meaning, value and motivation to persist in the face of adversity, thus finding meaningfulness.

Studies Underpinning This Chapter

Alexander-Passe (2016) notes a study of dyslexia and success, investigating $N=20$ adults with dyslexia (diagnosed by educational psychologists or specialist teachers) who identify themselves as successful. They were able to provide evidence of their success by being: mainly self-employed, degree-educated, some with master degrees and professionals, senior managers, entrepreneurs and business leaders in their chosen fields. An investigative interview script drew themes of: motivation, leadership qualities, attitudes towards risk and failure and, lastly, entrepreneurship. Questions were posed concerning their families and childhoods, looking at their school experiences as a means to understand their motivation to succeed post-school.

Alexander-Passe (2010) investigated $N=29$ adults with dyslexia (diagnosed by educational psychologists or specialist teachers), some with and some without a diagnosis of depression (some clinical). An investigative interview script was used to review childhood trauma and adult coping strategies (negative and positive). Whilst equal numbers of adults depressed to non-depressed were selected as a sample, the majority ($N=22$) indicated depressive symptoms: self-harm, avoidance, withdrawal, attempted suicide and/or risk behaviours.

Alexander-Passe (2009) studied $N=88$ adults and used the Adult Dyslexia Checklist (Vinegrad, 1994) to screen for the severity of possible dyslexia and two measures of personality (Eysenck & Wilson, 1991; Eysenck & Eysenck, 1975), personally approved by Eysenck for use. $N=46$ self-reported adults with dyslexia ($N=21$ males and $N=25$ females, mean age 35.63 yrs., SD 11.543) and $N=42$ adult controls ($N=17$ males and $N=25$ females, mean age 43.41 yrs., SD 8.180) were recruited. The measures of Emotional Instability vs Adjustment and Introversion vs Extroversion were used to identify differing personality profiles for those with dyslexia vary according to its severity. It also allowed a comparison of gender and degree/non-degree education as a means to investigate dyslexia and academic success.

Success—Crucial Factors (Alexander-Passe, 2016)

This study of successful adults with dyslexia aimed to look at their childhood backgrounds to understand their motivations for post-school success. The results indicated several factors:

- Their parents were highly supportive, praising effort and not achievement.
- They coped at school by avoiding reading and writing as much as possible.
- They had the opportunity to find hobbies and subjects that they could excel in at school (e.g. art, design, sport, drama and information and communication technology (ICT)).
- They had experienced success as children, and thus retained a sense of worth at school.
- They find as adults that assistive technology is helping them immensely to deal with their difficulties associated with dyslexia.
- As adults they are highly motivated to gain a sense of 'self-worth,' coming from a need to prove themselves to others dating back to their teachers' low preceptions of them.
- Many have a chip on their shoulder from school, to prove to their teacher that they were not 'stupid and lazy.'
- Many have a healthy relationship with risk, as they believe they experienced huge risks at school for it not to be 'found out' that they could not read or write.

- They perceive failure in a positive light, that they are not afraid of failing in tasks; failure is seen as a journey and opportunity rather than something to wallow in.
- They have extreme work ethics, which means they are willing to put in 70 hour weeks or more to achieve what needs to be done; this extreme focus allows them to act faster to the needs of the market.

It is interesting that N=15 out of the N=20 sample were self-employed. They explained that only by working for themselves can they delegate the tasks they are not good at, buy in talent/skills to allow them to work to their strengths (e.g. selling and motivating) and be judged on what they can do and not on what they cannot do.

Unsuccessful–Crucial Factors (Alexander-Passe, 2010)

(Question) Do you feel that you are reaching your potential?

No! I think my opportunities to reach my potential were reduced by me being diagnosed too late. I think going back into education when I did, showed that I missed out on so much opportunity (Anita).

(Q.) Would you call yourself a successful adult with dyslexia?

No (Jean).

(Q.) What do you think you would need to call yourself a successful adult with dyslexia? A degree?

Well. I think a degree is just one milestone to complete. For me at this age, if at a young age I had achieved my degree it would have made an advantage in my life, which would be more than an achievement, to respect myself. A degree is to achieve something that I was not equipped to achieve [when I was younger]. It was not that I was not inspired and that people were not there for me, I just did not do it (Jordan).

(Q.) Would you call yourself a successful adult with dyslexia?

It is quite funny in this one. In the material world, I am a failure, because I cannot get a job, which is how most people measure themselves. But in the providing help to others I seem to be quite good at that, and that is helping me understand me, it means when people say 'thank you for helping me' that gives me a buzz (George).

The previously stated evidence helps one to understand the experience of many with dyslexia and how they perceive themselves as being unsuccessful. It is not just about academic achievement but about personal achievement and working towards one's potential. Very few people in life are lucky enough to work to their true potential, but, in the previously stated evidence, they do not feel they are not even close to it, maybe a 'million miles away' from it. School and lack of early diagnosis and intervention seem to be the root causes for many.

Personality factors (Alexander-Passe, 2009) were shown in Figures 8.1 and 8.2 (Table 8.1).

Discussion

Each of the three studies enhances this discussion, which aims to investigate not only a common variable of school failure but also how successful and unsuccessful groups have differently dealt with their failure.

Alexander-Passe (2016) talked about how successful adults with dyslexia can positively use their 'school-trauma' to drive them forward, and how, whilst they had positive parenting that focussed more on effort than achievement, they still had huge chips on their shoulders from being called stupid and lazy. They were lucky to have found strengths at school and enjoyed some success there, which helped to improve their self-worth. It could be argued that they went beyond the achievements of their peers post-school, and will keep on over-achieving as they developed a thirst to prove others wrong about themselves. Many were self-employed, allowing them to be highly creative and to delegate their areas of difficulty to others, mainly linear thinkers/people who did not experience dyslexia.

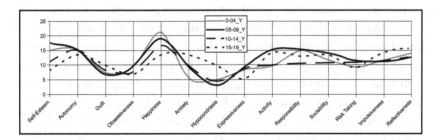

Figure 8.1 Degree Educated, Split by Traits (All Trait Groups), *N*=40
Source: Alexander-Passe (2009)

Table 8.1 Personality of Adults With Dyslexia (Academically Successful and Less-Successful)

Academically successful male adults with dyslexia	*Academically successful female adults with dyslexia*
Physically inactive and lethargic	Do not regret past actions/ behaviour
Casual, easy going and have less need for order	Cheerful, optimistic and mentally healthy
Resistant to irrational fears or anxieties	Resistant to irrational fears or anxieties
Confidence in themselves/abilities	Systematic, orderly and can be cautious
Enjoy freedom, independent and are realistic about abilities	
Careless, late and unpredictable	
Enjoy socializing and meets people easily	
Live dangerously, can be gamblers and enjoy taking risks	
Like ideas, discussions and speculations	
Do not regret past actions/behaviour	
Cheerful, optimistic and mentally healthy	
Less academically successful male adults with dyslexia	**Less academically successful female adults with dyslexia**
Careful, highly disciplined and finicky	Self-blaming and can be self-questioning of life
Easily upset by things that go wrong	Pessimistic, gloomy and depressed
Active and energetic	Easily upset by things that go wrong
Have low self-opinion and feel unattractive Failures	Can make hurried and premature decisions
Lack self-reliance and can be easily pushed around	
Reliable, trustworthy and a bit compulsive	
Few special friends and enjoys solo activities	
Prefer familiarity, safety and needs security	
Self-blaming, and self-questioning of life	
Pessimistic, gloomy and can be depressed	

   Interestingly many were social entrepreneurs and motivated to fix a perceived broken system, whether re-entering the education sector (their feared stimulus) to create the support that they once wished for, creating apps to help those with dyslexia, or doing support services for adults with dyslexia. Others said working for themselves allowed them to create and invent, as they constantly solved problems in their heads and most companies wouldn't invest in them. The Alexander-Passe (2016) study was in its analysis stage and further investigations with Interpretative Phenomenological Analysis and other models may uncover greater insights.

Alexander-Passe (2010) looked at depression, self-harm and attempted suicide. The evidence describes how many adults with dyslexia are diagnosed late in their lives, and that this delay in assessment had ramifications for them. Many mentioned that their dyslexia diagnosis was too late and they had gone through a grieving process, after a positive diagnosis, for the countless missed opportunities at school along with anger towards teachers who had missed sometimes very severe dyslexia symptoms. They ask, 'If I have achieved so much without the diagnosis, how much more with the help that a diagnosis would have brought at school?' However one could question whether they had achieved so much to date because they had this urge to prove to others that they were not stupid. When questioned about success, they talked about potential, namely missed potential, along with contentment. Many were questioned about whether a degree was enough to call an adult with dyslexia successful, and many thought not. Success for them was contentment and having their skills recognised.

Alexander-Passe (2009) investigated the personality traits of $N=88$ adults, most with symptoms of dyslexia. The screening measure was used to identify hidden dyslexia in the sample, and to understand the differences that come with the severity of dyslexia. Ten or more symptoms were perceived by Vinegrad (1994) to be enough to define severe dyslexia; however, some indicated 15+ symptoms. The ten to 14 symptom group was assessed compared to the zero to four symptom control group. The results indicated personality differences between adults with dyslexia with a degree (deemed as successful) and those without (deemed unsuccessful); whilst the term less-successful/unsuccessful was not ideal it was kept to aid understanding. This does not discount that many are successful without a degree and 'school-success does not always mean work-success'. In the case of those with dyslexia this is even more relevant (Morgan & Klein, 2003) as many are successful in vocational fields (e.g. plumbing, building, sales and training). Even with a degree, those with the most severe dyslexia (11+ symptoms) experienced higher levels of anxiety/hypochondria and lower self-esteem than the controls. Those without a degree, both in the group with severe dyslexia and those with the most severe dyslexia, had lower self-esteem, lower sociability, more anxiety and were more obsessive than the controls.

The profiles in Table 8.1 describes successful male and female groups who were highly resilient, resistant to irrational fears, optimistic and were willing to take risks for success (males only) and were systematic in their approach (females only). Those who were unsuccessful were more self-blaming, upset when things went wrong, made hurried decisions in life, were pessimistic/gloomy/depressive (females only) and had a low self-opinion of themselves/and felt a failure (males only).

Pulling the three studies together, both successful and less-successful adults with dyslexia experience similar experiences at school but each group cope differently and vary in support structures. However, both groups leave school with a need to find self-worth. It is not surprising that in leaving school (without support and with unidentified strengths) many were led into low paid and unfulfilling careers that could lead to self-harm (drugs, attempted suicide, etc.), carried out to improve a sense of control of their body. Depression and withdrawal was found as a means to cope defensively with their unfulfilling life, lacking the literacy/communication skills to find gainful, meaningful employment. Therefore, it could be argued that crime can be a strategy of self-survival in a community that does not judge individuals by academic achievement—one could argue that this is vocational success. Self-belief featured in all three studies, in that those who were successful believed in their gut that what they were doing was the right thing; however, the unsuccessful personality sample had self-doubt and this is hypothesised to come from the lack of successful childhood experiences.

Conclusion

This chapter began with a research question about the impact of school experience on the creation of post-school successful and unsuccessful adults with dyslexia. A wide literature review covered many topics: dyslexia, school experience/emotional coping, social exclusion, success, successful people with dyslexia, less-successful people with dyslexia, the disability paradox, dyslexia and depression/mental health and, lastly, post-traumatic growth. The reader is led to question why some adults with dyslexia can succeed, and to huge heights commercially, but still have experienced educational-trauma in school.

The three studies looked at success and the lack of success in different ways using a sample of successful people with dyslexia and a mix of people with dyslexia who were successful and less-successful, many manifesting depressive/mental health manifestations, argued to come from coping in literacy-based society. Lastly a personality investigation was conducted, looking at not only severity of dyslexia but also gender and attainment of a degree education. The result of the three studies indicates similar school experiences in all of those with dyslexia in mainstream education: late diagnosis, teachers without an awareness of barriers to learning caused by dyslexia and, lastly, humiliation from both peers and teachers due to their low academic attainment and, at times, their avoidance strategies.

What seems to separate the successful and less-successful group of adults with dyslexia were:

- the level of parental support as children,
- how they coped at school by avoiding reading and writing,
- opportunity to find hobbies and subjects that they could excel in at school,
- experience of success as children,
- use of assistive technology to help them cope with their difficulties associated with dyslexia,
- being highly motivated to gain a sense of 'self-worth',
- seeking to prove to their teacher that they were not 'stupid and lazy',
- having a healthy relationship with risk,
- perceiving failure in a positive light, as a journey and an opportunity,
- extreme focus on tasks or project.

Limitations

The Alexander-Passe (2009, 2012) personality data was sourced from self-disclosing individuals who identified themselves as experiencing dyslexia, thus caution should be used in generalizing from the data; however, generalized themes were its main intention.

References

Albrecht, G. L., & Devlieger, P. J. (1999). The disability paradox: High quality of life against all odds. *Social Science & Medicine, 48*(8), 977–988. https://doi.org/10.1016/S0277-9536(98)00411-0

Alexander-Passe, N. (2009). Dyslexia, gender and depression: Research studies. In P. Hernandez & S. Alonso (Eds.), *Women and depression*. New York, NY: Nova Science Publishers.

Alexander-Passe, N. (2010). *Dyslexia and depression: The hidden sorrow.* New York, NY: Nova Science Publishers.

Alexander-Passe, N. (2012). *Dyslexia: Dating, marriage and parenthood.* New York, NY: Nova Science Publishers.

Alexander-Passe, N. (2016). Dyslexia, success and post-traumatic growth. *Asia Pacific Journal of Developmental Differences, 3*(1), 87–130.

Antonovsky, A. (1987). *Unraveling the mystery of health—How people manage stress and stay well.* San Francisco, CA: Jossey-Bass Publishers.

British Dyslexia Association and HM Young Offender Institution Wetherby. (2005). *Practical solutions to identifying dyslexia in juvenile offenders.* London, England: British Dyslexia Association.

Connally, P. (1994). The California quality of life project: A project summary. In D. Goode (Ed.), *Quality of life for persons with disabilities: International perspectives and issues* (pp. 184–192). Cambridge, MA: Brookline Books.

Darwin, C., & Beer, G. (1996). *On the origin of species.* Oxford, UK: Oxford University Press.

Dowell, B. (2003, October 5). Secret of the super successful . . . they are dyslexic. *The Sunday Times.* Retrieved from www.thetimes.co.uk

Elliott, J., & Grigorenko, E. L. (2014). *The dyslexia debate.* Cambridge, UK: Cambridge University Press.

Emens, L. A. (2008). Cancer vaccines: On the threshold of success. *Expert Opinion on Emerging Drugs, 13*(2), 295–308. https://doi.org/10.1517/14728214.13.2.295

Eysenck, H. J., & Eysenck, S. B. G. (1975). *Manual of the Eysenck Personality Questionnaire.* London, England: Hodder and Stoughton.

Eysenck, H. J., & Wilson, G. D. (1991). *Know your own personality.* Harmondsworth, UK: Penguin Books.

Fink, R. P. (2002). Successful careers: The secrets of adults with dyslexia. *Career Planning and Adult Development Journal, 18*(1), 118–135. Retrieved from dyslexiahelp.umich.edu

Fitzgibbon, G., & O'Connor, B. (2002). *Adult dyslexia—A guide for the workplace.* Chichester, UK: Wiley.

Galton, F. (1895). *English men of science: Their nature and nurture.* New York, NY: D. Appleton and Company.

Gatewood, E. J., Shaver, K. G., & Gartner, W. B. (1995). A longitudinal study of cognitive factors influencing start-up behaviours and success at venture creation. *Journal of Business Venturing, 10*(5), 371–391. https://doi.org/10.1016/0883-9026(95)00035-7

Herrington, V., Hunter, G., & Harvey, S. (2005). Meeting the healthcare needs of offenders with learning disabilities. *Learning Disability Practice, 8*(4), 28–32. https://doi.org/10.7748/ldp2005.05.8.4.28.c1621

Hewitt-Main, J. (2012). *Dyslexia behind bars.* Benfleet, UK: Mentoring 4 U. Retrieved from www.lexion.co.uk

Krakovsky, M. (2014). *What we're missing when we study success.* Stanford, CA: Stanford Graduate School of Business.

Kruze, E. (2015). *Concerning the SID project in Sunderland.* Personal conversation, 26th October 2015. Sunderland, UK: University of Sunderland.

Lerner, D. J., Levine, S., Malspeis, S., & D'Agostino, R. B. (1994). Job strain and health-related quality of life in a national sample. *American Journal of Public Health (AJPH), 84*(10), 1580–1585. Retrieved from https://ajph.aphapublications.org/

Levine, S., Feldman, J., & Elinson, J. (1983). Does medical care do any good? In D. Mechanic (Ed.), *Handbook of health, health care, and the health professions* (pp. 394–404). New York, NY: Free Press.

Logan, J. (2001). *Entrepreneurial success: A study of the incidence of dyslexia in the entrepreneurial population and the influence of dyslexia on success* (Unpublished doctoral thesis). University of Bristol, Bristol.

Logan, J. (2009). Dyslexic entrepreneurs: The incidence; Their coping strategies and their business skills. *Dyslexia, 15*(4), 328–334. https://doi.org/10.1002/dys.388

Lowe, J. (1995). *Locke on human understanding*. London, England: Routledge.

Lundberg, O. (1997). Childhood conditions, sense of coherence, social class and adult ill health: Exploring their theoretical and empirical relations. *Social Science and Medicine, 44*(6), 821–831. https://doi.org/10.1016/S0277-9536(96)00184-0

Lys, K., & Pernice, R. (1995). Perceptions of positive attitudes toward people with spinal cord injury. *International Journal of Rehabilitation Research, 18*(1), 35–43. https://doi.org/10.1097/00004356-199501000-00004

Morgan, E., & Klein, C. (2003). *The dyslexic adult in a non-dyslexic world*. London, England: Whurr.

Pinker, S. (2003). *The blank slate: The modern denial of human nature*. London, England: Penguin Books.

Rack, J. (2005). *The incidence of hidden disabilities in the prison population: Yorkshire and Humberside research*. Egham, UK: The Dyslexia Institute. Retrieved from https://alippe.eu/

Ralph, P., & Kelly, P. (2014, July). The dimensions of software engineering success. In: *Proceedings of the 36th International Conference on Software Engineering* (pp. 24–35). New York, NY: Association for Computing Machinery (ACM). https://doi.org/10.1145/2568225.2568261

Raskind, M. H., Goldberg, R. J., Higgins, E. L., & Herman, K. L. (2003). Predictors of success in individuals with learning disabilities: A qualitative analysis of a 20 year longitudinal study. *Learning Disabilities Research and Practice, 18*(4), 222–236. https://doi.org/10.1111/1540-5826.00077

Scott, M. E., Scherman, A., & Phillips, H. (1992). Helping individuals with dyslexia succeed in adulthood: Emerging keys for effective parenting, education and development of positive self-concept. *Journal of Instructional Psychology, 19*(3), 197–204. Retrieved from https://search.proquest.com/

Stewart, W. H., Jr., & Roth, P. L. (2001). Risk propensity differences between entrepreneurs and managers: A meta-analytic review. *Journal of Applied Psychology, 86*(1), 145-153. https://doi.org/10.1037/0021-9010.86.1.145

Stiker, H. J. (1999). *A history of disability*. Ann Arbor, MI: University of Michigan Press.

Tanner, K. (2009). Adult dyslexia and the "conundrum of failure." *Disability and Society, 24*(6), 785–797. https://doi.org/10.1080/09687590903160274

Thomson, M. (1996). *Developmental dyslexia: Studies in disorders of communication* (3rd ed.). London, England: Whurr (Original work published 1990).

Vinegrad, M. (1994). A revised adult dyslexia checklist. *Educare, 48,* 21–24. Retrieved from https://dyslexiasupportservices.com.au/

Walmsley, B. J. (2012, June 28). *Education and training: People with hidden disabilities* (Hansard, HL Deb vol 738 col 385). London, England: UK Parliament. Retrieved from https://publications.parliament.uk/

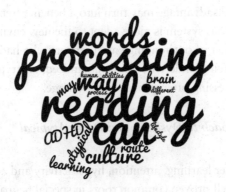

9 Multi-Sided Dyslexia

The Age of the Entrepreneurs With New Reading Abilities

Eva Gyarmathy

Introduction

It is high time for us to understand proliferating dyslexia's message instead of proliferating diagnoses. The emerging environment and culture should be analysed, and understanding atypically developing individuals could be of immense help in this process, because they are those who are more sensitive to the environmental factors.

The concept of evoked culture reveals the complex dance of gene-culture co-evolution. Transmitted culture is extremely important in explaining the changes in human behaviour, and can explain fashion, musical art, technology, science, culinary preferences, morals and many other things (Walsh & Yun, 2016). Evoked cultural behaviours are those that are the outputs of shared psychological mechanisms in response to environmental cues. On the other hand, transmitted cultural behaviours are those which are learned from one's social group, regardless of the environment.

Reading is a transmitted cultural behaviour, but the development of its neurological background functioning is also evoked by the environment. The atypical development of the nervous system can be a sign that the brain has already attuned itself to the new environment. This may cause trouble at school, where reading is taught (transmitted) according to the culture, but this disadvantage may turn into a benefit after leaving school because this nervous system is more adept to the new environment. There are a number of outstanding entrepreneurs who had difficulties in school but weren't hindered by dyslexia; indeed, an atypical way of information processing often proves an advantage.

A Holistic Approach to Dyslexia and Other Atypical Developments

Dyslexia and other learning, attention, hyperactivity and autism spectrum disorders have well-proven common roots in special neurological characteristics. They frequently co-occur in various combinations, which is indicative of their neurological relatedness.

Research results have shown that movement planning and coordination, sequentially, as well as rhythm-keeping may be problem areas in the case of dyslexia, Attention Deficit Disorder and Hyperactivity Disorder and autism spectrum disorder alike, and the same is true of deficits in inhibition and implementation functions, which play an important role in control (Denckla, Rudel, Chapman, & Krieger, 1985; Schonfeld, Schaffer, & Barmack, 1989; Barkley, Koplowitz, Anderson, & McMurray, 1997; Greenspan & Wieder, 1999; Piek, Pitcher & Hay, 1999).

According to Richardson and Ross (2000), the cause behind this frequent co-occurrence is a set of abnormalities in the production of fatty acids that play an important role in the cerebral neural transfer. Robert Melillo (2009) simply used the term 'Disconnected Kids'.

Kaplan, Crawford, Cantell, Kooistra, and Dewey (2006) stated that concepts such as atypical brain development and minor neurological dysfunction provide some possible explanations for the increased levels of co-occurrence of developmental disorders. Also, the *Diagnostic and Statistical Manual of Mental Disorders* seems to be following this viewpoint and learning, attention, hyperactivity and autism spectrum disorders have been categorised in a common section named 'Neurodevelopmental disorders'.

The basis for all the different forms of atypical developments is a common set of neurological characteristics, but idiosyncratic internal and external factors significantly influence cognitive deviations, which affect the acquisition of school skills and/or the control of attention and behaviour (Figure 9.1).

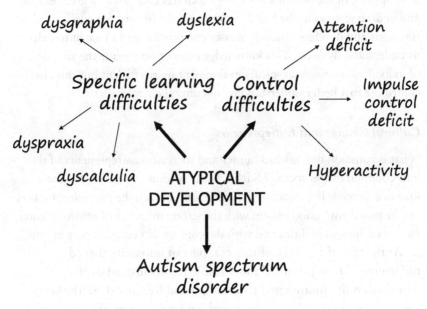

Figure 9.1 Types of Atypical Development

All forms of atypical development are characterised by the following:

- they are based on a different-from-normal neurological functioning,
- they constitute advantages and disadvantages throughout the individual's lifetime,
- they are independent of intelligence,
- they are environment-dependent.

All deviations have their own set of characteristics differentiating them from other forms of atypical development. At the same time, the previous list holds true for all of them. The gifted spectrum is only loosely connected to the other types of neurologically-based deviations, as not all criteria apply to it (it is not independent of intelligence) but, owing to similarities in neurological functioning, it shows some kinship with the neurological forms of atypical development under discussion. However, not all gifted development is characterised by neurological deviations, and not all cases of neurologically-based atypical development involve gifted development.

Twenty-first century changes have significantly increased the ratio of manifested atypical development. The environmental factors affecting the development of the nervous system—which has changed to a great extent and in diverse ways in the last decades—and the history of neurological functions and developmental processes can provide extra insight to help us understand dyslexia. This knowledge can not only make the support of individuals showing atypical development more efficient but can also contribute to a better understanding of cultural changes.

Cultural Change and Entrepreneurs

What is common to a nomad hunter and successful entrepreneurs of the info-communication society? Such a flashy section title may look like a joke or a prompt in a creativity training, but, in fact, the previous question can be posed with good reason with the strong influence of environmental factors on human abilities and with the concept of neurodiversity in mind.

At the end of the Palaeolithic era, part of humanity turned to farming, which promised more stable results instead of the more uncertain hunting and gathering-based livelihood. With the appearance of animal husbandry and land cultivation, the Neolithic era as a new culture proved to be a turning point in the development of the human brain as well (Figure 9.2).

The less predictable, and hence trial-and-error-like, hunter-gatherer lifestyle was superseded by the methodical, temporally segmented, planned and controlled farming lifestyle. Considering the gene-culture co-evolution theory (Walsh & Yun, 2016), this change in the culture manifested itself in

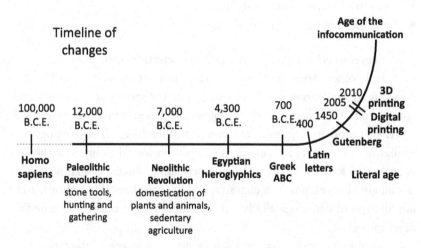

Figure 9.2 Cultural Changes

the genes. The new lifestyle changed the human nervous system in the few thousand years of the agricultural lifestyle.

The farming, the methodical, planned work, proved so successful that the human population started growing quickly, plus the brain's development laid down the neurological basis for literacy. Writing, as the sowing, goes in rows, orderly in one direction. There is a great deal of importance in keeping direction and rhythm in the work of the farmer, as in writing and reading.

Humanity invented writing, which meant the beginning of the age of written history and the end of the Neolithic era. The brain functions of humanity optimised originally over a million years to hunter-gatherer activities and underwent a significant change by switching to an agricultural lifestyle requiring methodicalness, planning and foresight. The characteristics of the new activities were virtually the opposite of those of the earlier, diametrically different ones.

The perception and the activities of hunter-gatherers are characterised by the following:

- spatial, visual, impulsive, and cooperative,
- doesn't store—acquires instead,
- searches, finds and selects,
- explores, gathers and moves along,
- conjectures, visualises and intuits,
- takes risks and proceeds on a trial-and-error basis.

The perceptions and activities of breeder-farmers are characterised by the following:

- time-bound, delimited, controlled and sequential,
- sows, tends, harvests and stores,
- foresighted, economical and methodical,
- place-bound and controlled work,
- plans and implements methodically,
- thinks systematically.

A nomad lifestyle corresponds to the learning style and activities of early childhood, while a farmer's lifestyle corresponds to the way of thinking to be acquired at school, all the functions that form the basis for literacy development during the preparation for activities connected with farming culture. This process is called the maturation of the nervous system, during which the 'hunter-gatherer' child gradually becomes suited for literacy and, ultimately, becomes literate.

Reading, writing and counting became essential knowledge for, and developed through, an agricultural lifestyle and, subsequently, more and more information communication activities came to build on these skills. In ancient hunter-gatherer cultures, brains characterised by the following proved useful for a million years:

- ready to solve spontaneously arising tasks,
- can adapt to an unknown future,
- its forte is problem-solving ability.

In contrast, an agricultural lifestyle requires a brain which:

- is able to carry out routine tasks,
- knows the process beforehand and plays it safe,
- its forte is vast professional knowledge.

School education serves to promote this process and essentially involves preparing children for methodical work. Of course, the most adaptive is to possess both kinds of thinking, as how much of each is needed is task-dependent. One is the leading approach to hunting, the other to husbandry. Which way of information processing is more useful depends on the specific stage of human culture.

By the twenty-first century, progress in information communication has reached a level bringing about a culture change. In the age of literacy, knowledge had to be planted, grown, harvested and stored like crops. In the info-communication age, it has become possible to 'hunt' for necessary information, and those who can will become more successful than those who continue to choose the lengthy process of knowledge cultivation and storage. An older function has become useful once again.

The epithet 'VUCA' is becoming widely used for our quickly changing age of vast information generation. The acronym 'VUCA' characterises situations that are:

- volatile,
- uncertain,
- complex,
- ambiguous.

The characterization of VUCA situations began in the American army. The end of the cold war brought about a dissolution of the clear, or at least clear-seeming, friend-or-foe picture. Soldiers must fight in situations which change constantly, which are uncertain and complex, where pre-learned solutions do not help. There is rarely an opportunity to methodically complete a process; one must instead grasp a situation quickly, improvise, interpret the circumstances at hand, find the relevant information and adopt the optimal attitude and activity. Based on the previously stated characteristics, the hunter-gatherer's brain is at an advantage in such a world.

The characteristics of the brain of a person with dyslexia are located in areas valuable for a breeder-farmer lifestyle and literacy. Its strengths are those of the hunter-gatherer ancestor. Paleolithic man can, with some exaggeration, be characterised as an individual with Attention-Deficit/ Hyperactivity Disorder (ADHD) and learning disorders, as Thomas Hartmann (1995) observed. Hartmann's intuition seems to be justified by the latest molecular biological and clinical studies.

The genetic correlation of ADHD—the 7R allele,—a version of the DRD4 gene, entered the human genetic material about 40,000 years ago (Arcos-Burgos & Acosta, 2007). The 7R allele of the DRD4 gene is associated with novelty-seeking and ADHD. The evolutionary biological studies of Eisenberg, Campbell, Gray, and Sorenson (2008) indicate that the DRD4/7R allele may be of greater advantage to nomads than settled shepherds. Nomads' subsistence relies on hunting, which is assisted by a nervous system inciting to search and motion. Patience is more rewarding for shepherds. Eisenberg and colleagues (2008) found that nomads with this allele have a better body-mass-index, while the opposite holds true for shepherds. So, the syndrome now getting a psychiatric diagnostic categorisation is advantageous for a nomadic hunter lifestyle.

The 7R allele constellation can only be identified as a part of the ADHD cases and is not accompanied by other neurologically-based deviations (Swanson et al., 2000; Hsiung, Kaplan, Petryshen, Lu, & Field, 2004). The above thus primarily demonstrates the potential advantages of atypical nervous systems from the point of view of dyslexia.

The co-occurrence of ADHD and reading disorder is, at the same time, fairly frequent. Germanò and Gagliano (2010), summarizing data from the literature, established that reading disorder appears in 18%–45% of ADHD cases, and ADHD syndrome accompanies about 40% of reading disorder cases. DuPaul, Gormley, and Laracy (2013), surveying 17 studies, found a rather big overlap of over 45%, hinting at the common roots of the two problems. Several people with dyslexia carry ADHD characteristics, and learning disorder often accompanies a diagnosis of ADHD. The genetic study conducted by Gialluisi et al. (2019) corroborates the hypothesis on the partly shared genetic etiology of developmental dyslexia and ADHD. Sánchez-Morán et al. (2018) found a significant association between dyslexia and ADHD in their Spanish population, but they found that the significance depends on the particular phenotypic groups compared.

A Change in Neurological Maturation

We are not aware of the exact effect that chemicals, drugs, cleaning products, additives, petrol fumes, lead and light- and noise pollution have on the developing nervous system, but we do know that they have some effect. In some people, even a small amount of exposure has a strong influence, while there is no perceptible effect on others.

Brain functions that are newer in an evolutionary sense are less stable than those that became strengthened during millions of years, and so the former are more susceptible to environmental effects. The process necessary for the acquisition of school skills, called neurological maturation, involves the development of cognitive functions that constitute the newest genetic innovations of humanity. As such, if anything happens to the brain, these are the cognitive processes that are affected the most. Smaller brain traumas before, during, or after birth, and environmental effects or deviations due to genetic makeup, can lead to a once adaptive cognitive constellation we can call the hunter functioning. This constellation might have been useful once, and in certain environments can still prove adaptive although it is certainly disadvantageous in terms of school conformity.

According to the person-environment fit (Caplan & Harrison, 1993), a prerequisite for successful adaptation is the agreement and efficient interaction between personal characteristics (biological and psychological needs, values, goals, abilities and personality) and environmental characteristics (task, work, role expectations, cultural values and social environment). Building on the concept of person-environment fit, Verheul et al. (2015) has shown, for example, that higher education students showing signs of ADHD will more probably become entrepreneurs than their peers without ADHD characteristics.

Twenty-first century entrepreneurs may get success in business life despite having had problems at school; among other things, they may struggle with reading disorders, be it because they carry the hunter genes or because they didn't become farmer-breeders for some other reason. Their nervous system does not tolerate constancy well, their brains are in constant motion; they also perceive the world in flux as well as three-dimensionally.

Entrepreneurs and Business Executives

Many successful entrepreneurs turn out to have struggled with dyslexia, and it is often the special way of information processing responsible for their dyslexia, or the battle with learning, that helped them on the way to success.

IKEA founder Ingvar Kamprad (Egan, 2016; Fredén, 2020) made navigation easier for himself using different simplifications, thereby also making his enterprise more efficient. For example, since his brain mixed up codes, he gave real names to pieces of furniture, thereby—as learning methodology tells us—exploiting the help of association. Meanwhile, having rivers, islands and other existing names identify their pieces of furniture has also become a trademark of IKEA.

Card (2019) cites Carlene Jackson, founder and CEO of Cloud9 Insight, who experiences dyslexia herself and who sees dyslexia as nothing but a gift. 'I consider my dyslexia to be a gift that's helped me in business', she says; 'If you're dyslexic, you can never truly fail because you simply accept that succeeding the first time may not happen so you're going to have to find a way around the problem' (Card, 2019).

Steven Spielberg, who fell 2 years behind his peers in reading development, escaped from shaming and bullying early on into filmmaking (Bullock, 2017, citing Friends of Quinn, 2012). Sometimes, defiance helps. Ben Way's teachers said he could never be successful because of his dyslexia, so he decided to prove them wrong. At the age of fifteen, he became one of the first dot-com millionaires, only to quickly lose everything; but he did not give up. He tried and tried and ultimately climbed back again into the rows of millionaires as an entrepreneur (Farmer, n.d.).

Field (2018) describes the entrepreneurial development of Barbara Corcoran. The entrepreneur grew up with her nine siblings in New Jersey and became a real estate icon. Being a child with dyslexia, she struggled with reading. Her teacher told her that 'she would always be seen as stupid if she didn't learn to read.' The author cites Corcoran as saying: 'My burning desire to prove that I was not stupid is the key to why I was so successful and continue to be.' Corcoran continues: 'I'm still insecure about it. I don't ever want to be embarrassed again and have someone look at me as a loser, and so I get a lot of ammunition out of that injury.' Field notes that after she sold her company, The Corcoran Group, for $66 million in 2001, Barbara Corcoran started to mentor the next generation of entrepreneurs. She looks for founders who have overcome adversity in their lives and who exhibit the long-term grit needed to survive in business (Field, 2018).

Entrepreneurs list excellent communication abilities, the ability to delegate tasks, creative solutions and spatial-visual-holistic awareness as profits gained from their struggle with dyslexia (Fitzgibbon & O'Connor, 2002). However, many entrepreneurs with dyslexia achieve highly without especially outstanding communication abilities or delegation of tasks abilities. There are as many ways to cope as there are people who experience dyslexia, but there still must be common aspects that make entrepreneurs with dyslexia so successful.

What seems certain is that dyslexia—more precisely, the factors associated with it—are a definite advantage in business. While the prevalence of dyslexia is 5%–20% in the entire population, 35% of entrepreneurs (Logan, 2009), and half of the biggest entrepreneurs, experience dyslexia (Feloni, 2018). Logan's (2009) study also reveals that only 1% of corporate managers experience dyslexia, which suggests that dyslexia may be an advantage in entrepreneurship but a disadvantage, if not a preclusion, when it comes to managerial work.

This huge difference is no coincidence: It is vital data. The difference between the two types of management mirrors the difference between people with dyslexia and without dyslexia, and shows moreover that motivation or excellent ability is not enough for success. These are necessary but not sufficient factors, as success is determined by the interaction of internal and external circumstances. Efficiency primarily requires a neurological functioning suited to the tasks set by the environment. Take the previously mentioned 7R allele, which evolved in the same period as the farmer lifestyle and was necessary because even farming required the conquest of new areas. However, carriers of the hunter gene were only successful if they did not try to be shepherds, but went forth and explored as dictated by their inner drive—a beautiful case of the person-environment fit.

Entrepreneurs, especially in a VUCA world, can gain much with their restlessly exploring mind while methodical, systematic executive work is required of a manager. Entrepreneurs who experience dyslexia innovate and push forward while managers, like good farmers, can control production well. In a changing, complicated world which needs new solutions by the minute, being able to use hunter-type cognitive areas is a decidedly adaptive response. Many elements of the ancient nomad brain functioning have become advantageous in the twenty-first century and are gaining prominence.

At the same time, all of what the methodical, agricultural, literacy-based approach developed in the human brain continues to remain indispensable because a certain amount of analytical, step-by-step thinking is necessary not just at school but also for higher-level, synthesising, critical thinking. Entrepreneurs cannot be successful in the twenty-first century by building only on their hunter's brains. The great task of education is to reconcile ancient human abilities with innovations of culture, such as literacy.

The Change in Reading Abilities

Learning to Read and the Reading Disorder

Since the development of the reading skill requires diverse abilities and processing modes, the disorder can likewise have diverse roots and locations. Reading disorder emerges if information processing modes necessary for a given phase are not available.

Frith (1985) identified three levels of reading skill development: Logographic, alphabetic and orthographic. Ehri (1999) differentiated four phases and emphasised a continuous rather than stages-based development of reading:

- **Pre-alphabetic phase**—reading words by memorising their visual features or guessing words from their context.
- **Partial-alphabetic phase**—reading is supported by recognising some letters of the alphabet and using them together with context to remember words by sight.

- **Full-alphabetic phase**—possession of the grapheme-phoneme correspondence which makes possible to analyse the words, that way decoding unfamiliar words and storing fully analysed sight words in memory.
- **Consolidated-alphabetic phase**—consolidated knowledge of grapheme-phoneme blends into larger units that recur in different words.

Note that the literacy of humankind went through a similar progress. Hieroglyphics are visual symbols, and the ancient languages, like Chinese or Japanese kanji, are logographic writing systems. Phoenician alphabet, the predecessor of the Greek alphabet, could be considered a partial alphabetic system. It was limited to consonants, and more languages kept that way. However, in the Greek language, certain consonants were adapted to express vowels. The use of both vowels and consonants makes Greek the first real alphabet. We can step forward in a thought experiment and consider the reading specialties like dyslexia at the beginning of the twenty-first century, a next step in the reading development of the humankind. Following the development of the human alphabet, we realise that the progress went through parallel processes and it went along different ways. The multiple routes to reading appeared among the reading models too.

Multiple Routes to Reading

To understand dyslexia as a symptom of this age, a suitable model needs to be developed. Peterson, Pennington, and Olson (2013), studying subtypes of dyslexia on a big sample, analysed two models of the development of the reading ability in detail: The Connectionist model of Harm and Seidenberg (1999) and the Dual Route Cascaded model of Coltheart, Rastle, Perry, Langdon, and Ziegler (2001). Their results supported both models partially, but neither one fully. This and the overview they provide can help us draw up a minimal model which can explain reading acquisition and the development of the different types of dyslexia alike.

The proposed minimal reading- and reading disorder (dyslexia) model is based on the phases captured by Frith (1985) and Ehri (1999), but they are arranged along with two dimensions. In other words, the model is not linear but triangle-shaped. In reaching the various levels, at least four modes of information processing are encountered: Visual-holistic, phonological, sensory-motor and semantic. The usual, and thus expected, type of learning to read requires all four processing types in the previously stated order. If any are missing or under-functioning, it leads to a disorder in the development of the reading ability—by definition, dyslexia. In most cases, reading develops despite the disorder, even if not in the expected form.

We can differentiate and describe two routes to the acquisition of reading ability based on the previous theoretical model (see Figure 9.3):

1. Logographic-orthographic route—currently not accepted in the Western culture, but as a reading mode, it clearly exists since antiquity. At the pre-alphabetic phase, word images are symbols bearing a meaning. The symbols are stored in and can be recalled from the mental lexicon through visual-holistic and semantic processing, and, as such, reading could progress to a kind of orthographic reading. This is a direct route to learning to read, the direct lexical route, in which phonology does not play a significant role. To read a new or a rarely used word, guesses will be needed usually using the context. Certainly, there is a good chance to err

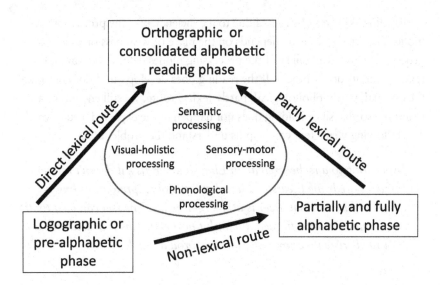

Figure 9.3 There Is More Than One Route to Reading—A Minimal Model Explaining the Acquisition of Reading

in that way. This is how small children with strong visual-holistic processing start to read very early on, and some adults with dyslexia also employ this route to reading.

2. Logographic-alphabetic-orthographic route—a currently widely used, accepted and expected analytical reading mode. At the pre-alphabetic phase, in visual-holistic processing, words appear as images and as symbols of a meaningful element. Parallel to this is another route, where visual elements (letters) signify sounds but do not carry meaning. This route requires the availability of phonological processing. In this case, any words, even non-words, can be read letter by letter. Building words and sentences from letters also require sensory-motor processing. This ensures the precise recognition of sequences, directions, visual and auditory details and, thereby, precise word-reading. Frequently encountered words and expressions get stored in the mental lexicon. To reach the consolidated-alphabetic phase, visual-holistic processing is once again necessary. If this route works correctly, there is no need to decipher words, merely a phonological check takes place. This is a partly lexical route since text decoding happens in tandem with phonological processing. To read a new or rarely used word, the phonological processing will be more dominant on this route.

Reading skill gets obstructed due to a deficiency of some processing mode. The type of dyslexia depends on the place of weakness or lack of a processing way. Availability of the processing modes defines the way of the reading and its development. If the reading does develop but it does not take the optimal, partly-phonological, partly-lexical route, we still encounter a reading disorder, since reading does not happen in the expected, usual way. The following weird text can help us understand the problem:

> *Aoccdrnig to a rscheearch at an Elingsh uinervtisy, it deosn't mttaer in waht oredr the ltteers in a wrod are, the olny iprmoatnt tihng is that the frist and lsat ltteer is at the rghit pclae. The rset can be a toatl mses and you can sitll raed it wouthit porbelm. Tihs is bcuseae we do not raed ervey lteter by it slef but the wrod as a wlohe.*

The previous text can be easily read with the usual reading abilities taking the partly-lexical, partly-phonological route to read when all necessary processing modes are available.

If somebody is not able to read the meaningless groups of letters but the phonological processing is intact, guesses can help to find the meaning of the text. It happens in cases when the reader saw/heard words in diverse ways when learning to read—owing to their weak sensory-motor processing—and so could not build up a stable lexicon whence they could safely recall words based on their phonological characteristics. The problem is thus that owing to an uncertain perception of directions and relations induced by sensory-motor processing errors and to letter mix-ups, individuals are unable to decipher words when learning to read, whereby words are perceived differently each time, and so word images do not form, get mixed up, or are unstable. Stably recallable verbal units are necessary for proper reading.

In this case, somebody who uses the direct-lexical route to reading for the previous text will find it unmanageable, as it also requires phonological and sensory-motor processing, which is not part of reading in their case.

Culture Change Brings Reading Change

While the previous model is suitable for analysis of reading disorders, it also makes understanding different reading modes possible. Moreover, the model brings to light the connection between different reading modes and different cultures.

Both genetic and cultural traits can change through time and produce functional psychological mechanisms for facing adaptive challenges (Moya & Henrich, 2016). The cultural changes at the beginning of the twenty-first century brought new reading methods. The brains with dyslexia may be the forerunners in a way, and successful people who experience dyslexia are the best sources for the research of successful adaptivity.

Fink (1998) studied the reading and the reading development of 60 successful people with dyslexia. It turned out that they progressed best through reading materials belonging to their sphere of interests. When reading about a specific topic, they got familiar with the specialised vocabulary, the typical expressions and concepts. Reading about a favourite topic enlarged their background knowledge and made it possible to get a reading experience, which in turn promoted more fluent reading and the development of the necessary abilities. While they could interpret even complicated texts, they still lagged behind in some basic abilities, although they compensated for the deficiencies well. Based on partly compensated errors, two groups could be identified: One group only made spelling errors, while the second group showed weaknesses in word recognition and word reading, too, besides spelling.

The first group presumably struggled with the sensory-motor processing, while the second group had difficulties in the phonological processing and could therefore only read familiar words stably and quickly. Successful individuals could read efficiently despite a potentially severe level of dyslexia, indicating that there can be different viable routes to reading. The reading techniques of skimming and scanning are well-known from learning methodology. The way successful individuals with dyslexia read is in many respects based on these techniques. They guess at the meaning of the text from relatively few words, and they look for relevant information. They can thereby process written materials quite quickly using efficient semantic processing. Skimming and scanning are hunter-gatherer ways of reading, while the methodical, step-by-step, detailed reading is the farmer type of reading.

Especially in the twenty-first century, there are many advantages of the skimming and scanning mode of reading (see Figure 9.4). Even without dyslexia, effective people use these methods to process a large amount of written information. Using the good old in-depth reading will not be enough to process the growing amount of available reading material. To see the big picture and to spot the relevant information is crucial, and these are where a successful entrepreneur is good.

Here we encounter entrepreneurship and dyslexia. You do not have to experience dyslexia to have the ability to see the big picture and be

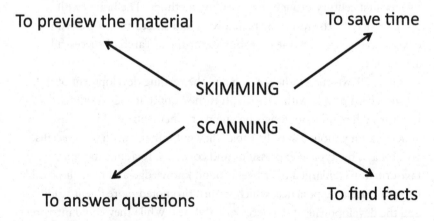

Figure 9.4 The Advantages of Skimming and Scanning Types of Reading

able to find the important aspects; moreover, dyslexia is not sufficient to be successful. However, a bright brain with dyslexia is an advantage in a world full of fuzzy and changing information, which is the everyday experience of an entrepreneur.

Conclusion

As Kitayamama and Uskul (2011) wrote, the human genome is a million-year collection of evolutionary wisdom. Culture is used to select genetic variants, and the variants motivate their carriers to choose from cultural practices.

The most ancient reading modes correspond to Ehri's pre-alphabetic reading phase. Direct reading, which entirely or mostly disregards phonology, is characteristic of early cultures, where symbols corresponding to expressions are stored in the mental lexicon without letter-to-sound correspondence. A newer invention of humanity is the use of letters symbolising sounds, making it possible for writing to construct an infinite number of words from a finite number of elements. The most common reading mode today combines letter-to-sound correspondence and the use of images stored in the mental-orthographical lexicon.

Persons who carry the genes from a previous culture may be confronted with difficulties, but the same genes may be advantageous when a new culture arises. Modes of processing information useful in a prior culture, namely in the hunter-gatherer culture, have become more frequent and may be advantageous. The fact is that due to the bio-psycho effects on the nervous system, children show a different development than the previous group that we perceived as normal.

The environmental impacts affect which reading paths children's minds choose. Visual-holistic processing, which is rather a hunter-gatherer style, became stronger and phonological and detail- and relation-oriented processing, a farmer style, became weaker. Because of this, an increasing number of children will show delayed readiness for reading and other skills expected in school.

Reading instruction awaits alphabetic readers' brains in vain, children use the processing available to them, that is visual-holistic processing, and they learn to read by guessing. Their grapheme-phoneme awareness can develop but they use the visual-lexical path as the primary way of reading. Spatial-visual, holistic processing, the big picture orientation, enhances holistic reading. The successful entrepreneur is just like that, and the irregular way of reading, called dyslexia, is therefore characteristic of this population.

By the twenty-first century, humanity is producing an immense quantity of text, reading which is impossible even in possession of the best reading skills. Electronic info-communication tools churn out materials, in the processing of which reading skills continue to play a role but not necessarily in the way they did in previous millennia. The hallmark of good reading is not fluency but the efficiency of extracting information.

Efficient methods of reading have appeared. Reading methods like skimming and scanning are important ways to process literal information in the twenty-first century. Successful people with dyslexia employ these methods usually without anyone having taught them to. Genes, abilities and culture affect each other in a complex interaction, and the massive appearance of a given specialty can indicate the direction of changes. It is high time to reconsider reading, reading instruction and reading modes. An insight into how people with dyslexia and with outstanding performance read can add to this reconsideration.

References

Arcos-Burgos, M., & Acosta, M. T. (2007). Tuning major gene variants conditioning human behaviour: The anachronism of ADHD. *Current Opinion in Genetics & Development, 17*(3), 234–238. https://doi.org/10.1016/j.gde.2007.04.011

Barkley, R. A., Koplowitz, S., Anderson, T., & McMurray, M. B. (1997). Sense of time in children with ADHD: Effects of duration, distraction, and stimulant medication. *Journal of the International Neuropsychological Society, 3*(4), 359–369. https://doi.org/10.1017/S1355617797003597

Bullock, P. (2017, March 5). The generation of writers: Spielberg, dyslexia and the written word. *Medium*. Retrieved from https://medium.com/

Caplan, R. D., & Harrison, R. V. (1993). Person-environment fit theory: Some history, recent developments, and future directions. *Journal of Social Issues, 49*, 253–275. https://doi.org/10.1111/j.1540-4560.1993.tb01192.x

Card, J. (2019, June 12). Dyslexia is a gift that's helped me in business. *Minutehack*. Retrieved from https://minutehack.com/

Coltheart, M., Rastle, K., Perry, C., Langdon, R., & Ziegler, J. (2001). DRC: A dual route cascaded model of visual word recognition and reading aloud. *Psychological Review, 108*(1), 204–256. https://doi.org/10.1037/0033-295X.108.1.204

Denckla, M. B., Rudel, R. G., Chapman, C., & Krieger, J. (1985). Motor proficiency in dyslexic children with and without attentional disorders. *Archives of Neurology, 42*(3), 228–231. https://doi.org/10.1001/archneur.1985.04060030042008

DuPaul, G. J., Gormley, M. J., & Laracy, S. D. (2013). Comorbidity of LD and ADHD: Implications of DSM-5 for assessment and treatment. *Journal of Learning Disabilities, 46*(1), 43–51. https://doi.org/10.1177/0022219412464351

Egan, J. (2016). *1000 inspirational facts.* Morrisville, NC: Lulu Publishing Services.

Ehri, L. C. (1999). Phases of development in learning to read words. In J. Oakhill & R. Beard (Eds.), *Reading development and the teaching of reading: A psychological perspective* (pp. 79–108). Oxford, UK: Blackwell Science.

Eisenberg, D. T. A., Campbell, B., Gray, P. B., & Sorenson, M. D. (2008). Dopamine receptor genetic polymorphisms and body composition in undernourished pastoralists: An exploration of nutrition indices among nomadic and recently settled Ariaal men of northern Kenya. *BMC Evolutionary Biology, 8*(1), 173. https://doi.org/10.1186/1471-2148-8-173

Farmer, D. (n.d.). Ben Way. A story of success. *Total Prestige Magazine.* Retrieved from www.totalprestigemagazine.com/

Feloni, R. (2018, February 7). 3 of the 6 'Shark Tank' investors are dyslexic— And they credit it for their success as entrepreneurs. *Business Insider.* Retrieved from www.businessinsider.com/

Field, S. (2018, January 31). Barbara Corcoran on dyslexia, the power of empathy and Oprah as President. *Forbes.* Retrieved from www.forbes.com/

Fink, R. P. (1998). Literacy development in successful men and women with dyslexia. *Annals of Dyslexia, 48*, 311–346. https://doi.org/10.1007/s11881-998-0014-5

Fitzgibbon, G., & O'Connor, B. (2002). *Adult dyslexia: A guide for the workplace.* London, England: Wiley.

Fredén, J. (2020, January 16). *How Kamprad became king of IKEA.* Stockholm, Sweden: The Swedish Institute. Retrieved from https://sweden.se/

Frith, U. (1985). Beneath the surface of developmental dyslexia. In K. Patterson, J. Marshall, & M. Coltheart (Eds.), *Surface dyslexia, neuropsychological and cognitive studies of phonological reading* (pp. 301–330). London, England: Lawrence Erlbaum.

Germanò, E., & Gagliano, A. (2010). Comorbidity of ADHD and dyslexia. *Developmental Neuropsychology, 35*(5), 475–493. https://doi.org/10.1080/87565641.2010.494748

Gialluisi, A., Andlauer, T. F. M., Mirza-Schreiber, N., Moll, K., Becker, J., Hoffman, P., . . . Schulte-Körne, G. (2019). Genome-wide association scan identifies new variants associated with a cognitive predictor of dyslexia. *Translational Psychiatry, 9*(1), 1–15. https://doi.org/10.1038/s41398-019-0402-0

Greenspan, S. I., & Wieder, S. (1999). A functional developmental approach to autism spectrum disorders. *Journal of the Association for Persons with Severe Handicaps, 24*(3), 147–161. https://doi.org/10.2511/rpsd.24.3.147

Harm, M. W., & Seidenberg, M. S. (1999). Phonology, reading acquisition, and dyslexia: Insights from connectionist models. *Psychological Review, 106*(3), 491–528. https://doi.org/10.1037/0033-295X.106.3.491

Hartmann, T. (1995). *ADD success stories.* Grass Valley, CA: Underwood Books.

Hsiung, G. Y., Kaplan, B. J., Petryshen, T. L., Lu, S., & Field, L. L. (2004). A dyslexia susceptibility locus (DYX7) linked to dopamine D4 receptor

(DRD4) region on chromosome 11p15.5. *American Journal of Medical Genetics, 125B*(1), 112–119. https://doi.org/10.1002/ajmg.b.20082

Kaplan, B. J., Crawford, S., Cantell, M., Kooistra, L., & Dewey, D. (2006). Comorbidity, co-occurrence, continuum: What's in a name? *Child Care, Health and Development, 32*(6), 723–731. https://doi.org/10.1111/j.1365-2214.2006.00689.x

Kitayamama, S., & Uskul, A. (2011). Culture, mind, and the brain: Current evidence and future directions. *Annual Review of Psychology, 62*, 419–449. https://doi.org/10.1146/annurev-psych-120709-145357

Logan, J. (2009). Dyslexic entrepreneurs: The incidence; Their coping strategies and their business skills. *Dyslexia, 15*, 328–334. https://doi.org/10.1002/dys.388

Melillo, R. (2009). *Disconnected kids: The ground-breaking brain balance program for children with autism, ADHD, dyslexia, and other neurological disorders*. New York, NY: Perigee Press.

Moya, C., & Henrich, J. (2016). Culture-gene coevolutionary psychology: Cultural learning, language, and ethnic psychology. *Current Opinion in Psychology, 8*, 112–118. https://doi.org/10.1016/j.copsyc.2015.10.001

Peterson, R. L., Pennington, B. F., & Olson, R. K. (2013). Subtypes of developmental dyslexia: Testing the predictions of the dual-route and connectionist frameworks. *Cognition, 26*(1), 20–38. https://doi.org/10.1016/j.cognition.2012.08.007

Piek, J. P., Pitcher, T., & Hay, D. A. (1999). Motor coordination and kinaesthesis in boys with attention deficit-hyperactivity disorder. *Developmental Medicine and Child Neurology, 41*(3), 159–165. https://doi.org/10.1017/S0012162299000341

Richardson, A. J., & Ross, M. A. (2000). Fatty acid metabolism in neurodevelopmental disorder: A new perspective on associations between attention-deficit/hyperactivity disorder, dyslexia, dyspraxia and the autistic spectrum. *Prostaglandins, Leukotrienes and Essential Fatty Acids (PLEFA), 63*(1–2), 1–9. https://doi.org/10.1054/plef.2000.0184

Sánchez-Morán, M., Hernandez, J. A., Duñabeitia, J. A., Estévez, A., Bárcena, L., González-Lahera, A., . . . Carreiras, M. (2018). Genetic association study of dyslexia and ADHD candidate genes in a Spanish cohort: Implications of comorbid samples. *PLoS ONE, 13*(10), e0206431. https://doi.org/10.1371/journal.pone.0206431

Schonfeld, I., Shaffer, D., & Barmack, J. (1989). Neurological soft signs and school achievement: The mediating effects of sustained attention. *Journal of Abnormal Child Psychology, 17*, 575–596. https://doi.org/10.1007/BF00917723

Swanson, J., Oosterlaan, J., Murias, M., Schuck, S., Flodman, P., Anne Spence, M., . . . Posner, M. (2000). Attention deficit/hyperactivity disorder children with a 7-repeat allele of the dopamine receptor D4 gene have extreme behavior but normal performance on critical neuropsychological tests of attention. *Proceedings of the National Academy of Sciences of the United States of America (PNAS), 97*, 4754–4759. https://doi.org/10.1073/pnas.080070897

Verheul, I., Block, J. H., Burmeister-Lamp, K., Thurik, R., Tiemeier, H., & Turturea, R. (2015). ADHD-like behaviour and entrepreneurial intentions. *Small Business Economics, 45*, 85–101. https://doi.org/10.1007/s11187-015-9642-4

Walsh, A., & Yun, I. (2016). Evoked culture and evoked nature: The promise of gene-culture co-evolution theory for sociology. *Frontiers in Sociology, 1*, 8. https://doi.org/10.3389/fsoc.2016.00008

Part III
Education

10 Entrepreneurship Education and Dyslexia

Pedagogies and a Pilot Study

Barbara Pavey

Introduction

A few years into the twenty-first century saw widespread economic crises affecting both Europe and the USA, with global implications. Entrepreneurship became positioned as a means for economic survival and reconstruction. Major international organisations turned their attention to entrepreneurship education, with a view to encouraging the growth of entrepreneurship. At the same time, developing academic interest saw the topic of entrepreneurship become embedded in business courses in universities and in business studies syllabuses in schools. Business studies as a field began to recognise the value of personal narratives and testimonials for increasing understanding of the entrepreneurial process and the implications for entrepreneurship education (Rae, 2000, 2005).

The development of disability activism championed the expectation that disabled people would be involved in the matters that concerned and affected them. Prior to this, many studies had gathered data from existing sources without considering the impact of disability, and without talking to people who experienced disabilities themselves. Once recognised, research began to develop wherein disability was considered as a factor, and the circumstances of entrepreneurs who experienced dyslexia became more apparent.

Entrepreneurship Education Policy: Directions and Recommendations

The development of entrepreneurship education policy is an example of the 'Punctuated Equilibrium' model of policy change described, as one of several, by Cerna (2013). Citing Baumgartner and Jones (1991), Cerna describes the model:

> [o]nce an idea gets attention it will expand rapidly and become unstoppable. Many ideas are competing for attention but then something happens at some point. The process comes about from external events that disrupt the political system, particularly the ones that are big enough to disrupt or punctuate its equilibrium.
>
> (Cerna, 2013, p. 9)

This describes quite well the growth of attention to entrepreneurship and, consequently entrepreneurship education, following the financial disruption and recession during, and subsequent to, 2008.

The European Commission had produced its *Green Paper, Entrepreneurship in Europe*, in 2003; this noted less 'entrepreneurial dynamism' in Europe than in the USA (Commission of the European Communities, 2003, p. 9) and promoted innovation, internationalisation and entrepreneurship as a means of social benefit beyond business implications. Subsequently the economic downturn triggered an increased interest in entrepreneurship education. International research, policy development and advisory groups became proactive in trying to create and support educational conditions for entrepreneurship. Policy documents were developed without any deep interrogation of the concerns regarding theory, definition, or pedagogy described in the academic literature. Policy was concerned primarily with promoting the dissemination of entrepreneurship concepts and programmes.

The European Commission continued its support for entrpreneurship with the Entrepreneurship 2020 Action Plan, and this included the recommendation to member states that they should,

> Establish and run entrepreneurship education schemes for the unemployed to enable them to (re-)enter business life as entrepreneurs based on successful models from a number of Member States, in partnership with education and training systems as an engagement route into second chance education.
>
> (European Commission, 2013, p. 27)

Here was a new focus on entrepreneurship as a solution for unemployment. Key action points included education and training and provided the impetus for the subsequent development of the Entrepreneurship Competence Framework (EntreComp).

Advisory and policy groups interested in entrepreneurship also involved themselves in considerations of entrepreneurship education; an example was Valerio, Parton and Robb's 2014 report for The World Bank, *Entrepreneurship Education and Training Programmes Around the World*. By this time, independent providers had entered the field and entrepreneurship pedagogy was no longer the province of schools, universities and colleges; this expanded the field of entrepreneurship education and training. Valerio et al. (2014) acknowledged a wide variety of clients and students for the programmes, including self-employed individuals with reduced literacy, implying, at last, a wider acknowledgement of sole traders and self-employed individuals working in traditional trades and also people who might experience dyslexia.

Entrepreneurship education, as it stands, follows a range of approaches, concerning itself with understanding the nature, the process, or the real-time application of entrepreneurship principles and practices. Among these multiple purposes, the EntreComp seeks to draw entrepreneurship education together, providing a comprehensive answer to the question of what an entrepreneurship curriculum might offer if the broad rather than the narrow definition of entrepreneurship is used.

The competencies described in the EntreComp cover three areas—those of ideas and opportunities, resources and the capacity to translate these into action (Bacigalupo, Kampyis, Punie, & van den Brande, 2016, p. 6). The document states: '[t]he framework aims to establish a bridge between the worlds of education and work and to be taken as a reference de facto by any initiative which aims to foster entrepreneurial learning' (Bacigalupo et al., 2016, p. 5). Within its framework, the document describes 15 competencies and includes a detailed analysis of how these may be understood and translated into learning outcomes. These are expressed as 'I can' statements, reinforcing their potential for education and training since pedagogies commonly make use of learning outcomes for which evidence must be provided by learners.

Provision and Pedagogy in Entrepreneurship Education

The development of entrepreneurship education has attracted a number of academic reviews, as noted by Mwasalwiba (2010). The global position regarding entrepreneurship education is also tracked by the Global Entrepreneurship Monitor, reporting annually. Amongst reviews, an early example by Dainow (1986) described the growth in entrepreneurship courses in a relatively new academic area, seeking more empirical practice and cross-disciplinary links. These themes remained evident, as pointed out by Gorman, Hanlon and King (1997) when they took the review process up to 1997. These authors noted the growth in the field of entrepreneurship education. However, Pittaway and Cope's review (2006) reported a fragmented field of study, lacking research in some areas and lacking also a clear paradigm and an agreed pedagogy. The authors noted also that links between policy and the provision and practice of entrepreneurship were underdeveloped.

While considering that progress had been made in establishing the field of study, Mwasalwiba's (2010) review concluded that it still lacked congruity and was still uncertain in its pedagogy; he noted the large number of academic articles discussing pedagogy but offering no consensus. From among 26 articles, Mwasalwiba (2010) identified 13 key teaching methods, dividing them into traditional or passive, and innovative or active methods. Ranked from most to least used, these were:

- lectures and theory based,
- case studies,
- discussions and group work, (tied with. . .)
- business simulations,
- videos and filming,
- role models and guest speakers, (tied with. . .)
- business plan creation,
- projects,
- real venture setting up, (tied with. . .)
- games and competitions, (also tied with. . .)
- workshops,
- presentations,
- study visits.

The most commonly used methods identified were lectures, case studies and group discussions; all methods which are relatively cheap in resource terms and straightforward matters for the lecturer. However, they are also likely to have a heavier demand for reading and written work.

Mwasalwiba's study was concerned with describing the field and identifying impact factors, but in considering the implications for students with dyslexia and with entrepreneurial interest, his analysis of pedagogical methods is valuable; he concludes,

> [m]ost scholars are of the opinion that there is a need to be more innovative on designing modules that will enable learners to achieve their predetermined outcomes in learning by either for, about or in entrepreneurship. The objectives and type of audience have to be matched with the course contents and teaching methods.
>
> (Mwasalwiba, 2010, p. 40)

This does not negate the importance of theory and traditional scholastic approaches, but given that the purpose and content of entrepreneurship education courses is by no means agreed it shows that, at the time of writing, there was a need for diversity to be recognised.

Since Mwasalwiba's review, further reviews of entrepreneurship education have taken place, and different approaches to pedagogy have been offered. Pedagogical suggestions, all of which offer interesting and meritorious ideas, include Blenker et al. (2012), who recommend a personalised entrepreneurship pedagogy; Huq and Gilbert (2017), who wish to see the application of design thinking to entrepreneurship education; Man and Farquharson (2012), who discuss team projects; and Neck and Corbett (2018) who propose a curriculum based on andragogy (methods and principles for adult learning) and heutagogy (self-directed learning carried out by adult learners). The range of even this small number of examples demonstrates the heterogeneity of the field.

It is within this context that entrepreneurship education was reviewed by Lackéus (2015) in order to inform the development of the EntreComp (Bacigalupo et al., 2016). In their background paper, they describe the range of terminology, as well as the range of definitions in use, noting the dichotomy of having both wide and narrow definitions in play. Similarly to Mwasalwiba, Lackéus points out that entrepreneurship programs can be through, for, or about entrepreneurship. He expresses this as a continuum of entrepreneurship practice reaching from the wider, personal development focus to the narrower, business focus (Lackéus, 2015, p. 8). The author bases his conclusions on the broad definition of entrepreneurship, considering the key function of entrepreneurship to be that of producing value for others. This function he places ahead of venture creation; that is, the creation of new businesses.

Lackéus (2015) offers an analysis of entrepreneurship teaching and learning or, as he terms it, entrepreneurial education, and suggests 'tools' which are intended to bring about 'innovative and iterative value creation' (p. 30). These include active and interactive approaches applied to real-world and solution-focussed concepts, in a progression model that sees the processes as being built upon personal and social development. The potential for curriculum reform based around such concepts is acknowledged.

However, a different point of view is presented by Neck and Corbett (2018), who researched the views of an expert panel of entrepreneurship educators. There was overlap in the two perspectives; Neck and Corbett's (2018) panel agreed that entrepreneurship was 'a life skill for the 21st century' (p. 30), but their conclusion was that new venture creation was at the heart of entrepreneurship education rather than value creation. This view relates, in effect, to contrasting broad and narrow definitions of entrepreneurship.

Of particular interest in Neck and Corbett's research is the panel's doubts regarding their teaching effectiveness. Being themselves from research backgrounds in areas such as business studies, entrepreneurship and economics, and functioning at the professorial level, they felt the lack of educators' professional knowledge. The authors note:

> A disconnect exists between what we want and expect from our students when compared to what the students actually produce. We heard that students were not prepared, do not engage, fail to do high-level work, are distracted in class, and are often leery to engage with stakeholders outside the school. Who is to blame? We tend to blame students but is it time to turn the mirror on ourselves?
>
> (Neck & Corbett, 2018, p. 33)

The panellists described students in universities or business schools, and it is the sense of frustration engendered by these attitudes that led panel members to believe that they are in need of educators' skills.

It is clear that much of the discussion regarding entrepreneurship and entrepreneurial education remains at the theoretical and definitional level. There is less focus upon effective content, and it is this gap that the EntreComp seeks to fill. The document does not go so far as to offer specific teaching and learning methods for effectuating the content, and this, rather than the content itself, is the area where Neck and Corbett's expert panellists feel themselves to be disadvantaged.

It is apparent that the development of entrepreneurship knowledge, attitudes and skills has become the big educational idea for the first part of the twenty-first century. Indeed, such is the enthusiasm for entrepreneurship that Farny, Fredericksen, Hannibal, and Jones (2016) compare it to a cult in its attention to deities (successful entrepreneurs), rituals (the accepted processes of being an entrepreneur) and salvation, the inherent belief that, 'Individuals can reach emancipation, self-realisation and find true happiness through enterprise' (Farny et al., 2016, p. 527). It is the concern of the authors that, unexamined, these characteristics combine to form a hidden curriculum that needs to be challenged in order to broaden understanding of entrepreneurship and make it more accessible to a wider range of potential entrepreneurs.

In spite of any limitations, entrepreneurship education has become an important area of policy worldwide, in both educational and industrial contexts. While the academic focus is on theory and definition, the policy focus seeks practical, educational expressions of something that is already accepted as a public good, overriding or disregarding unresolved theoretical views. Nevertheless, Lackéus (2015) concludes his review of entrepreneurship education with a warning:

> Despite its promising effects on students and society, it is important to keep in mind that the field of entrepreneurial education is in a quite early stage of development. It is still regarded as an innovative but marginal pedagogical approach spurring much interest but also much confusion among various stakeholders.
>
> (Lackéus, 2015, p. 35)

A Pilot Study

One recognisable characteristic among the efforts to understand, theorise, define and interpret entrepreneurship education, is that the field does not address itself to questioning what the subjects of this work, the entrepreneurs, would offer in the way of suggestions for effective teaching and learning. While the intersection of dyslexia and entrepreneurship is acknowledged, discussion does not extend to considerations of about how best to help young people with dyslexia who have entrepreneurial interests in order for them to benefit from entrepreneurship education in general. The assumption seems to be that literacy boosting and access arrangements will be of sufficient assistance to allow entrepreneurship education to continue to follow established methods.

A small pilot study asked five individuals, four men and one woman, for their views about how best to help young people who might experience both dyslexia and entrepreneurial flair, through education in schools, colleges and universities (Pavey & Adkins, 2010). This was a volunteer sample, found by asking people who had identified themselves as experiencing dyslexia and who had built their own businesses, whether they were willing to be interviewed about how to help such young people in schools and universities. The questions were:

Q 1. Are you dyslexic?

Q 2. Was this formally identified or did you work it out for yourself?

Q 3. Would you describe yourself as an entrepreneur?

Q 4. Do you think that there are young people with dyslexia who might become entrepreneurs if they had the right sort of input at school?

Q 5. (If 'yes' to school), what would be the right sort of support or lessons in school?

Q 6. What about in universities?

Q 7. Do you think there is anything universities could do to help young people with dyslexia who want to be entrepreneurs—or do you think they would not be useful?

Q 8. Is there anything universities can do to help to make the move from school to further study (to college or university) for young people with dyslexia who would like to be entrepreneurs?

Q 9. What about trading games where you build a business, have you heard of these? Do you think they could be used to develop entrepreneurship or not?

Q 10. Is there anything else we could do to encourage and support entrepreneurship?

Q 11, Is there anything else you would like to tell me about this (dyslexia and entrepreneurship)?

The researchers were aware that the respondents did not benefit directly from this research, but they kindly gave their time because they believed the project to be worthwhile for others. All respondents framed their answers in terms of their personal experience and knowledge, providing thought-provoking information about their experiences with dyslexia in school, college and university.

In terms of their own school input, respondents described:

- school failure,
- anger,
- lack of attention, help, or concern from schools,
- undermining of self-belief,
- lack of information about entrepreneurship as a career route,
- lack of engagement with traditional teaching and learning styles,
- lack of practical experiences,
- lack of engagement with themselves by schools.

In schools, respondents wanted to see:

- nurturing of self-belief,
- explanation about dyslexia,
- constant stimulation to try new things,
- opportunities to take charge of own learning,
- non-traditional teaching and learning styles,
- workshops,
- a rich panoply of tools, skills and experiences, including practical opportunities,
- social and other interaction/experience,
- opportunities to meet entrepreneurs.

In universities and colleges, respondents wanted to see:

- buddying of students who experience dyslexia with students who do not,
- signposting of the help available,
- specific enterprise courses with role-model speakers,
- contact with entrepreneurial activities and entrepreneurs for all students,
- centres, incubators and all-in resource bases made available,
- hands-on, real business-building experience.

In suggesting ways of helping the move from school to college and/or university, respondents were divided between those wanting to highlight dyslexia as a disability with entitlements under the UK Equality Act of 2010 and those who felt that difference should not be seen as a disability and that dyslexia could be an asset. Respondents agreed that there was a need for dyslexia-aware staff and policies and that evidence of these should be made plain. They called for the reconsideration of conventional examination qualifications for admission to courses, and of paper-based methods of assessments within courses; they felt that both of these methods disadvantaged young people who experience dyslexia.

Asked if they thought that trading games could help, the entrepreneurs with dyslexia were generally doubtful; and only half of the respondents had used such games. Respondents felt that games might have a role for trying out new ideas, modelling particular aspects and transactions, but they were not a substitute for reality—people should try a real, small business instead.

Respondents considered that there should be much more support, more opportunities and more suitable resources in entrepreneurship education. They wanted to see something other than traditional approaches, such as:

- mixed groups, with collaborative and cooperative working,
- more recognition and more help,
- mentoring,
- practical experience including apprenticeships,
- attainable role models,
- multisensory methods.

Respondents told of their frustrations in their educational settings. They felt that this experience, which was often negative, may have helped them to develop the grit and resilience that they needed to survive in the business world. Nevertheless, they felt that it was important that educators should continue to try to reach and support young learners with dyslexia who experienced, or might experience, entrepreneurial flair.

Subsequent to this overview, the answers from one more entrepreneur with dyslexia were added to the previous responses, extending the pilot study to encompass a sample of six, and the results were re-analysed in greater detail for the purpose of this chapter. It was noticeable that there was very little congruency amongst the answers made by respondents, so that many, indeed most, of the points offered in this analysis came from individuals. There was common ground but there was also a plethora of ideas and a great deal of variety in the responses. Respondents seem to appreciate the chance to talk about ways in which to help young entrepreneurs who experience dyslexia, and the questions sparked a great many comments, suggestions, and individual points.

In coding the responses, it was possible to determine some overarching categories, within which were recurring points that crossed between different answers. The points that respondents wanted to make about entrepreneurship education were identifiable as falling within the following broad categories: Theory/paradigm; practice; pedagogy, both in terms of pedagogical structure and specific methods; and personal and social education, with separate categories for personal and social aspects. Comments made by respondents were distributed between categories, although this sometimes meant that a conversational response was broken up into different themes.

Furthermore, different respondents made similar points in different ways, with different word choices, and in response to different questions. One respondent might say a great deal about one area while another focussed differently, each making many points, some of which overlapped while others contrasted. It is possible that questions were not clear enough, or distinct enough, to differentiate the answers fully. There were, however, topics to which the respondents were sensitive, so that they continued to engage with the overall matter of their entrepreneurship experience, in all its aspects and ramifications. For the entrepreneurs with dyslexia, these matters seemed important, and urgent.

Within the category of **theory/paradigm**, there was recognition of foundational concepts within business studies for entrepreneurship, but there was also a wish for the breaking down of barriers and the integration of entrepreneurship concepts across boundaries. Taken together, the respondents wanted to see theoretical and paradigm foundations and functions intensified. They wanted a focus on dyslexia and entrepreneurship, and possibly specific courses; they wanted centres of excellence, but also a shared vision. While respecting the place of theory and links with business studies, there was a sense of frustration about aspects of provision that reflected traditional academic style, and a silo mentality. Most particularly, respondents wanted links and integration outside of the university course, and more flexible thinking on the part of course providers:

> *That is a special sort of vision that reaches across, it's nothing to do with the departments, it's taking responsibility.*
>
> *(Respondent 4)*

In terms of the **practice** within such courses, empirical experience was seen to be an important part of provision for potential entrepreneurs who experience dyslexia. Respondents wanted students to be building their own businesses and helping other businesses from the earliest stages, although one respondent supported the view that theory should form the basis for this work. Real-world practice figured strongly in responses, with support for charitable fundraising, community projects and not-for-profit organisations being seen as useful opportunities for this:

> *So maybe for someone to become an entrepreneur, students need to go out and help local businesses, so that they become maybe consultants in that businesses, helping someone improve their business. It's more hands-on.*
>
> *(Respondent 6)*

Practice would take place under the shelter of the university course, and one respondent suggested that university finance could be a source of investment in such small new businesses. Mentoring by entrepreneurs was seen to be valuable; and for the respondent who was self-employed and working in a traditional trade, this was related to apprenticeship, involving both craft and finance aspects of the new business:

> *They should make everyone do apprenticeships, that's what I think, the shortage is absolutely unbelievable, my kids will be learning trades.*
>
> *(Respondent 1)*

This respondent saw the need for apprenticeship and/or mentoring that covered the management of business, describing clearly the working arrangements in place for numbers of entrepreneurs who experience dyslexia and self-employed individuals working in traditional trades (see Logan & Martin, 2012, p. 63):

> *I've just stuck to what I know now, I am struggling on the business side of things but luckily I've got my wife backing us at home, she does all the books, she pays all the bills, I've got my business card, I buy what I want.*
>
> *(Respondent 1)*

Pedagogical aspects were expressed in terms not only of programme structure but also of teaching and learning methods. Experiential, practical aspects were affirmed as important. Pedagogical changes were sought at both school and university levels. Some respondents wanted more practical aspects; in addition to improved geographical/locational provision, they wanted also to see more awareness of dyslexia:

> *Universities and Colleges should be centres of excellence for*
> *entrepreneurship, and dyslexia, and recognising it.*
>
> *(Respondent 2)*

At the structural level, respondents generally wanted an intensification of many aspects of educational provision for entrepreneurship. They wanted school students to have experienced entrepreneurship and to have studied the basic skills and tools for business. They wanted more favourable conditions for potential entrepreneurs with dyslexia, including admission and assessment arrangements that did not disadvantage them:

> *[h]ow can the dyslexic student access university? 'A' levels? Not*
> *the best assessment of someone who's bright but can't express their*
> *depth of knowledge and understanding on paper and maybe doesn't*
> *comprehend the question in the first place . . . forget the bloody bits*
> *of paper—these say nothing about entrepreneurial intent or ability.*
>
> *(Respondent 5)*

Regarding pedagogical methods, respondents wanted experiential and discovery-based learning within interactive or live environments. They wanted a chance for students of entrepreneurship who experience dyslexia to meet and to work together with established entrepreneurs. While there was a strong wish for students to be taught in ways that were inclusive, there was also some support for a more focussed, positive approach for learners with dyslexia, including specific courses and settings. Once again, the view was expressed that more should be understood about dyslexia and its impact upon pedagogy and learning, for example recognising the slower processing speed experienced by learners with dyslexia.

One respondent pointed out that educators were still not doing enough to make the accommodations and adjustments to which students who experience dyslexia are entitled. Another voiced the opinion that traditional business school approaches did not suit learners with dyslexia, while a third challenged conventional expectations about thinking processes:

> *I think equally the dyslexic way of thinking is normal. If we, the dyslexics, try and enforce our way of thinking on 'normals', they'd be going 'Oh this isn't quite right, I'll have to think like this'! I do think there's a major difference.*
>
> *(Respondent 6)*

In the matter of specific activities, respondents had some interesting ideas. One respondent wanted to see workshops that would help students to understand their own dyslexia, how it related to their entrepreneurial interests and how they could use information technology to support their work. Respondents generally wanted to see more active and interactive learning, and could see a role for games as part of this process:

> *Negotiation skills, game theory (simple), importance of integrity and honesty, all these need to be introduced but again in games and group interactive projects, in other words it needs to be applied live learning.*
>
> *(Respondent 5)*

Regarding **personal and social aspects** of education for potential entrepreneurs who experience dyslexia, respondents wanted to talk about the characteristics of individuals with this profile. They saw support for individual development as being important, especially support for confidence and motivation; one noted that the time of transition from school to university could be difficult in this respect. Respondents wanted students to know about their own personal characteristics of dyslexia and to be encouraged in creative practices. They wanted opportunities for students to carry out practical, entrepreneurial work.

Alongside a greater awareness of learning needs relating to dyslexia within provision, respondents wanted to see more use of adaptations and techniques to support dyslexia. One respondent saw advantages in the ability to be able to use a wider range of means and methods; at the same time, another warned against creating a climate where dyslexia might be offered as an excuse for lower achievement—they felt that standards must be maintained. Together, respondents sought greater sensitivity to the needs of students with dyslexia in the matter of confidence and self-esteem. This sensitivity should extend to awareness that while entrepreneurship students who experience dyslexia may think differently from their peers, this need not be interpreted negatively.

Respondents found social-interactive techniques, and opportunities for social interaction, to be important. They believed that collaboration between people was helpful, enabling things to develop and happen. Another thought that gaining a new network of friends was an entrepreneurial way of working, while a third thought that:

> *A lot of the time with entrepreneurism it's spotting the opportunities and playing the game, and its (getting) the right timing, and the right game. If you don't know the game or if you can't spot the opportunity—it doesn't happen.*
>
> *(Respondent 6)*

As a group, respondents spoke in terms of their thoughts, feelings, ideas and personal experiences in bringing together their beliefs about how best to help young students with dyslexia who might be potential entrepreneurs. In the process of answering the questions, respondents spoke about their own education experience, how they began their business and planned its development, occasions when they were audacious, experiences that hurt them and what approaches worked for them, or did not work. They spoke about the impact of their dyslexia, their coping strategies and what they considered to be important, especially for the future entrepreneurs on whom the research was focussed. In doing so, several consistent aspects emerged, not necessarily linked to any specific questions. In summary, respondents wanted to see:

- a more vivid focus on factors which would affect learners who experience dyslexia, including a more specific input in terms of available courses. They acknowledged the importance of theory and basic concepts but wanted these moved away from a more traditional academic style towards something more impactful. Within this more specific focus they included a wish for wider learning opportunities,
- a greater use of interactive opportunities with existing entrepreneurs who were working currently; these would include input for

the courses but also a focus on mentoring, work experience opportunities and apprenticeships,

- a move away from an emphasis upon written work for entrance requirements, course requirements and assessment. They wanted more support, including financial support, for the development of businesses under the shelter of entrepreneurship education,
- more knowledge and understanding about dyslexia amongst those who taught them, including knowledgeable and appropriate use of adjustments and accommodations and information technology. Respondents acknowledged that students also needed input to help them understand their own dyslexia, and to benefit from positive aspects of their own dyslexia characteristics.

Conclusion: The Pedagogy of Entrepreneurship Education

In the entrepreneurship literature, entrepreneurship courses are described as focusing on one or more of several possible purposes—being by, for, about, or through the activity of entrepreneurship. To increase the effectiveness of programmes for students who experience dyslexia, the purposes of the programmes need to be clear in the administrative documents supporting the courses, and in the prospectuses, the recruitment of staff and students, the outlook of the practitioners and the pedagogical strategies used in the programmes.

In the pilot study, entrepreneurs with dyslexia seemed to seek a reduction in academic conventions, yet conformance to these is a critical part of the accreditation process and cannot be forgone. Research is needed to advance understanding of how best to conduct entrepreneurship education for this group, and for entrepreneurship students in general, and this needs to be embedded in established research protocols in order to be considered valid and reliable. Without this, there is the over-reliance on anecdotes and narratives found in journalistic accounts. Although respondents in the pilot study wanted more practical experience and less paperwork, they recognised the foundational importance of theory and they were not seeking to move entrepreneurship education away from the Higher Education sector.

The question of access to practicing entrepreneurs is perhaps more easily raised than effectuated. It is quite possible that entrepreneurs who experience dyslexia would prefer to be engaged in entrepreneurial activity rather than in academic activity, especially where teaching and learning has been difficult in their own lives. Similarly, finding placements has its own difficulties. With these issues it is easy to see how standard transmissive teaching and learning techniques could come to be relied upon.

Nevertheless, there is more that could be done in education to help potential entrepreneurs who experience dyslexia. Accommodations and adjustments in line with disability and equality legislation should be the province of all Higher Education staff, just as they are expected to be the province of school teaching staff. However, making adjustments for the range of students' learning needs, and making learning more interesting and accessible generally, takes time, money, attention and commitment. This should be acknowledged and allowed for within pedagogical arrangements.

It is clear from the pilot study that what is being sought by entrepreneurs with dyslexia is a much more powerful pedagogical impact than has sometimes been the case, in their experience. In the study, there is no mention of different purposes in entrepreneurship education; the respondents' emphasis is all upon potential entrepreneurs who happen to experience dyslexia having better opportunities to be entrepreneurial, through the recognition of, and attention to, their particular learning characteristics. This moves pedagogical requirements into areas addressed by the Universal Design for Learning and Dyslexia-Friendly Movements (Appendix One), designed to increase the accessibility of teaching and learning for all. However, it also highlights the personal limitations acknowledged by some entrepreneurship educators. Further discussion about how pedagogical methodology can aid potential entrepreneurs who experience dyslexia, and by extension all students, will be found in the concluding chapter to this volume.

References

Bacigalupo, M., Kampyis, P., Punie, Y., & Van den Brande, G. (2016). *EntreComp: The entrepreneurship competence framework* (No. JRC101581). Brussels, Belgium: Joint Research Centre, European Commission. Retrieved from http://publications.jrc.ec.europa.eu/

Baumgartner, F., & Jones, B. (1991). Agenda dynamics and policy sub-systems. *Journal of Politics, 53*(4), 1044–1074. https://doi.org/10.2307/2131866

Blenker, P., Frederiksen, S. H., Korsgaard, S., Müller, S., Neergaard, H., & Thrane, C. (2012). Entrepreneurship as everyday practice: Towards a personalized pedagogy of enterprise education. *Industry and Higher Education, 26*(6), 417–430. https://doi.org/10.5367/ihe.2012.0126

Cerna, L. (2013). *The nature of policy change and implementation: A review of different theoretical approaches.* Paris, France: Organisation for Economic Cooperation and Development (OECD). Retrieved from http://search.oecd.org/

Commission of the European Communities. (2003). *Green paper, entrepreneurship in Europe.* Brussels, Belgium: Commission of the European Communities. Retrieved from https://eur-lex.europa.eu/

Dainow, R. (1986). Training and education of entrepreneurs: The current state of the literature. *Journal of Small Business and Entrepreneurship, 3*(4), 10–23. https://doi.org/10.1080/08276331.1986.10600245

European Commission. (2013). *Communication from the Commission to the European Parliament, the Council, the European Economic and Social Committee and the Committee of the Regions. Entrepreneurship 2020 action plan: Reigniting the entrepreneurial spirit in Europe.* Brussels, Belgium: The European Commission. Retrieved from https://eur-lex.europa.eu/

Farny, S., Fredericksen, S., Hannibal, M., & Jones, S. (2016). A CULTure of entrepreneurship education. *Entrepreneurship and Regional Development, 28*(7–8), 514–535. https://doi.org/10.1080/08985626.2016.1221228

Gorman, G., Hanlon, D., & King, W. (1997). Some research perspectives on entrepreneurship education, enterprise education and education for small business and management: A ten-year literature review. *International Small Business Journal, 15*(3), 56–78. https://doi.org/10.1177/0266242697153004

Huq, A., & Gilbert, D. (2017). All the world's a stage: Transforming entrepreneurship education through design thinking. *Education + Training, 59*(2), 155–170. https://doi.org/10.1108/ET-12-2015-0111

Lackéus, M. (2015). *Entrepreneurship in education: What, why, when, how* (Entrepreneurship 360 Background Paper). Paris, France: Organisation for Economic Cooperation and Development (OECD). Retrieved from www.oecd.org/

Logan, J., & Martin, N. (2012). Unusual talent: A study of successful leadership and delegation in entrepreneurs who have dyslexia. *Journal of Inclusive Practice in Further and Higher Education, 4*(1), 57–76. Retrieved from www.brainhe.com/

Man, T. W. Y., & Farquharson, M. (2012). Psychological ownership in team-based entrepreneurship education activities. *International Journal of Entrepreneurial Behavior & Research, 21*(4), 600–621. https://doi.org/10.1108/IJEBR-11-2012-0126

Mwasalwiba, E. (2010). Entrepreneurship education: A review of its objectives, teaching methods, and impact indicators. *Education + Training, 52*(1), 20–47. https://doi.org/10.1108/00400911011017663

Neck, H., & Corbett, A. (2018). The scholarship of teaching and learning entrepreneurship. *Entrepreneurship Education and Pedagogy, 1*(1), 8–41. https://doi.org/10.1177/2515127417737286

Pavey, B., & Adkins, P. (2010, August). *Dyslexia-Friendly entrepreneurship: What do dyslexic entrepreneurs say?* [Presentation at Inclusive and Supportive Education Congress (ISEC)]. Belfast, Northern Ireland: Queen's University.

Pittaway, L., & Cope, J. (2006). *Entrepreneurship education: A systematic review of the evidence* (National Council for Graduate Entrepreneurship Working Paper 002/2006). Sheffield, UK: Sheffield University Management School Enterprise and Regional Development Unit. Retrieved from www.ncge.org.uk/

https://journals.sagepub.com/doi/abs/10.1177/0266242607080656

Rae, D. (2000). Understanding entrepreneurial learning: A question of how? *International Journal of Entrepreneurial Behaviour and Research, 6*(3), 145–159. https://doi.org/10.1108/13552550010346497

Rae, D. (2005). Entrepreneurial learning: A narrative-based conceptual model. *Journal of Small Business and Enterprise Development, 12*(3), 323–335. https://doi.org/10.1108/14626000510612259

Valerio, A., Parton, B., & Robb, A. (2014). *Entrepreneurship education and training programs around the world: Dimensions for success*. Washington, DC: The World Bank. Retrieved from https://elibrary.worldbank.org/doi/abs/10.1596/978-1-4648-0202-7

11 Developing Entrepreneurs With Dyslexia Through Higher Education (HE) in Wales

Matthew Armstrong and
Margaret Meehan

Introduction

This chapter discusses the development and current position of entrepreneurship in Wales. Wales is a bilingual country, and the 2018 Welsh language standards built on the 1993 Welsh Language Act (Welsh Government, 2018) gives clarity to Welsh speakers about what services they could expect to access in the Welsh language. All public institutions, including universities, must comply with the Welsh Language Act and be consistent in their provision in both Welsh and English. Certainly most Welsh universities have increased the number of courses taught through the medium of Welsh, especially in the area of health science, but the percentage of courses is still small. The Special Educational Needs (SEN) Code of Practice for Wales (National Assembly for Wales, 2002) included the right of the child to a diagnostic assessment in their preferred language of English or Welsh. This is subject to the availability of diagnostic tests in the Welsh language. It may be that young Welsh speaking potential entrepreneurs are at a disadvantage if such tests are in English, and this may also be the case for Welsh speaking adult entrepreneurs.

In the rapidly changing landscape of Higher Education (HE), cuts in the Disabled Students Allowance (DSA) have been made in England with an emphasis on inclusion of disabled students by universities and the use of assistive technology to support students in their studies. Many universities have site licenses for text to speech, concept mapping and recording of lectures software which allows students to better access the curriculum, but the lack of availability of such software in the Welsh language may also impede Welsh speaking student entrepreneurs who experience dyslexia. While the Welsh government has not reduced its DSA budget, there are fewer Welsh speaking specialist tutors to support Welsh speaking university students who experience dyslexia.

HE in Wales is a devolved area, which means decisions made about HE in Wales are taken by the Welsh government with HE Funding Council for Wales (HEFCW) acting as its intermediary. HE Institutions (HEIs) generate income from these public funds in addition to student fees, research and increasingly, from important business activities. HEFCW's Draft Paper Welsh Government Higher Education Strategy to 2027 (HEFCW, 2016) sets out the Welsh government's stance over the next decade, which puts university graduates, businesses and underrepresented student groups, including students who experience dyslexia, at the heart of the plan.

Arguably, the unique selling point of a university education is the garnering and exploitation of information. Similarly in business, a strategic plan will seek to utilise information, position, or its products in order to gain an advantage over its competitors. This is why the HEFCW plan to associate business and HE has such potential for success, offering a much-needed additional income stream to Welsh HEIs in the short term and building a stronger economy over the course of the next decade and beyond. The Welsh government provision is well-rounded and comprehensive; it encompasses the Youth Entrepreneurship Strategic Action plan 2010–2015 (Welsh Government, 2010), the exploitation of potential benefits of the Welsh language through the Arfor Project (Welsh Government, 2019a) and the Supporting Entrepreneurial Women in Wales programme and good practice guide (Welsh Government, 2019b).

The challenge of any strategy of course is in the doing, and, in this case, there are two related aspects to the strategy in the form of the developing of the business-ready interior of Wales and the forging of appropriately skilled graduates to be employed in Wales or to start-up businesses in Wales.

The Welsh government will be seeking to build on previous strategies of inward investments supporting businesses in Wales. These have included incubating business start-ups, facilitating commissioning and procurement and developing supply chains. In addition, the Welsh government makes overt efforts to drive innovations and entrepreneurial activities; see for example, the Business, Economy and Innovation Planning and Strategy website, (Welsh Government, n.d.).

Monitoring Business Impact

Internationally, entrepreneurship is measured by the Global Entrepreneurship Monitor (GEM), with 49 economies reported as participating in 2018/2019, the twentieth anniversary of the research (Bosma & Kelley, 2018). This approach is very useful to compare performance with other economies meaningfully and accurately, track year-on-year progress of policy and identify new areas for the government to consider deploying policy. GEM researchers identify critical indicators of an economy's entrepreneurial potential, including personal characteristics and circumstances, early entrepreneurial stages and the likelihood of employees becoming entrepreneurs.

Individuals have a greater potential to become entrepreneurs if they are resilient to failure, acknowledging that starting a business is strewn with setbacks and focusing instead on the positive prospects of the new business. A person must possess a determined self-belief to overcome setbacks, but also to provide vision and drive to the new venture and its employees. Top-down policymaking will need to address these specific points in order to foster entrepreneurial activity and help to insulate individual entrepreneurs from the many hardships in early and later stages of business development. Government policy will need to include softer elements of business mentoring, as there is evidence that being recently exposed to a business start-up, or if there is a familial history of business, makes a person more likely to become an entrepreneurial business owner themselves (White, Thornhill, & Hampson, 2007; Hart, Bonner, Levie, & Heery, 2017).

Defining Entrepreneurship

Entrepreneurship is an elusive concept to define in relation to definite causal factors. According to Halfpenny and Halfpenny (2012), Logan

(2009) used Bolton and Thompson's (2000) approach. Their definition of entrepreneurship is first establishing a business and then growing the business successfully; this view returns the narrative to what is arguably the main purpose of business. However, when considering a global perspective, this definition may prove too narrow, potentially excluding from entrepreneurship measurement any non-registered businesses and also people who are in the idea/preparation phase before launching a business, the employed and those who maintain a mixed portfolio of employment status. Therefore, a truly global definition will need to encompass pre-business activity, look at potential entrepreneurs and recognise employed individuals as capable of entrepreneurial activity. GEM provides a broad definition, stating that entrepreneurship is 'Any attempt at new business or new venture creation, such as self-employment, a new business organization, or the expansion of an existing business, by an individual, a team of individuals, or an established business' (GEM, 2019).

On the face of it, this definition is business-focussed; however, GEM uses a broad definition of what constitutes business and, all-importantly, includes pre-business registration as entrepreneurial activity. Furthermore, business, and by extension entrepreneurship, is used in the occupational sense to encompass employees whose behaviour can be described as entrepreneurial—sometimes described as 'Intrapreneurship' when it happens within the employment of a company.

GEM measures entrepreneurial activity as two main components. The first is the phase where the entrepreneur is identifying their unique idea, including the potential market segment which is either unoccupied, under-serviced, or is ripe for disruption with their new product or service. A business plan (or business case when considering intrapreneurship) may be prepared, sources of funding are identified and legal perspectives are sought, all in preparation for the launch of the business—GEM describes this phase as 'nascent entrepreneurship.' Following this inception stage is the launch of the business, business activity, or project where the owner, manager, or employee puts their plan into place, pushing the project toward its intended goal, negotiating the pitfalls and selling the vision to those who will listen. 'owning-managing the new firm' is the descriptive term given to this stage and is reminiscent of Bolton and Thompson's (2000) expansion and establishing phase. GEM defines this as a 42-month period. Taking the number of nascent entrepreneurs and the number of owner-managers of a new firm and totalling them gives the key metric of Total early-stage Entrepreneurial Activity (TEA).

Key factors in Welsh entrepreneurial activity are the Welsh TEA and how this relates to England as a near and lead competitor. Also important is the history of how these relationships have developed over the period of available Welsh evidence, from 2010 to 2017. Of particular interest is how graduate and non-graduate entrepreneurial activity compares with that of the wider population, since graduates are in the unique position of being in receipt of enterprise training in Wales. They are the beneficiaries of joint ventures between HEIs and industry and have the access and skills to apply large quantities of good-quality evidence to their business aspirations.

Welsh TEA from 2002 through 2008 was affected by the period of economic deterioration known as the Great Recession starting in 2008, and by 2010, perhaps unsurprisingly, not much had changed. Wales was producing TEA of 5.8% compared with England's 6.7%, with the middle of the scales occupied by the UK as a whole at 6.5% (Hart & Levie, 2011). By 2016, Welsh TEA had rallied to 7.6%, showing strong recovery (Bonner, Hart, & Levie, 2017) but waning to a position of 6.3% in 2017 (Hart, Bonner, Levie, & Heery, 2018). Using this data, it can be calculated that England forged ahead to 9.1% with a percentage change of 36% in 2017. However, despite Welsh numbers initially rallying in 2016 with a percentage change of 31%, by 2017 they had returned to earlier values and a percentage change of just 8.6%.

A key weakness in the GEM reports for Wales is the sample sizes themselves, being only 2,995 in 2010 and 2,950 in 2016. This means that reliable or significant statistical comparisons of sub-sets are difficult to make for data such as graduate TEA. This matter is compounded by the constraints placed upon samples due to a change in the research methodology. However, this longitudinal study has garnered some 60,000 Welsh respondents since 2002 and should be viewed over the longer-term to establish trends (Hart et al., 2017).

The cause of the stalling performance of entrepreneurship in Wales is difficult to define; we must examine the data for the interior economic context in Wales to understand it. GEM's global measurement of entrepreneurial potential is measured by four interrelated statements of belief with which non-entrepreneur respondents agree or disagree (GEM, 2017). Does the respondent know of a business start-up in the last 2 years and do they have a positive perception of this? Does the respondent believe themselves to possess the necessary skills to succeed in a start-up, and would they ignore personal fear of failure in establishing their own start-up? The purpose of these questions is to explore entrepreneurial activity across the globe and how individuals view and engage in entrepreneurship. The Welsh government needs to ensure that there is accessible mentorship for younger entrepreneurs and promote the embedding of entrepreneurship in HE.

Young People Approaching Entrepreneurship in Wales

Graduates appear to dominate the entrepreneurial scene in the UK, including Wales, and have done so over the recorded period of the GEM studies available at the time of writing (2010–2016). In 2010, the TEA for graduates in Wales was 6.2% with non-graduates represented at approximately 5.9%. In England, the TEA for graduates was 8% with non-graduates delivering only 5.5%. In 2016, Wales had made impressive improvements with a graduate TEA of 9.1% and a non-Graduate TEA of 6.9%. But by 2017, graduate TEA in Wales had been reduced to 7.5% and non-graduate TEA reduced, correspondingly, to 5.5%. Meanwhile in England in 2017, the graduate TEA had increased to approximately 11.0% with non-graduate data showing 7.5%, this being the only UK home nation to show a statistically significant improvement. Wales' diminishing performance in 2017 can be calculated and summarised by the graduate TEA percentage change of 21% while the non-graduate TEA took a retrograde step of minus 7.0% (Hart et al., 2017).

The 18–24 age range is an important category, as it represents 66% of the student body in Wales in 2017/2018 (Higher Education Statistics Agency, 2019) with a university's main product arguably the generation of knowledge and the development of skills. It could be argued that graduates are successful entrepreneurs because they have access to large amounts of information and research evidence, and are able to leverage it to recognise and create opportunities. Students are in an environment where education overtly collaborates with industry, participating in knowledge transfer and joint working projects. Welsh HE students have access to specific enterprise training to develop the right skills and characteristics for success (Pickernell, Packham, Jones, Miller, & Thomas, 2011).

Nevertheless, a long-running theme in Wales is the significantly lower perception that there are good business start-up opportunities in the next 6 months, when compared with the UK at large. When analysing the data by age, it appears that significantly fewer 18–24 year-olds believe there are good start-up opportunities in Wales, at just 25% in comparison to the UK's 35%. These views are compounded further when only 28.9% of Welsh 18–24 year-old respondents thought they had the right knowledge, skills and experience to begin a start-up business, in stark contrast with 40.6% of non-entrepreneurs of all ages in the UK (Hart et al., 2017).

Necessity Entrepreneurship, Opportunity Entrepreneurship and Innovation

As discussed earlier, entrepreneurship can elude explicit definition, partly since individuals carry with them the experiences and beliefs informing their personal definition and partly since certain activities conform more easily to given definitions. Areas of conflict will always include whether an employee can be an entrepreneur in their employment, which can be described as intrapreneurship or as employee entrepreneurial activity (Hart et al., 2017), and whether activity which has no innovative leap can be considered entrepreneurship, since innovation is considered to be tacit but intrinsically characteristic of entrepreneurship.

In order to disaggregate entrepreneurship, we can consider inaugural activity as either necessity- or opportunity-based. Necessity entrepreneurship is where there are no better alternatives to work; for example, a painter and decorator sets up a business to sell his skills and competes in the market place with other painters and decorators. In contrast, opportunity entrepreneurship occurs when someone identifies an opportunity to create a new market segment, or disrupt an established segment, with a new product or service. For example, if the same painter and decorator developed a new paint delivery system, they would have started from necessity but moved into the area of opportunity. If this new paint delivery system brought novel benefits to customers, for example using environmentally-sound ingredients, which conformed to an ethic that customers wanted to support, the painter and decorator's entrepreneurship would have moved into the area of innovation.

GEM recognises innovation as a concept associated with opportunity entrepreneurship; this concept describing the point where other businesses do not offer this same product or service and where no, or relatively few, customers would have seen a similar product or service. GEM sees innovation as indicative of innovative, that is developed, economies. Innovative entrepreneurship is measured by the innovation rate, itself measured as a percentage of TEA and combines with opportunity TEA to describe the cutting-edge of new business entrepreneurial behaviour. Opportunity and innovation TEA describe more precisely the true definition of entrepreneurship, and this is the arena in which Welsh graduates now stand out.

Perhaps counterintuitively, Wales had the highest level of necessity TEA of any Great Britain nation in 2010 at 1.08%. A high necessity TEA is not desirable, as it is a proxy for the unavailability of suitable jobs; this explains the higher necessity TEA throughout the Great Recession. However, by 2017, necessity TEA had fallen to 0.9%, the lowest in the UK; this is likely to have been due to wider improvements seen in TEA and the support of the Welsh government. Furthermore, opportunity TEA was 4.14% in 2010, representing the greater proportion of TEA in Wales, and growing sustainably to 5.1% by 2017. These measures of entrepreneurship need to be understood in the context that Wales, like other nations, is still recovering from the Great Recession and from the fiscal policies put in place to counter its effects by the UK central government. Despite this, overall TEA has grown; opportunity TEA has grown by 0.96%, with this value most likely powered by graduate increases in TEA, thus counteracting the effects of the Great Recession. Further gains could be made by attracting 18–25 year-olds into Welsh HE and inputting the necessary skills, experience and knowledge to link with, and realise, the available opportunities.

Welsh Government Support for Entrepreneurship

The Welsh government is creating policy to shape the right parameters for business and is preparing graduates to be skilled in this new environment. Business-focussed policies include:

- a suite of support mechanisms to enhance business start-up and growth,
- focussing on small to medium sized enterprises,
- access to the Welsh development fund,

- elbow-to-elbow mentorship from business leaders,
- free commissioning and procurement support,
- access to their online platform (Sell2Wales),
- assisting business with intellectual property protection,
- access to expertise Wales innovation projects,
- free support from Superfast Wales (broadband) to keep growing businesses that are lean and agile, with good accesses.

The Welsh government also helps new businesses to find their feet internationally, at the time of writing participating in Enterprise 2020 and the European development fund. The sum effect of these measures depends upon the working-age population having the right skills to take up the opportunities identified.

In keeping with other areas of the UK, access to goods and services for students in Wales should not be restricted because of disability; this is based on the protected characteristics of the Equalities Act 2010. There is a special onus on HEIs to be anticipatory in making provision, and this requirement is inclusive of students who experience dyslexia when it is deemed to be disabling.

Enterprise Training in Welsh Higher Education (HE) and its Implications for Welsh Entrepreneurship

The draft HEFCW HE Strategy 2027 requires university fee and access plans to exploit effectively the knowledge base. This is to be done through working with businesses and employers, contributing to the future Welsh economy, raising skill levels of the Welsh work force and supporting businesses to become increasingly innovative and competitive (Higher Education Funding Council for Wales [HEFCW], 2016). This shows how the Welsh government has given impetus to universities to embed entrepreneurship across Wales in a two-pronged approach.

The dividing lines between entrepreneurship, enterprise and innovation are poorly understood. 'Enterprise' describes the skills needed to be entrepreneurial (planning, idea creation, skills, resilience to failure, working in a group and conflict and skill mix), and innovation is the inception of something new. It is easy to see the place of Welsh education and its HE students in this triad with the role of the university as facilitator. Universities in Wales are now running discrete courses in enterprise as well as embedding enterprise into existing modules.

For example, the skills obtained in enterprise include planning, which Welsh HE students develop in conducting research and in preparation for assessments. While they are at university, students are able to leverage existing data to inform their own ideas or use opportunities to develop their own data.

Following enterprise principles, collaboration between students amplifies the effects of idea creation, utilising learning opportunities in group work and preparing them for their role in collaborative partnerships in the future. A critical pathway in collaboration is identifying risk and developing appropriate mitigation, and, on those occasions when conflict must occur, developing the management skills to make it productive. Recognition of a student's own skills and the skills of others are essential in working toward a common goal. Students in HE undertake group work which mimics real life-ventures, being assessed on their individual contribution and on the results of the whole. Enterprise seeks to develop character to withstand the shocks of failure and resilience to continue leading in difficult times.

Widening Entrepreneurship Discussion in Welsh Higher Education (HE)

It is useful to consider whether discussions about entrepreneurship, and about entrepreneurship courses in HE, will change as the gender balance changes. Gender balance in HE has become uneven in favour of women in Welsh universities, with an increasing percentage of HE enrollments being female, according to data available from 2013/2014 to 2017/2018 (Higher Education Statistics Agency [HESA], 2019). This trend is mirrored by a corresponding 10% increase in female entrepreneurs globally. Although males have made up the greater proportion of entrepreneurs over the long term, running at 4.5 males to 1 female in 2017, this appears to be changing, reflecting the higher numbers of women in HE generally.

A great deal of the narrative around entrepreneurs has focussed upon the nature of entrepreneurship; however, it is also useful to think about the identity of entrepreneurs given that growing numbers are female (Hart et al., 2017), may be of non-UK origin (op.cit.) and/or may experience dyslexia. Entrepreneurial activity amongst immigrants to Britain and citizens across a range of ethnicities suggests an encouraging picture showing a rise in TEA to 14.5% with 12.9% of the former in the early stages of entrepreneurialism compared to 8.2% of UK-born individuals

(Global Entrepreneurship Monitor (GEM), 2017). In the case of students with dyslexia, there is a long-established notion that dyslexia is synergistic with entrepreneurship. This is undoubtedly founded upon how people who experience dyslexia think, experience and take part in the world, how their specific learning difficulty has an impact upon their learning and occupation and how people who experience dyslexia circumvent imposed limitations.

Some Shared Characteristics Among Students With Dyslexia in Welsh Higher Education (HE): Nursing and Entrepreneurship

It is not within the scope of this chapter to discuss whether dyslexia directly impinges on the developmental character traits of individuals or whether people who share common adversity develop common working solutions. We have observed that people who experience dyslexia are heavily represented in entrepreneurial circles (Franks & Frederick, 2013), and we have peer group leaders who experience dyslexia and are captains of industry such as Richard Branson, Bill Gates and the late Steve Jobs; so there is some anecdotal evidence for such a tendency.

The statistics for the number of people who experience dyslexia in the population, and therefore HE, will depend on the definition of dyslexia used, but is thought to be around 10% (Rose, 2009), rising to 14% when considering certain occupations like nursing (H. Taylor, 2003; Hartley, 2006). Logan and Martin (2012) have established that 30% of entrepreneurs sampled in the USA experienced dyslexia and, by contrast, 19% of entrepreneurs in the UK experienced dyslexia, a staggering triple and double of the prevalence rates in the UK in general. Logan (2009) herself suggests that people who experience dyslexia do not thrive in restrictive, process-driven environments. Nor do they excel in occupations heavy in finance, management, science and computing (K. E. Taylor & Walter, 2003), although of course there are exceptional people in all fields.

The greater numbers of people who experience dyslexia in occupations like nursing is, at first glance, perplexing. The answer to this and also the reason for greater numbers of people who experience dyslexia in nursing itself could lie in the coping strategies deployed. Working to one's strengths and minimising exposure to one's weaknesses is a sound approach, so seeking out opportunities to talk rather than write would explain the leaning toward nursing.

Adjusting the environment and mode of learning, including metacognition, are key methodologies deployed in special education in HE in Wales. It is no surprise perhaps that entrepreneurs who experience dyslexia seek out the ultimate in occupational adjustment by establishing a business that reflects their own propensities and preferences—in their own image (Logan, 2009). Nursing in Wales is an all-graduate profession. What is not explained is why, since it is assessed academically mainly via essays and the profession itself is heavily structured and evidence-based in its practice, people who experience dyslexia still choose this arena? The answer to this, and also to the question of why people who experience dyslexia make such good entrepreneurs, may be found in the intrinsic characteristics of an entrepreneur and of a person who experiences dyslexia.

Entrepreneurs are clearly opportunity seeking and determined, can be highly motivated and self-reliant and have a high risk tolerance (Franks & Frederick, 2013). People who experience dyslexia on the other hand are often visual thinkers with strong spatial skills, are resilient to failure and are expert delegators with natural problem-solving skills (Franks & Frederick, 2013). Reading this skills mix, it is clear that all of these traits would be beneficial in the establishment of a new business venture, particularly if it is innovative and therefore has additional difficulty and risk. Entrepreneurs and people who experience dyslexia are also often considered to be both proficient, verbal communicators, employing conceptual thinking and highly influential orators, working best when mentored (Franks & Frederick, 2013). Entrepreneurs are typified by their ability to see something that no one else can see, which leads to opportunities in the creation and ultimately innovation in new business, or leads to intuition when nursing a patient. When speaking to entrepreneurs about a new opportunity, it is easy to be infected by their enthusiasm and captured by their vision. Dig a little deeper, however, and it can be difficult to get numbers onto a page to independently verify the validity of the business potential.

One of the authors spoke to an entrepreneur recently about his business; he was finding it difficult to write his business plan and to carry out other written aspects of his application for funding. The entrepreneur, of non-UK origin, said he did not need a degree, as his own technical knowledge had surpassed that of what was provided in the degree course. The author pointed out that HE would have equipped him to write structured, evidenced and persuasive pieces, a skill he could have leveraged on his application, but the entrepreneur remained unconvinced. The author went on to point out that students have access to more information than non-graduates. They become more adept at opportunity identification and evidence application, and are the net beneficiaries of HE/Industry partnerships. The final conversation was around referring the hopeful entrepreneur to one of the Welsh government's rapid development programmes, of which he was unaware. The programme could provide mentor support, seed money, access to a network of other entrepreneurs and opportunities such as direct routes to market, for example accessing the National Health Service, a major procurer of goods and services in the UK.

The need for achievement is a key motivating factor in entrepreneurs but not necessarily in entrepreneurs who experience dyslexia or 'Dyspreneurs', which casts doubt on their viability as business start-up catalysts (Franks & Frederick, 2013). However, it is time we reframed the notion of achievement, given that Dyspreneurs will start up more businesses than their entrepreneurial peers who do not experience dyslexia, employ more staff and own or operate multiple businesses (Franks & Frederick, 2013). In addition to their named degree programme, people who experience dyslexia and who enter HE in Wales will participate in a programme of individualised study-skill building, which is designed to overcome unhelpful traits that may be characteristic of dyslexia; and they will graduate from Welsh universities as independent graduates. People who experience dyslexia in this arena tend to be determined to succeed, which is the trait that brought them to the degree programme in the first place, and they are dedicated to graduating and obtaining the career opportunity of their choice. This dedication is arguably an analogue of the desire for success and the demonstration of single-mindedness.

Having a known literacy weakness, living in a literacy-centric society and taking on elite education in Welsh universities is a demonstration of that single-mindedness and the need to succeed. Perhaps we are therefore asking the wrong question of Dyspreneurs, not, 'Do you have the need to succeed?' but rather, 'tell us what you have done to succeed this far?' Only then will we see their true desire to succeed, perhaps only filtered through the lens of low self-efficacy and low self-esteem, most likely due to languid, patchy, insufficient support earlier in the education system

(National Assembly for Wales Enterprise and Learning Committee, 2008).

If early diagnosis could be improved, then appropriate earlier, and persistent, support could be provided in order to see more individuals meet their HE potential in Wales. Indeed, adopting a systematic approach, with an individual learning plan of evidence-based methods, improves both soft and hard outcomes for students in HE who experience dyslexia, helping them to develop compensatory strategies which can be valuable in the remainder of their career, whether that be as the instigator of a rapid-growth start-up or as an intrapreneur in a Welsh business.

Since there are greater numbers of people entering HE because of their strategic plans and wishes, it is reasonable to assume that better, earlier detection would see higher numbers of entrepreneurs, female entrepreneurs and entrepreneurs who experience dyslexia graduating into Welsh communities with a business-positive outlook, bringing about a corresponding increase in business start-ups. If support for people who experience dyslexia was removed or severely restricted because of what is defined as dyslexia, and therefore students who experience dyslexia no longer received support through the equality legislation, the effects would be felt in only a very few years through lower students numbers and fewer dyspreneurs graduating. The effects of such a move would be felt for a generation, having a knock-on effect since both entrepreneurs and dyspreneurs benefit from exposure to start-up businesses and ongoing elbow-to-elbow mentorship. The lack of such exposure would make the starting of new businesses more difficult and less likely.

Graduate entrepreneurial activity is decisively linked to new businesses, new employment, innovative products and services, higher employment figures and new taxation, so a prosperity manifesto in Wales needs to place graduate entrepreneurs at the centre of its plan. For maximum benefit, the Welsh government will need to be resolved in their support of HE and entrepreneurial activity but also be long-sighted in supporting people who experience dyslexia throughout the education system. In Welsh universities, it is likely to be graduate entrepreneurs who experience dyslexia who will deliver the most joined up, advanced, fastest-growing and concurrent businesses. The Welsh economy is subject to the market forces of the UK government, the European Union and its own internal economy; the only force which the Welsh government can truly control is the internal market.

Supporting our entrepreneur graduates who experience dyslexia is the surest, longer-term investment.

Conclusion

This chapter discusses the development and current position of entrepreneurship in Wales. The Welsh government recognises the importance of entrepreneurship to the economy and makes funding available to support young entrepreneurs, and, more recently, female entrepreneurs and Welsh-speaking entrepreneurs. Entrepreneurship is difficult to define but is explored here in relation to TEA along with enterprise and innovation.

Some of the characteristics of entrepreneurs, nurses and individuals who experience dyslexia are discussed and compared; most notably, resilience and the need to succeed displayed by entrepreneurs and individuals who experience dyslexia are highlighted as necessary traits for success. Thus, dyspreneurs, that is, entrepreneurs who experience dyslexia, are in a good position to make the most of the market.

In the rapidly changing landscape of HE, cuts in the DSA have been made in England, but, so far, Wales has not reduced this budget. University students who experience dyslexia are supported by the DSA, so it is in Wales' best interest to identify individuals who experience dyslexia at an early age and to support undergraduate entrepreneurs who experience dyslexia as part of its long-term strategy.

References

Bolton, B., & Thompson, J. (2000). *Entrepreneurs: Talent, temperament, technique*. Oxford, UK: Butterworth-Heinemann.

Bonner, K., Hart, M., & Levie, J. (2017). *GEM UK: Wales report 2017*. London, England: Global Entrepreneurship Research Association. Retrieved from https://gov.wales/

Bosma, N., & Kelley, D. (2018). *Global entrepreneurship monitor 2018/2019 global report*. London, England: Global Entrepreneurship Research Association. Retrieved from www.c4e.org.cy/

Franks, K., & Frederick, H. (2013). Dyslexic and entrepreneur: Typologies, commonalities and differences. *Journal of Asia Entrepreneurship and Sustainability, XI*(1), 95–115. Retrieved from http://hdl.handle.net/

Global Entrepreneurship Monitor (GEM). (2017). *Global report 2016/17*. London: Global Entrepreneurship Research Association. Retrieved from https://www.gemconsortium.org/

Global Entrepreneurship Monitor (GEM). (2019). *How GEM defines entrepreneurship*. London, England: Global Entrepreneurship Research Association. Retrieved from www.gemconsortium.org/

Halfpenny, J., & Halfpenny, C. (2012). *In their element: The case for investing in dyslexic entrepreneurs*. Leadhills, Scotland: Halfpenny Development Ltd. Retrieved from https://s3.amazonaws.com/

Hart, M., Bonner, K., Levie, J., & Heery, L. (2017). *Global entrepreneurship monitor United Kingdom 2017 monitoring report*. London, England: Global Entrepreneurship Research Association. Retrieved from www.enterpriseresearch.ac.uk/

Hart, M., Bonner, K., Levie, J., & Heery, L. (2018). *Global Entrepreneurship Monitor United Kingdom 2017/18 monitoring report*. London: Global Entrepreneurship Research Association. Retrieved from https://www.enterprise research.ac.uk/ https://gov.wales/sites/default/files/publications/2019-05/global-entrepreneur ship-monitor-gem-uk-wales-report-2017.pdf

Hart, M., & Levie, J. (2011). *Global entrepreneurship monitor United Kingdom 2010/11 monitoring report*. London, England: Global Entrepreneurship Research Association. Retrieved from www.researchgate.net/

Hartley, J. (2006). What are UK schools of pharmacy providing for undergraduates with disabilities? *The Pharmaceutical Journal, 276*, 444–446. Retrieved from www.pharmaceutical-journal.com/

Higher Education Funding Council for Wales (HEFCW). (2016). *Draft Welsh government higher education strategy to 2027*. Caerphilly, UK: Higher Education Funding Council for Wales. Retrieved from www.hefcw.ac.uk/

Higher Education Statistics Agency (HESA). (2019). *Who's studying in HE? Personal characteristics*. Cheltenham, UK: Higher Education Statistics Agency. Retrieved from www.hesa.ac.uk/

Logan, J. (2009). Dyslexic entrepreneurs: The incidence; Their coping strategies and their business skills. *Dyslexia, 15*(4), 328–346. https://doi.org/10.1002/dys.388

Logan, J., & Martin, N. (2012). Unusual talent: A study of successful leadership and delegation in entrepreneurs who have dyslexia. *Inclusive Practice, 4*, 57–76. Retrieved from www.cass.city.ac.uk/

National Assembly for Wales (NAW). (2002). *Special educational needs code of practice for Wales*. Cardiff, UK: National Assembly for Wales. Retrieved from www.snapcymru.org/

National Assembly for Wales Enterprise and Learning Committee. (2008). *Support for people with dyslexia in Wales*. Cardiff, UK: National Assembly for Wales. Retrieved from www.assembly.wales/

Pickernell, G., Packham, G., Jones, P., Miller, C., & Thomas, B. (2011). Graduate entrepreneurs are different: They access more resources? *International Journal of Entrepreneurial Behaviour & Research, 17*(2), 183–202. https://doi.org/10.1108/13552551111114932

Rose, J., Sir. (2009). *Identifying and teaching children and young people with dyslexia and literacy difficulties*. Nottingham, UK: Department for Children, Schools and Families (DCSF). Retrieved from www.thedyslexia-spldtrust.org.uk/

Taylor, H. (2003). An exploration of the factors that affect nurses' record keeping. *British Journal of Nursing, 12*(12), 751–758. https://doi.org/10.12968/bjon.2003.12.12.11338

Taylor, K. E., & Walter, J. (2003). Occupation choices of adults with and without symptoms of dyslexia. *Dyslexia, 9*(3), 177–185. https://doi.org/10.1002/dys.239

Welsh Government. (2010). *Youth Entrepreneurship Strategy (YES) action plan 2010–15*. Cardiff, UK: Welsh Assembly Government. Retrieved from https://businesswales.gov.wales/

Welsh Government. (2018). *The Welsh language standards (no. 7) regulations 2018*. Cardiff, UK: Welsh Government. Retrieved from www.legislation.gov.uk/

Welsh Government. (2019a). *Arfor*. Cardiff, UK: Welsh Government. Retrieved from www.rhaglenarfor.cymru/

Welsh Government. (2019b). *Supporting entrepreneurial women in Wales*. Cardiff, UK: Welsh Government. Retrieved from https://businesswales.gov.wales/

Welsh Government. (n.d.). *Business, economy and innovation planning and strategy*. Cardiff, UK: Welsh Government. Retrieved from https://gov.wales/

White, R. E., Thornhill, S., & Hampson, E. (2007). A biosocial model of entrepreneurship: The combined effects of nurture and nature. *Journal of Organizational Behavior, 28*(4), 451–466. https://doi.org/10.1002/job.432

12 Post-Traumatic Growth (PTG)

A New Way of Understanding the Experience of Successful People With Dyslexia

Neil Alexander-Passe

This chapter will investigate dyslexia and success, looking at the motivations and processes that a person experiences with dyslexia through school, turning childhood school oppression into adulthood workplace success.

The journey from school is long and hard for many individuals with dyslexia, and it should be recognised that many who have been through this journey have been unsuccessful, with many ending up in prisons. They have struggled through the lack of awareness, screening, diagnosis and interventions at school; resulting in leaving school with few, if any, qualifications to their name. However, this chapter looks at those who have been through similar journeys at school, many leaving without a diagnosis, who have used the trauma positively as motivation to prove their teachers, peers and society wrong about them. Developing the awareness of their strengths and talents to become successful in a wide range of careers and entrepreneurship is one such avenue chosen.

School—Emotional Coping in People Who Experience Dyslexia

Scott (2004), Edwards (1994) and Alexander-Passe (2015) suggest young people with dyslexia commonly experience adversity, both educationally in school and socially through exclusion and bullying from peers due to their learning differences. Hulme and Snowling (2009) note that those with difficulties in phonological processing, spelling, grammar, reading and writing are at a distinct disadvantage in mainstream education. Dyslexia Action (2013) reported that teachers lack the skills to effectively differentiate for those with dyslexia and other different learners in their classes, highlighted through the lack of special educational needs training for new teachers and infrequent continual professional development of current teachers.

Humphrey and Mullins (2002) and Humphrey (2003) comment on the low self-esteem in school-aged persons with dyslexia, with Scott (2004) and Alexander-Passe (2010, 2015) arguing that bullying by both teachers, in their lack of differentiation/understanding, and peers, through ostracising and exclusion, can lead to depression, withdrawal, self-harming and Post-Traumatic Stress Disorder (PTSD).

Lackaye and Margalit (2006) and P. L. Morgan, Fuchs, Compton, Cordray and Fuchs (2008) found those with dyslexia and reading disabilities can suffer from low self-concept, self-efficacy, engagement and other emotional coping that can have a significant bearing on a child's motivation. Many conceal/camouflage the true nature of their reading difficulties from their teachers, resulting in underachievement (Wadlington, Elliot, & Kirylo, 2008).

Fitzgibbon and O'Connor (2002), Armstrong (2010), E. Morgan and Klein (2003) and McLoughlin, Leather, and Stringer (2002) argue that for too long the main focus has been on the causes of dyslexia, with little understanding of the emotional effects of having such a long-term disorder (their experiences/secondary effects), especially in adults.

School–Social Exclusion

How was your time at primary school?

I always felt left out, on the outside.

By your teachers or peers?

I felt I did not fit, I felt they were doing things I could not do. So it was like a two-way process, if I felt I could join in, I would, and thus if I did not join in they just left me alone. Teachers generally tended to be rather supportive without really understanding what the problem was.

(George, in Alexander-Passe, 2010)

When you were at primary school, did you feel you fitted in, due to your learning difficulties?

No, I never felt normal, I have always felt other really, that is from beginning to end (of my school life) and to now.

You were talking about being different from your peers, did you like being different?

I   appreciate it much more now.

So you liked being different now, but not growing up?

I was happy to be different but I did not like the reactions it caused. . . . I was upset that my not liking what they liked, caused me to be ostracised and bullied and that sort of thing.

Were you being physically bullied?

Yes, a couple of times.

You did not fight back?

I was and still am, four foot nine inches, so no.

(Kirsty, in Alexander-Passe, 2010)

Young people with dyslexia, like other groups who are unable to fit into socially accepted norms of school, or even their own families, can feel excluded by society (Alexander-Passe, 2010), a view supported by Morgan and Klein (2003) and Scott (2004). Research into families of those with dyslexia and non-dyslexia siblings interestingly support the view that unless one parent also had dyslexia (especially the mother), their child with dyslexia could develop a low self-image and question their place in the family unit. Unfair sibling comparison can be extremely painful for young people with dyslexia, creating anxiety and stress in addition to that which comes from their low academic output (Alexander-Passe, 2008).

Post-Traumatic Stress Disorder (PTSD)

Definition: PTSD, or post-traumatic stress disorder, is an anxiety problem that develops in some people after extremely traumatic events, such as combat, crime, an accident or natural disaster. People with PTSD may relive the event via intrusive memories, flashbacks and nightmares; avoid anything that reminds them of the trauma; and have anxious feelings they didn't have before that are so intense their lives are disrupted.

(American Psychiatric Association, 2015)

PTSD is a relatively new term and was identified in the study of those who returned from war zones, formerly the conditions to define similar traits were called shell-shock. In more recent times, the term has been the focus of many research studies, and has been identified in the latest Diagnostic and Statistical Manual of Mental Disorders (DSM-5) guidelines.
These include PTSD in children younger than six years old and PTSD with prominent dissociative symptoms; either experiences of feeling detached from one's own mind or body or experiences in which the world seems unreal, dreamlike or distorted (American Psychiatric Association, 2015).

In the case of people with dyslexia, Scott (2004) and, more recently, Alexander-Passe (2010, 2015) have argued that many people with dyslexia can suffer from PTSD from their adverse schooling. Alexander-Passe found in a study of *N*=29 adults with dyslexia that in many with depressive symptoms, PTSD was evident when they needed to return to school for their own children. Symptoms included: Resentment and anger towards teachers, severe anxiety when seeing and being made to sit on primary school chairs, smelling floor cleaners, sitting waiting outside the Headmaster's office, hearing their child's teacher not listening to their concerns about their child with possible dyslexia and seeing children's work being pinned to the wall as their own was never deemed good enough.

Post-Trauamtic Growth (PTG)

Definition: The term refers to positive psychological change experienced as a result of the struggle with highly challenging life circumstances.

(Calhoun & Tedeschi, 2001)

PTG was introduced by the American Psychiatric Association in 1980. With examples documented from the last century (e.g. Roosevelt's renewed empathy when struck down with Polio, then becoming President of the USA, cancer sufferers and air craft crash victims being moved to have a renewed love of life and focus, and Holocaust survivors being moved to share their traumatic and life-changing experiences on a world-wide stage), Linley and Joseph (2004) argue that 30%–70% survivors of trauma say they have experienced positive change in one form or another. The term has recently been used to understand the growth gained through trauma and adversity (Calhoun & Tedeschi, 2006; Weiss & Berger, 2010) as a related positive psychology stance (Seligman, 2011).

Tedeschi and Calhoun (2004) argue that major life crises typically result in unpleasant psychological reactions; however, PTG happens when attempts are made to adapt to highly negative sets of circumstances engendering high levels of psychological distress. Tedeschi and Calhoun (2004) argue that growth is more frequent than psychiatric disorders following high levels of trauma; however, growth and personal distress often coexist, and stories over the centuries point to growth from distress (e.g. Christianity: after Jesus's death, his disciples, whilst traumatised, go on to create a powerful new religion; Islamic: Mohammed's suffering is instrumental to his great work).

Examples of PTG have been documented in those surviving/suffering from: bereavement, HIV infection, death of a child, heart attack, sexual assault and sexual abuse and combat.

Tedeschi and Calhoun (2004) and Schoulte et al. (2012) argue that PTG's typical manifestations are positive psychological change, discovery of meaning, positive emotions and positive reinterpretation. Tedeschi and Calhoun (2004) argue that the growth part of PTG comes not as a direct result of the trauma, but rather from the individual's struggle with the new reality in the aftermath of trauma; this defines whether PTG is occurring. They use the metaphor of an earthquake, in that it is not the shake that causes the psychological trauma but the effects of the shake in the building, the loss of life, the change from predictable to unpredictability of life and the changes to their regular life pattern which are traumatic.

It is argued with PTG that it is not a return to baseline levels of activity that defines whether an individual has PTG or not, it is the improvement that is experienced, and it is more common in adolescents and adults than children because PTG implies an established set of values changed through trauma. Joseph and Linley (2008) noted that individuals are intrinsically motivated towards processing new trauma-related information in ways to maximise their psychological well-being. Using the metaphor of a shattered vase, imagine that one day you break it by accident. You can either try to piece it together, to try to badly re-form the original shape, or you use the pieces to create a beautiful new mosaic. If your perspective is to bin the pieces and give up, or try and rebuild in its entirety as the original vase, then this is an impossible task as it will still be fractured, vulnerable and prone to break again. But if you take on board that a return to the original will be impossible and that you need to create a new use for the pieces, then you are more realistic and a new use can be considered.

In the case of individuals who experience dyslexia, there is very little evidence to date. Alexander-Passe (2010) argues that a pre-school child is normally taught through multisensory activity (e.g. play and hands on learning with the need to read or write). However, when a child with dyslexia starts school, they come with an established set of rules (a belief system and assumptions about themselves in the world which has guided them successfully to this point) about learning and believe themselves to be normal learners. At the point that phonics, reading and writing is introduced, there is a change and a realisation that they may or may not be able to develop in line with their peers. The first trauma takes place in that they see their peers understanding and learning a new language of learning and they are unable to. The second and longer trauma is the ongoing effect of their inability to learn like their peers.

Summary

The empirical review suggests that people with dyslexia are affected as much as by their learning differences as by the way that society views their difference. Such differences go beyond reading and writing and affect their interactions with others. Trauma at school is a common experience for young people with dyslexia and it is argued that this trauma is both distressing and continuous, occurring over a ten year school career (resulting in post-traumatic stress). It is argued by this author that people who experience dyslexia either rebuild positively from their school/post-school lives (PTG) or remain shattered and fragile, which can result in unsuitable careers or a path ending up in prison.

This chapter looks at an investigative qualitative study of dyslexia and success, to understand the personal histories of many successful adults with dyslexia and relate these to their personal childhood histories of possible school trauma.

Methodology

This study used a qualitative investigative interview study of $N=20$ successful adults with dyslexia, selected from a pool of $N=56$ successful adults with dyslexia (participants from the online survey who offered to be interviewed).

Investigative Interview Study

$N=20$ successful adults diagnosed with dyslexia were interviewed using an investigative script of six main items with a number of sub-items. The interviews were conducted using Skype or FaceTime, allowing for facial prompts to be used and participants to be put at ease through facial empathy. The interviewer disclosed his own dyslexia in order to put participants at ease and to explain his own school background. This was felt to be important as trauma was likely to be discussed.

Participants were selected subject to diagnosis by either an educational/clinical psychologist or specialist teachers. Evidence was sought to support their diagnosis claims. Before each interview, the interviewer gave an overview of the project and confirmed that the interview could be stopped at any time by the participant; however, none took this option. Interviewees were asked if they wished to proceed with the interview and all agreed. Names were changed to provide anonymity.

The interviews were digitally audio-recorded and transcribed. The transcripts were then sent to participants to check and correct/ amend if needed. They were advised that their interviews would not be used in their entirety and would be cut up into themes. All quotes were anonymised. The interview data was split into questions and sorted, so themes could be located within the data. Quotes were highlighted and combined to create themes, which were then compared to previous empirical studies for reflection. Interpretative Phenomenological Analysis (Smith, 2004) was used to create useful themes for further investigation.

The 20 participants included:

- $N=11$ male, $N=9$ female,
- $N=1$ (10–20yrs), $N=1$ (21–30yrs), $N=7$ (31–40yrs), $N=5$ (41–50yrs), $N=6$ (51–60yrs),
- $N=18$ based in the UK, $N=2$ based in the USA,

- $N=15$ diagnosed by an educational psychologist, $N=5$ diagnosed by a specialist teacher,
- $N=1$ diagnosed in pre-school, $N=3$ diagnosed in primary school, $N=5$ diagnosed at secondary school, $N=4$ diagnosed at university, $N=7$ diagnosed at work,
- $N=15$ no signs of mental health issues, $N=5$ had mental health issues.

From the sample selected, the following abridged evidence was given of their success:

- multi-entrepreneur, started at 13 years old,
- owns a successful information technology (IT) website design company,
- owns an IT project consulting company,
- owns a consultancy for police forces,
- owns a foreign exchange trading company, multi-entrepreneur,
- a social entrepreneur, owns a building company, who gained the Member of the Order of the British Empire (MBE) award from the Queen,
- social entrepreneur, television (TV) apprentice participant,
- award winning TV and film producer,
- winner of an apprentice TV show, inventor,
- retired Lieutenant Colonel of the US Marines,
- one of the youngest Head teachers in the UK.

The sample evidence also found seven had gained a first degree, and eight had gained a master's degree in addition to a first degree. The previous evidence of their success and their academic success was deemed sufficient to describe the sample as successful adults with dyslexia, according to the criteria indicated earlier.

Results—Interview Study

School: General

- *When I went into 1st grade the wheels came off and I had a rotten teacher. When she is dead I will dance on her grave, not just once. She was horrible (TBA)!*

- *The more you hear how stupid you were, and lazy you are, the more it becomes your reality. Lazy & dumb. So I went on, trundled through school, it was horrible. A never ending stream of misery (PSS).*
- *I was sent to a school for dyslexics, but it just turned out to be a school for un-academic children (JBB).*
- *We talk about PTSD about soldiers coming back from combat. I have been in combat, but my issues are still with my time at school. I have bad dreams (nightmares) about being in college and thinking about how I will cope. My dreams as a soldier are positive but my dreams of school are never happy, they are dark (TBA).*
- *Being told by a teacher 'There's not a lot going in there is there? (referring to his brain)' (PAT).*
- *Copying from the board: it was horrendous, I hated it. It was a waste of time for me because I could never take things down fast enough. An absolute waste of time (PUY).*
- *I have memory of being taken to the front of the class and asked to demonstrate how useless I was at using scissors (NHN).*
- *Many teachers were abusive and unpleasant, and wanted to tear me down. I used to plot their destruction and petty ways of hurting them (GHD).*
- *Extremely traumatic, I would go as far as to say abusive, getting consistent reinforcement that you are failing time after time without the teachers asking why and helping you (ESA).*

In summary, eight enjoyed school, 12 found school traumatic and the majority (17) felt they were unsupported at school, while only three felt supported. The evidence supports the concept that many in this sample experienced traumatic school experiences and felt misunderstood by teachers on a daily or hourly basis. Several noted how they plotted their teacher's deaths as a result of the trauma they had caused them. What is also evident is the lack of understanding by teachers and the humiliation that many experienced, with only eight enjoying school and 17 feeling unsupported by teachers.

School: Avoidance of Tasks

- *I tried to do as little as possible, sit at the back of the class or keep one's head down and just hope that, you know, they didn't spot you and say 'will you read the next two paragraphs?' Oh God, I hated that. So yes, I was consciously trying to avoid reading aloud (JBB).*

- *You just made sure you didn't catch the teacher's eye (TPE).*
- *I would shy away from writing (PSS).*
- *I think it suited me to be the cheeky one at the back of the class making everyone laugh (PAT).*
- *My whole life at school was about not being discovered, keeping my head down and out of trouble, and that fear has stayed with me for 35 years (JEA).*
- *The worst nightmare was reading around the class, so that was a question of distraction to stop it getting to me, not misbehaving, but asking the teacher to explain something, and then something else (JEA).*

Evidence suggests that the participants in this sample were creative in their means to survive the continual trauma of mainstream education, in that they used avoidance of reading, writing and spelling to maintain their self-esteem. Seeking to avoid discovery is noted in several of the quotes, and using camouflaging to avoid detection; fear is noted by many.

Motivation

- *It's not (about) money, its actually proving a point now. That I can be as successful as all my contemporaries in the city, but one step better, better because it's my business and I am running it and I'm CEO, and that's my satisfaction every day. To prove to people that this is what I am doing and I am capable of doing it (JBB).*
- *It definitely comes from when I was young. Being frustrated at school and feeling a sense of purpose and ability that came from working outside school and earning money, which was more satisfying than sitting down and doing homework (JBB).*
- *I love the fact that I can control my own world, and that means more to me than anything else (JBB).*
- *I seek recognition of my skills and abilities, and this goes right back to childhood and school. I will work extremely hard to achieve things, but it's recognition I seek most of all. I have a chip on my shoulder about not achieving at school (NHN).*
- *I seek self-worth, I always had a sense of wanting to be known to be good at something (PSS).*

- *It's not about money, its gaining self-respect. It just makes me think one of my teachers didn't waste her time on me. It always links back to my school days, being under-rated (AP).*
- *It's not about money, it's about helping children who are stuck in the school system not being supported properly. I want to make a difference (AHD).*

This section also relates to a later section on 'entrepreneurship', which discusses what motivates individuals to be successful and to do well in business. Evidence suggests that they are motivated to prove themselves, not just to themselves that they are as good as the next person but also to those who doubted their abilities when they were children at school. Many are motivated to change the world for the better and to provide the support and the services they would have wanted as children. This sense of a chip on their shoulders is a strong motivating force that should not be discounted in understanding the make-up of successful adults with dyslexia.

Personality

How would someone describe you?

- *Participating leader, nurturing, tolerant, trustworthy, loyal, hardworking (PAT).*
- *Down to earth, humble (PUY).*
- *Creative, determined, happy, positive, different, quirky (TPE).*
- *Very unpredictable, totally non-linear, won't follow rules, quite short-tempered, emotional, determined, intelligent, charismatic, tenacious, generous (GHD).*
- *Global thinker, perfectionist, poor attention to detail, good listener, a broad-brush man (ASG).*
- *Confident, outgoing, a stickler for detail. I'm pretty headstrong, what you see is what you get (PSS).*

Several themes were evident: determination, enabler of people, hard-working, people-skills, global thinking but challenging to work with due to non-linear thinking and the inability to play by traditional rules.

Traits: Dealing With Risk

- *I will take risks, damn right, I will take risks that people would consider somewhere close to effing horrendous. I don't focus on consequences. You evaluate risk, so I have a high tolerance for risk (ASG).*
- *One of the biggest risks is not trying at all. Actually if you don't try, you'll never know if it was a good idea (TPE).*
- *Risk is good, however risk without thought is dangerous (PAT).*
- *I think risk is something I don't like, but I think it's unavoidable for dyslexics. Your whole life is waiting to be 'found out' at any moment. You're so familiar with what it feels like, either to anticipate it or to be in that horrible moment when the wheels just come off in life. Your fear, it drives you (JLA).*
- *I don't avoid it, I would say I have calculated risk. I take more risks than most (PSS).*
- *I'm a risk-taker without a shadow of doubt, I think 'what have I got to lose' (JBB).*

Traits: Coping With Failure

- *I always say, in order to succeed in life, you must fail first because you will never understand the taste of success unless you fail. For me, failure is an experience. In order to celebrate success, you must go through the depths of failure (PUY).*
- *Those who have never failed at school find failure as an adult really hard, as they never had the opportunity to fail as children. I think failure is bad, but at least I've done it a lot so at least I know it's not life threatening (TPE).*
- *Failure is important. I think I have more grit for long-term projects and perseverance, because I don't expect to be the best at something when I begin, or expect to get it right the first time. I have spent many many years being forced to do things I'm not good at [at school] that I'm adamant about not being in that position again (ESA).*
- *Peter Stringfellow said one of the best things that happened to him was leaving school without any qualifications, because there were no expectations of him. He could try whatever he wanted and failure wasn't a big deal because he wasn't expected to achieve anything (SDE).*

- *I think I was simply driven to bounce back from failure. I got used to failing, and I got used to picking myself up again as best I could, because I hated it. That's what drove me as a child and a young adult (JLA).*

In summary, 16 felt that failure was an essential part of success, two did not and two were undecided.

The ability for many of this sample of individuals with dyslexia to deal with risk and cope with failure is evident. Most indicate the willingness to take on risk, and some relate this to their childhood and schooling in that they learnt to effectively cope (emotionally) with risk and failure. Some have the lifelong fear of being found out as experiencing dyslexia in school and in the workplace and expecting to be fired as a result. Others see failure as part of a learning journey as many had failed so much at school that they had almost become immune to the negative emotional effects of failure. Interestingly, they note that they were more willing to risk to gain success compared to their peers without dyslexia, who were risk-adverse and were less successful in life and where failure was avoided at all costs. The majority, however, note that failure was an essential aspect of their later success in life.

Traits: Hard-working/Passionate

- *One of my biggest strategies is to work until it's done. It's not uncommon for me to work until 2–3 in the morning. Occasionally I work all night (JLA).*
- *I am pretty persistent (TPE).*
- *My whole life is setting a goal and doing it. Why else get out of bed in the morning (TBA).*
- *I've got a relentless drive to work past stubborn people who say 'no' to me, and wear them down or go around them. If they say 'no' because it's never been done that way before, 'we have always done it this way,' or 'no because I out-rank you,' then that's not good enough for me (NHN).*
- *I get very frustrated when people give excuses as to why they haven't done things (JBB).*

All noted their willingness to work extremely hard to achieve success in life. Their persistence to not give up and to work until the job is done is a testament to why they have achieved in life. The term 'passion' sums up an all-consuming need to understand and solve problems that go beyond the normal 'call of duty' of most people/employers. Their willingness to work extremely long days demonstrates their determination in life.

Traits: Are People With Dyslexia Over-Achievers?

- *Yes, and I can't just do one thing, I'll always have new ideas. When dyslexics achieve a degree, they often feel even more driven to do more. I want to show everyone they were wrong about me and how bright I am, as we can cope with more than one thing at a time (PUY).*
- *I would say I'm an over-achiever but sometimes also a perfectionist. My friends tell me I'm doing too much, everyone tells me I don't get enough sleep because I work too hard (SDE).*
- *I find it very hard to multi-task and a few years ago I burnt myself out taking too many things on (PAT).*

In summary, ten thought that adults with dyslexia were over-achievers and five did not, the rest were undecided. This question found that whilst many of the successful adults with dyslexia in this sample could be described as over-achieving, very few of them recognise it in themselves. However, the survey data only found that 50% felt that adults with dyslexia tend to be over-achievers in life.

Post-Traumatic Growth (PTG): Trauma as a Life Motivation

- *People say I'm unpredictable, but I say this is learned behaviour from school. I would just fight back if I was bullied or teachers unfairly picked on me. If people question me in a certain way, I emotionally just start seeing that chain of events starting again. It's just a feeling of being picked on again (GHD).*
- *Some dyslexics I've met have gone to the n'th degree to prove that they are not stupid (SDE).*
- *Looking back to my trauma at school, I always say I have to thank them because I would never have done as well as I have without that experience (PUY).*
- *Every time I failed at school I was able to say that Richard Branson also failed at school and has built a hugely successful company. That's really what got me through the worst of it and where I am today (ESA).*

- *It's a bit of a nag at the back of my head, being told at school I can't do it and now I say 'Look at me now' (PSS).*
- *Yes I have a chip on my shoulders about not doing well at school. I'm described as a workaholic, but is it because of school (ASG).*

Evidence points to school-failure being a motivating element in this sample's success, that there was a need to show self-worth and to not only prove others wrong but to shove it in their faces that they harshly miss-judged them. It is recognised that trauma at school was never good; it could be argued it was a main motivating force for them. However, was school-trauma the only factor in their success?

Post-Traumatic Growth (PTG): What Could I Have Been Without School-Trauma?

- *If I would have been happier at school I would have ended up being a completely different person, content with life and being in a normal job, and focussing on normal relationships (GHD).*
- *What would I have been if I would have been supported and un-traumatised by school, just a housewife with seven children, just like my mother? So not a successful author and playwright (PMS).*

Questioned about the possibilities if they hadn't experienced school trauma, two noted that they would possibly not have been as successful but likely to have been more contented with life. So was their school trauma the key factor in their success?

Workplace: Why Am I Successful? (Online Survey Data)

- *Hard work, perseverance, creativity, computers (OFC).*
- *Entrepreneurial, enthusiastic and creative thinker (OTB).*
- *I started a business aged 13; I've been in over 100 magazine and newspapers in three years, good pals with lots of celebrities (OMB).*
- *I have persevered, despite times of utter exhaustion, to do my job well. I have displayed grit (OAC).*
- *More by accident than deliberately I have been able to create a life/work style that happily accommodates my dyslexic weaknesses and delight in my dyslexic strengths, and extremely hard work (OGD).*

- *Coped with dyslexia, proved people wrong who said I couldn't do things (OPN).*
- *I have achieved a degree and 2 master's degrees (my last one gaining a distinction for my dissertation). I also was appointed as one of the youngest head teachers in the country 3 years ago. I was a finalist in the UK's young composer of the year competition (OKN).*

In summary, 19 call themselves successful and 20 are called successful by others. 13 were self-employed, five were senior managers, four were professionals. 13 worked for themselves and seven worked for others.

The previous survey data quotes describe why they described themselves as being successful, and it is easy to agree with them that they have achieved success by most standards. Some point to fame, others to proving self-worth, still others, lastly, to create paid employment that works to their strengths. Success is subjective, but 19 call themselves successful with the majority (13) recognising that being self-employed was the means for their success, as Frank Sinatra sang: 'Doing it my way.'

Discussion and Conclusions

The study used an online survey to firstly recruit interview subjects for an in-depth study and gain a wider sense of success amongst adults with dyslexia. 56 volunteered to be interviewed, and a pilot study of 20 participants is detailed in this chapter.

The results tell a message of trauma and hardship at school, with most reporting humiliation and the lack of understanding by school educators. However, a minority experienced support from individual teachers, many turning into lifelong mentors. School was found by both studies to be a harsh place for young people with dyslexia to exist in, with many feeling unsupported.

The interview evidence supported the hypothesis that most (but not all) successful adults with dyslexia experience a troubled schooling, creating the motivation to prove themselves. School can be a harsh environment for a person with dyslexia who has difficulty reading, writing and spelling, amongst many other difficulties.

Evidence suggests high avoidance strategies to camouflage such difficulties (e.g. hiding in class, forgetting books/homework); the other option is to either submit to the humiliation of not being able to read effectively as their peers or to use distraction (e.g. being the class clown) or truancy (e.g. calling in sick to avoid tests). This taught many adults with dyslexia to be creative and divergent to maintain their self-esteem; however, the evidence still suggested school-trauma was experienced. Both Fitzgibbon and O'Connor (2002) and Albertson (2001) note the camouflaging of difficulties by young people with dyslexia in school, and Belzberg (2013), Foss (n.d.), Bort (2014) and Tickle (2015) echo the humiliation, by teachers, that they experienced at school.

Many point to school as being their motivation to do so well in life (e.g. *'to return to school in a Rolls Royce to show them they were wrong about me'*). This indicates the need to demonstrate self-worth to those whose opinion mattered to them: their peers and their parents. Maybe they felt a need to also show their parents that they were in fact able to hold down a job and be a success. However, evidence also indicates that many were over-achievers, working long hours on a multitude of projects and businesses to keep on achieving beyond the level of their peers, thus keeping on fighting even when they have proven their self-worth to others. The need to go beyond such levels is likely to come from proving to themselves their own potential and self-worth.

Abilities to create a vision and pull people along and the problems in delegating effectively due to communications problems were evident; however, despite this, some were very effective in building large organisations. Those who were good at delegating, appreciating their own lack of abilities and the better skills of others, were the ones with greater growth, as also found by Clarkson (2015) and Logan (2009, 2010).

Interview evidence suggests that successful adults with dyslexia can be highly creative (Tickle, 2015; West, 2009) and are able to come up with many solutions to everyday problems, but also have difficulty turning off such problem-solving (e.g. in the evening after work and at bed time). One participant identified that the only way of really coping with his creative abilities was to work for himself, as companies were unwilling to pay him to express his creativity and develop various products. The majority of the sample were self-employed, as only they believed in themselves with their need for their constant experimentation of ideas. This also led them to create a working environment that was Dyslexia-Friendly and conducive to business growth (Inskeep, 2007).

The majority of the interview study participants solved problems using gut intuition, many in three dimensions, reflecting the work by Thomas West (2009) and his book *In the Mind's Eye*, using intuition and empathy to effectively manage staff and spearhead decisions (also reported by Fink, 2002), leading to clear unique differences between them and their peers—giving them a unique edge. Results indicated advanced three dimensional modelling (visual-spatial) and the ability to think differently (also found by Logan, 2010). Many noted the ability to solve problems faster by going from A to Z in seconds rather than having to go through each step separately (as also noted by Bort, 2014). Whether this is through creative or divergent logic is another question.

This study indicated that successful adults with dyslexia were far more willing to take risks, some large ones, as failure was not feared, as they experienced so much of this growing up and had developed resilience as a result. Logan (2010) and others have also highlighted this factor. This also relates to the persistence that Kopf (2013), Alexander-Passe (2015) and Fink (2002) noted in their studies, to not give up and to have the determination to drive concepts into fruition.

The links to school were still evident as successful adults, leading to questions about PTG. Was suffering in mainstream school a positive element in their success as adults? The results do seem to suggest that school suffering was a main element; however, other factors such as supportive parents and experiencing success surpassing their peers were also important.

References

Albertson, C. (2001). Backwards and wearing heels: Conversations about dyslexia, ceramics and success. *Marilyn Zurmuehlen Working Papers in Art Education, 2001*(1), Article 2. Retrieved from https://ir.uiowa.edu/

Alexander-Passe, N. (2008). The sources and manifestations of stress amongst school-aged dyslexics, compared with sibling controls. *Dyslexia, 14*(4), 291–313. https://doi.org/10.1002/dys.351

Alexander-Passe, N. (2010). *Dyslexia and depression: The hidden sorrow*. New York, NY: Nova Science Publishers.

Alexander-Passe, N. (2015). *Dyslexia and mental health: Helping people to overcome depressive, self-harming and other adverse emotional coping strategies*. London, England: Jessica Kingsley Publishers.

American Psychiatric Association. (2015). *Post-traumatic stress disorder* (Fact sheet APA_DSM-5-PTSD.pdf). Washington, DC: Author. Retrieved from www.psychiatry.org/

Armstrong, T. (2010). *Neurodiversity: Discovering the extraordinary gifts of autism, ADHD, dyslexia, and other brain differences*. Philadelphia, PA: Da Capo Press.

Belzberg, L. (2013, April 22). Can dyslexics succeed at school or only in life? *Huffington Post*. Retrieved from www.huffpost.com/

Bort, J. (2014, July 24). Cisco CEO John Chambers: My dyslexia is a weakness AND a strength. *Business Insider.* Retrieved from www.businessinsider.com/

Calhoun, L. G., & Tedeschi, R. G. (2001). Posttraumatic growth: The positive lessons of loss. In R. A. Neimeyer (Ed.), *Meaning reconstruction and the experience of loss* (pp. 157–172). Washington, DC: American Psychological Association. https://doi.org/10.1037/10397-008

Calhoun, L. G., & Tedeschi, R. G. (2006). *The Foundations of posttraumatic stress: An expanded framework.* Mahwah, NJ: Lawrence Erlbaum Associates Inc.

Clarkson, N. (2015, February 15). As an entrepreneur, one of the key things you have to learn to do is delegate. If you struggle with this, check out Richard Branson's advice. *Virgin.* Retrieved from www.virgin.com/

Dyslexia Action. (2013). *Dyslexia and literacy difficulties: Policy and practice review.* Evesham, UK: The Dyslexia-SpLD Trust. Retrieved from www. thedyslexia-spldtrust.org.uk/

Edwards, J. (1994). *The scars of dyslexia: Eight case studies in emotional reactions.* London, England: Cassell.

Fink, R. P. (2002). Successful careers: The secrets of adults with dyslexia. *Career Planning and Adult Development Journal, 18*(1), 118–135. Retrieved from dyslexiahelp.umich.edu

Fitzgibbon, G., & O'Connor, B. (2002). *Adult dyslexia—A guide for the workplace.* Chichester, UK: Wiley.

Foss, B. (n.d.). *The road to success.* Westport, CT: Smart Kids with Learning Disabilities Inc. Retrieved from www.smartkidswithld.org/

Hulme, C., & Snowling, M. J. (2009). *Developmental disorders of language and cognition.* Oxford, UK: Blackwell/Wiley.

Humphrey, N. (2003). Facilitating a positive sense of self in pupils with dyslexia: The role of teachers and peers. *Support for Learning, 18*(3), 130–136. https:// doi.org/10.1111/1467-9604.00295

Humphrey, N., & Mullins, P. (2002). Personal constructs and attribution for academic success and failure in dyslexics. *British Journal of Special Education, 29*(4), 196–203. https://doi.org/10.1111/1467-8527.00269

Inskeep, S. (Host speaker). (2007, December 26). *Does dyslexia translate to business success?* (Radio broadcast with transcript). Washington, DC: National Public Radio (NPR). Retrieved from www.npr.org/

Joseph, S., & Linley, P. A. (2008). Psychological assessment of growth following adversity: A review. In S. Joseph & P. A. Linley (Eds.), *Trauma, recovery, and growth: Positive psychological perspectives on posttraumatic stress* (pp. 22–36). Hoboken, NJ: John Wiley & Sons.

Kopf, B. (2013, November 13). From dyslexia to CEO: How my learning disabilities taught me to be a successful entrepreneur. *Entrepreneur, The Next Web (TNW).* Retrieved from http://thenextweb.com/

Lackaye, T., & Margalit, M. (2006). Comparisons of achievement, effort, and self-perceptions among students with learning disabilities and their peers from different achievement groups. *Journal of Learning Disabilities, 39,* 432–446. https://doi.org/10.1177/00222194060390050501

Linley, P. A., & Joseph, S. (2004). Positive change following trauma and adversity: A review. *Journal of Traumatic Stress, 17*(1), 11–21. https://doi. org/10.1023/B:JOTS.0000014671.27856.7e

Logan, J. (2009). Dyslexic entrepreneurs: The incidence; Their coping strategies and their business skills. *Dyslexia, 15*, 328–346. https://doi.org/10.1002/dys.388

Logan, J. (2010). *Unusual talent: A study of successful leadership and delegation in dyslexic entrepreneurs.* London, England: Cass Business School, City University of London. Retrieved from www.cass.city.ac.uk/

McLoughlin, D., Leather, C., & Stringer, P. (2002). *The adult dyslexia: Interventions and outcomes.* London, England: Whurr.

Morgan, E., & Klein, C. (2003). *The dyslexic adult in a non-dyslexic world.* London, England: Whurr.

Morgan, P. L., Fuchs, D., Compton, D. L., Cordray, D. S., & Fuchs, L. S. (2008). Does early reading failure decrease children's reading motivation? *Journal of Learning Disabilities, 41*(5), 387–404. https://doi.org/10.1177/0022219408321112

Schoulte, J., Sussman, Z., Tallman, B., Deb, M., Cornick, C., & Altmaier, E. M. (2012). Is there growth in grief: Measuring posttraumatic growth in the grief response. *Open Journal of Medical Psychology, 1*(3), 38–43. https://doi.org/10.4236/ojmp.2012.13007

Scott, R. (2004). *Dyslexia and counselling.* London, England: Whurr.

Seligman, M. E. P. (2011). *Flourish.* New York, NY: Free Press.

Smith, J. A. (2004). Reflecting on the development of interpretative phenomenological analysis and its contribution to qualitative research in psychology. *Qualitative Research in Psychology, 1*(1), 39–54. https://doi.org/10.1191/1478088704qp004oa

Tedeschi, R. G., & Calhoun, L. G. (2004). Posttraumatic growth: Conceptual foundations and empirical evidence. *Psychological Inquiry, 15*(1), 1–18. https://doi.org/10.1207/s15327965pli1501_01

Tickle, L. (2015, January 15). Dyslexic entrepreneurs—Why they have a competitive edge. *The Guardian.* Retrieved from www.theguardian.com/

Wadlington, E., Elliot, C., & Kirylo, J. (2008). The dyslexia simulation: Impact and implications. *Literacy Research and Instruction, 47*(4), 264–272. https://doi.org/10.1080/19388070802300363

Weiss, T., & Berger, R. (Eds.). (2010). *Posttraumatic growth and culturally competent practice: Lessons learned from around the globe.* Hoboken, NJ: Wiley.

West, T. (2009). *In the mind's eye: Visual thinkers—Gifted people with dyslexia and other learning difficulties* (2nd Rev. ed.). Amhurst, NY: Prometheus Books.

13 Dyslexia and Entrepreneurship Education: What do Students who Study in Higher Education (HE) Say?

Margaret Meehan, Paul Adkins,
Barbara Pavey and Angela Fawcett

Introduction

Entrepreneurship is essential to the health of the UK economy, and supporting young entrepreneurs into business is an important strategy for sustaining the necessary momentum for growth and for wealth creation (McFarlane, 2016). As prospects for employment are a key factor in student university choice and university ranking, embedding entrepreneurship into the curriculum across all disciplines has become imperative, resulting in an expansion of entrepreneurship education in Higher Education (HE). As Guillies noted in her 2015 Kaufman Foundation State of Entrepreneurship address (Guillies, 2015), the fastest growing programmes on campuses are entrepreneurial in nature across various disciplines. However, entrepreneurial education needs to move from a mainly behaviourist pedagogical method of passive transfer of knowledge (lectures, coursework, etc.) to a more experimental, experiential and participatory constructivist pedagogy (Nabi, Linán, Faycolle, Krueger, & Walmsey, 2017, citing Neergaard, Tanggaard, Krueger, & Robinson, 2012) in order for students to move beyond entrepreneurial intention to business start-up, (Nabi et al., 2017). Zulfiqar, Sarwar, Aziz,

Chadia, and Khan (2019) note that educators need to reform curricula so that students are given practical training to develop business skills and abilities to move on to business start-up. Business simulation games could be seen as a practical as well as creative and innovative way to enhance student learning (Mawhirter & Garofalo, 2016), bridging theory and practice (Hughes & Scholtz, 2015) and allowing an interactive and experiential way of exploring possible business scenarios in a risk-free environment, encouraging 'out of the box' thinking (Zulfiqar et al., 2019).

In encouraging entrepreneurial activity, universities become anchor institutions that are rooted in their local community, supporting local small business enterprise (Smallbone & Kitchling, 2019). This has had a key impact in Wales, where one of the universities in this study is situated. The Welsh government has encouraged and supported entrepreneurship through the promotion of various projects. The Youth Entrepreneurship Strategy Action Plan 2010–2015 (Welsh Assembly Government, 2010) was introduced to promote entrepreneurship to young people by empowering them, for example, by providing experiential learning workshops in schools and giving young graduates paid project placements through the Go Wales initiative. Local business enterprise is being encouraged in the 'Arfor at Work' project promoting entrepreneurship in Welsh-speaking areas (Welsh Government, 2019a). Female entrepreneurs are being promoted in a programme, Supporting Entrepreneurial Women in Wales and the Good Practice Guide (Welsh Government, 2019b). It has been suggested previously that there was a link between Welsh language-speakers and entrepreneurial activity but such a relationship has not been supported (Jones-Evans, Thompson, & Kwong, 2010). Nevertheless, there has been an acknowledged interest in Welsh entrepreneurship.

Entrepreneurship is a slippery concept, according to McFarlane (2016). Its definition depends on the objectives of the group using the term (Hornsby, Messersmith, Rutherford, & Simmons, 2018) and the culture and context of its application (Khajeheian, 2017; Giones & Brem, 2017). One definition describes an initial stabilising phase after start-up, followed by expansion of the business. This parameter Halfpenny and Halfpenny (2012) suggest is used by Logan (2009) citing Bolton and Thompson (2000) in her study of dyslexia and entrepreneurship. These studies, amongst others, claim a higher incidence of entrepreneurs with dyslexia than the general population.

It may be that individuals who experience dyslexia develop strategies to overcome educational obstacles which build up transferable skills (Fitzgibbon & O'Connor, 2002) as well as emotional resilience, which could be advantageous in a business start-up. Miller (2014) also suggests that a tough upbringing, where hardships are overcome, promotes a more ruthless and possibly successful approach to entrepreneurship.

Dyslexia, similarly to entrepreneurship, has different definitions and these are reflected in its diagnosis (Ryder & Norwich, 2017). However it is defined, dyslexia is recognised in UK legislation as a Specific Learning Difficulty (SpLD) initially in the Disability Discrimination Act (1995), and extended to HE in the Special Education Needs Disability Act (2001), and the Equality Act (2010), with further updates in England with the Special Educational Needs and Disability Code of Practice: 0 to 25 Years (Department for Education and Department for Health, 2015). Students in HE are supported by the Disabled Students Allowance (DSA). Additional reasonable adjustments that are recommended for each student who has disclosed their dyslexia are identified by an educational psychologist or a qualified teacher and an Assessor of Needs, and these are expected to be anticipatory.

The current importance of inclusion in UK HE is propelled by the cost of government funding for the DSA. This cost is increasing each year and thus government funding bodies are handing over the responsibility of supporting students to the universities to fund through existing inclusion funding within their budgets. Indeed the dissolution of the DSA Quality Assurance Group (QAG) as a consequence of changes to the delivery of the DSA shows how important inclusion will become in England. Currently HE Statistics Agency (HESA, 2019) figures for 2017–2018 are that 15% of university students in the UK have a disability, SpLDs account for the highest proportion at 39%, and mental health difficulties at 24%. Although there is a wish that inclusion will eliminate any need for extra support, observation of inclusion policies is sometimes overlooked inadvertently. Extra support will be needed by some disabled students, most particularly for students with multiple and complex disabilities. There comes a point for individuals where the university budget for inclusive measures is insufficient. In addition, Kendall (2018) [N=20] stated that training for lecturers is not keeping pace with the numbers and diversity of students accessing third level courses. For inclusion to be successful, mandatory training for academic and professional staff is necessary. The implementation of the principle of inclusion impacts the educational experience of individuals who experience dyslexia, and they may influence student experience and retention. This may in turn impact on the potential for entrepreneurial activity in students with dyslexia.

Following a small pilot study undertaken by Pavey and Adkins (2010), a larger pilot study was undertaken with HE students who experience dyslexia studying business either as their main degree discipline or alongside another discipline. Their views were sought regarding the development of entrepreneurship skills amongst young people who experience dyslexia and the ways in which educational opportunities at university level may be improved for them.

This chapter focuses on analysing and discussing the answers to two from amongst a range of questions put to the HE students who participated in the study. Respondents were asked: What could universities do to support entrepreneurs who experience dyslexia? They were also asked whether they had played business simulation games and whether they found them helpful in their studies, particularly as they have a more practical nature. These were sub-questions of the overarching research question regarding the development of entrepreneurship skills and the ways in which educational opportunities may be improved for them.

Methodology

Semi-structured interviews were undertaken with two small groups of students, undergraduates or postgraduates, who experienced dyslexia. All students in the sample were studying business (either a business degree or business modules as part of their degree) in each of two HE Institutions. Eight interviews were carried out in an English university (rural) and nine interviews were carried out in a Welsh university (city).

Students were recruited for the study by responding to an invitation via email, with an information sheet detailing the study attached, sent to all students who had disclosed dyslexia to the university and thus were self-selected. The recorded interviews were transcribed, validated by two colleagues and analysed thematically using a modified phenomenological approach (Hycner, 1985). This approach is based on emphasising the role of personal knowledge and experience. The authors have complied with the expectations of the British Educational Research Association (BERA; 2004) ethical guidelines, with the Market Research Society Code of Conduct and with the ethical codes of their respective universities.

Any responses that enable the identification of a specific course or individual student have been considered to be unusable data.

In order to maintain anonymity but to still be able to discriminate between individuals for the purposes of the analysis, respondents will be referred to by number. Numbers 1–8 refer to students from an English rural university and numbers 9–17 refer to students from a Welsh city university.

Participants

The sample was made up of a total of ten male and seven female students: Four male plus four female students from an English university and six male plus three female students from a Welsh university. 12 students were undergraduates and five postgraduates: Seven undergraduates (two at level one, two at level two, one at level three final year and two at level four final year) and one postgraduate (at level three final year) were from the English university whereas five undergraduates (three at level one, one at level two, and one at level three final year) and four postgraduates (one at level one, and one on a one year course; one at level three of four; and one PhD on writing extension) were from the Welsh university.

The students' ages ranged between 18 and 33 years old with the majority under 30 years old. All the students were British except two international students and, thus, 15 of the 17 had experienced the British education system (see later). 11 students were studying business courses and six were studying business modules as a minor part of their degree alongside their main discipline.

It is important to note that in this study all students had a formal diagnosis of dyslexia: Four students were first assessed at primary school, three at secondary school, four during A Level study, and six at university. This contrasts with Logan's (2009) study where participants were self-identified using a screening checklist, the Adult Dyslexia Checklist (Smythe and Everatt 2001), and they had to meet a number of criteria that Logan put in place but not all of them, which left some ambiguity as to the recognition of dyslexia. Here a more precisely defined understanding of dyslexia is set as the criteria for diagnosis. All students had been awarded the DSA and they had availed themselves of learning support.

This chapter analyses the answers of two from a range of questions, namely: How could universities help entrepreneurs who experience dyslexia? and Have you played business simulation games and how did they help your studies?

Results and Discussion

There were several recurring themes which wove in and out of the responses for each of the questions asked of the participants. Not all respondents provided answers to all questions. Nonetheless, the questions were meaningful to the students and many interesting issues were brought forward and explored. Since this was the case also for the earlier Pavey and Adkins (2010) study, it might suggest a weakness in the question structure or wording. Alternately, it might say something about the styles of thinking and communicating amongst the interviewees, who all experienced dyslexia. This requires further research but does not undermine the validity of the individual comments made.

Respondents' voices were respected even though they did not fall neatly into the questions' format. In answering the questions put to them, there was no unanimous agreement amongst participants, within or across universities, on any particular point, but some views were shared whilst others were unique, that is, expressed only by one student. In particular, one shared theme was that in educating entrepreneurs who experience dyslexia, practical experience should be emphasised over theoretical input. This could be because practical tasks are a perceived strength in individuals who experience dyslexia, which may contrast with their confidence in academic writing and reading as well as other difficulties they experience at university (Callens, Tops, Stevens, & Brysbaert, 2014). In Callens et al.'s (2014) study ($N=100$), average individuals who experience dyslexia at university had persistent difficulty with reading, spelling, phonological skills, mental arithmetic, rapid naming and possibly the retrieval of information from long-term memory.

Question 1: How Could Universities Help Entrepreneurs Who Experience Dyslexia?

15 of the 17 participants answered the question on what universities could do to support entrepreneurs who experience dyslexia. 12 students made practical suggestions because, as one student stated, a lot of practical knowledge is necessary to be good in business, and:

> *I don't think anyone who sat that course or went to that business school . . . would be a successful entrepreneur. . . . you obviously need*

a lot of practical knowledge to be good in business but I think there should be a lot of emphasis on experience.

(Respondent 10)

Kuratko and Morris (2018) state that universities should prepare students for entrepreneurship by using practical and extra-curricular activities to cultivate the entrepreneurial mindset, and Hornsby et al. (2018) report a trend for experiential learning in entrepreneurial curricula. Students suggested changes in course curriculum (including the addition of a business start-up project), course format, assignments and assessments as well as wanting more extracurricular events to be applied to the management/entrepreneurial aspects of their degree courses. Many responses on entrepreneurship were based on students' personal experiences of general education, primary, secondary and tertiary levels, whether positive or negative.

Although the participants expressed various views, these could be grouped under three main themes: Business start-up, course improvements to develop practical skills needed by entrepreneurs, and employment.

Business Start-Up

Logan (2009) found that individuals who experience dyslexia tended to have multiple business start-ups, and to grow their businesses rapidly with the ability to delegate and take risks, which together with the less structured environment of a start-up allowed them to play to their strengths. As already stated, 15 students in this study were enthusiastic about starting their own business and three of these wanted to start a business as soon as possible. One respondent suggested that a new module could be designed where students would be supported in taking the risk of starting a business, which would give a more experiential type of education (Shirokova, Tsukanova, & Morris, 2017).

However, Guerrero, Urbano, Cunningham, and Gajón's (2017) study suggests that support for students such as entrepreneurial accelerators and incubators have little effect on start-up after graduation, so support for this is mixed. Nonetheless, four students thought that universities could provide money to help students start a business or incentivise them to gain experience. No particular sum was stated but universities are businesses and would probably need to be circumspect in offering such sums, especially when first year cohorts in management schools can be very large. However, some universities do provide start-up funds (Hornsby et al., 2018) and some pair up entrepreneurial student teams with mentors (Ahsan, Zheng, DeNoble, & Musteen, 2017), so there are some models available which could be replicated in some fashion across HE.

This is not to minimise the importance of gaining knowledge of the fundamentals of business start-up in order to facilitate the transition from theory to practice because knowledge is needed to initiate a new venture. This corresponds to one of the recommendations of Kuratko and Morris (2018).

Apart from providing the business opportunity, financial support and the necessary knowledge to start a business, several respondents recognised that students need confidence to start a business and may need encouragement especially to take risks. As one student stated,

> *If you don't feel confident . . . you're not going to put your neck on the line and say I'm going to start my own business and go and look for that business opportunity that is there but nobody's noticed it yet.*
>
> (Respondent 11)

This was reiterated by another student's comment,

> *If you don't try it you will never know if you can succeed.*
>
> (Respondent 2)

O'Byrne, Jagoe and Lawler (2019) noted in their study of university students who experience dyslexia that a lack of self-confidence is a barrier to success. Cameron (2016) also notes that the reflective diaries of her research participants indicated a constant self-monitoring and feelings of not belonging in academic spaces. Encouraging the development of entrepreneurs could be achieved by the university supporting them to become more employable from the start of their degree and promoting entrepreneurial groups where students can generate ideas and gain assurance and self-belief from their peers. A lack of confidence could prevent students from fulfilling their potential if experiencing dyslexia made them feel a failure, so university courses/staff should show students that they are capable of starting a business,

> *It [Dyslexia] shouldn't hinder you a huge amount to become an entrepreneur. . . . I do think you should be shown, you can do this.*
>
> (Respondent 11)

Practical Classes and Internships

Respondents focussed on the need for improving and increasing the practical aspects of a degree course in order to prepare them for running a business. Thus, they suggested that adjustments to current courses could include the incorporation of practical entrepreneurial tasks which mimic the skills required in business, for example, contacting and liaising with others. Navalenny, Logan and Carawan (2018) made a similar proposal for college students who experience dyslexia to prepare them for the world of work, and would develop their self-efficacy. Bandura (1989, cited in Navalenny et al., 2018) defined self-efficacy as the confidence that one can complete a certain task in a particular context. This attribute, according to Li, ur Rehman, and Asim's (2019) model, 'mediates the relationship of entrepreneurship education, business incubation and entrepreneurial intention' (Li, ur Rehman, & Asim, 2019, p. 1).

The practical suggestions put forward by respondents would have the potential to improve students' self-efficacy. These included building more talks by other entrepreneurs about both their successes and failures into modules (Respondent 11) because, as another respondent stated, after a graduate talk,

> *He managed to get a first degree and he ran a business whereas, getting a degree in the first place is going to be hard but the fact he could do it with something else on the side, proves it's not impossible.*
>
> (Respondent 12)

Also,

> *Examples help, it shows potential. . . .*
>
> (Respondent 8)

Business competitions as part of a degree course between student groups could be promoted or a day where students have to come up with a business idea and find ways to implement it could be planned so that students could hone their business skills because, as one respondent stated,

> *Understanding how a functioning company works that's half the battle for starting your own.*
>
> (Respondent 16)

As a stepping-stone towards a business start-up, students could run a business within the university, for example, the student bar or the planning and organising of a money-spinning task. A good example would be offering to clean cars for people, as a student recounted they had done in the first year of university.

All these practical tasks would build up the students' self-efficacy. Kuratko and Morris (2018) report that such practical tasks implemented across disciplines would benefit students and staff even when the administration and delivery of the entrepreneurship programme lies within the subject specific department. In this way, the academic status of the individual disciplines would be maintained.

The authors suggest that this is important where entrepreneurship is embedded across curricula. Different course formats could be considered, for example, a one year apprenticeship or a sandwich course. One student suggested that universities should be more proactive in supporting students to obtain internships. This supports Navalenny et al.'s (2018) suggestion that adults who experience dyslexia would benefit from work internships.

Employment

Family background can be a driving force in the development of entrepreneurship. Four students worked in the family business at some time and 10 students had at least one parent who owned their own business. In addition, one student, whose parents were not in business, had other family members in business and another said their mother was entrepreneurial but due to legislation was not able to follow her desire to start a catering business, at least at the moment. This was a trend that Logan (2009) reported and it is echoed here: Individuals who experience dyslexia were more likely than the control group to be influenced by a role model within a family business.

15 of the 17 participants wanted to start a business and one expected to be self-employed. Another respondent intended to join the armed forces and, if they were accepted, would apply any business acumen they had gained at university to the military environment. Although 15 students were keen to start up a business, 12 expected to go into employment for one to three years for various reasons, for example, to gain capital or to research the market after graduation and prior to pursuing a business

start-up; and so comments on employment were pertinent to students' future plans.

Indeed, one student who was keen to start a business, stated that it was necessary to consider employment after graduation as a back-up plan in case a business start-up does not take off. University employability rankings are important to enhance the degree status for the student and their prospective employment once graduated. Most universities run employability fairs where students can meet different companies who are looking to employ graduates.

Final year students might be able to share their final year project/ dissertation experience and be offered internships or recommended to send the company their curriculum vitae. One respondent thought universities needed to better promote employability fairs where students can pitch to the various companies who come to the university because not many students seem to be aware of how advantageous they can be, what they might learn and the contacts they might make.

Question 2: Have You Played Business Simulation Games and How Did They Help Your Learning?

All but one of the students provided a response related to business simulation games. Although some students shared very similar views, there were no clear themes shared by all participants concerning business simulation games. This made it somewhat difficult in terms of thematic analysis of this question, and suggested that this question requires further investigation. Some respondents thought that business simulation games would help students to think practically about running a business, for example, by,

> helping people understand some economic concepts such as supply and demand.
>
> (Respondent 1)

This is corroborated by Zulfiqar et al. (2019). Other students thought that games provided limited help or they were no use at all because they gave no sense of risk or a *'sense of loss if all your money goes'* (Respondent 10) which is present in real situations.

16 of the17 students gave answers about business simulation games. 11 participants said they knew of business simulation games or had tried

them (two as part of a university module). Seven participants had either never heard of them or had not tried them. One student who knew of business games asked some pertinent questions: What do they assess? What do they give you? What tells you what is right or wrong? Do they measure that compared with how much effort you put in it? In other words, what is the purpose of playing business simulation games? Some of these questions are answered in the following analysis of respondents' answers.

In terms of helping entrepreneurs who experience dyslexia, five participants thought business games would be helpful, two thought not and three thought there were positives and negatives. They could help with a practical understanding of economics, for example, supply and demand, or be used in conjunction with other practical work; Zulfiqar et al. (2019) suggests that business games can transform the learning of economics and thus boost the entrepreneurial spirit. Such games enable students to see the outcomes of different experiments with a chance to make various changes, which, in the real world, would not be possible and takes the risk element out of a business. Simulation games make students think about everything in practical terms and this is borne out in Zulfiqar et al.'s (2019) study. They provide a context where a student can *'take learning from a textbook or listening to a lecturer'* (Respondent 12) and apply it to think for themselves via a game and consider dealing with such situations in business. However, the usefulness of business simulation games depends on how realistic they are.

Respondents considered that various skills needed in a business are absent from simulation games, for example, the lack of paperwork and filling in forms was a problem for one student because:

> *as a dyslexic that would be my biggest worry.*
>
> (Respondent 16)

Such games do not teach the skill of contacting people and speaking on the phone to them.

Two students had experienced business simulation games as part of their taught modules. One student had used a game as part of an entrepreneurial module; they enjoyed it but there were technical limitations and drawbacks and it ended with the group hating the game. Zulfiqar et al. (2019) report that there is a need for educators to learn new technologies and methods in teaching so that students can enjoy learning and perform well, most particularly as students' perceived value of simulation games, if positive, has a positive impact on the students' attitude toward entrepreneurial tasks. However, it is important that simulated games, as part of a group project, mimic what the real business world is like and indeed they might be more appropriate for secondary school or college-level students.

In summary, business simulation games are helpful to some respondents and not to others. Over half of the respondents (11) knew of or had tried business simulation games and half of these (5) thought them helpful. They could help with the economics of supply and demand as well as taking the risk out of experimenting with different business scenarios. However, the success of a business games would depend on how closely they mimicked real-world scenarios, and two respondents thought that they were not helpful because there was no real sense of loss if things went wrong.

Comparing the two universities, students in both universities knew of such games but in the English rural university only one student had tried them, and in the Welsh city university two students had played a game as part of a module and had difficulties with the technical sides of the games and all 17 students thought they gave no real sense of loss when money was lost.

Conclusion

This study adds to the literature on the links between entrepreneurship and dyslexia by examining the attitudes of students with a formal diagnosis of dyslexia in two universities in different settings. It is significant because embedding entrepreneurship into university curricula is spreading across the UK and is important for universities' ranking and in contributing to the UK economy.

The two questions explored and analysed in this chapter are: How could universities help entrepreneurs who experience dyslexia? and: Have you played business simulation games and did they help your studies? There was no unanimous agreement on a particular theme, but there were many shared themes both within and across universities and some interesting unique themes. Over all, respondents found university education systems to be too restrictive and advocated for more practical approaches to learning for potential entrepreneurs (12 respondents out of [N=17]). Suggestions ranged from including a module involving a business start-up with money provided by the university, and support and encouragement in taking such a risk, to outside lectures from entrepreneurs.

There were mixed responses to the question concerned with business simulation games. The main outcome was that some students thought they could be helpful to a certain extent but how helpful depended on how closely they mimicked real business scenarios.

References

Ahsan, M., Zheng, C., DeNoble, A., & Musteen, M. (2017). From student to entrepreneur: How mentorships and affect influence student venture launch. *Journal of Small Business Management, 56*(1), 76–102. https://doi.org/10.1111/jsbm.12362

Bandura, A. (1989). Human agency in social cognitive theory. *American Psychologist, 44*(9), 1175–1184. http://dx.doi.org/10.1037/0003-066X.44.9.1175

Bolton, B., & Thompson, J. (2000). *Entrepreneurs: Talent, temperament, technique.* Oxford, UK: Heinemann Butterworth.

British Educational Research Association (BERA). (2004). *Revised educational guidelines for educational research.* Southwell, UK: BERA. Retrieved from www.bera.ac.uk/

Callens, M., Tops, W., Stevens, M., & Brysbaert, M. (2014). An exploratory factor analysis of the cognitive functioning of first year bachelor students with dyslexia. *Annals of Dyslexia, 64*(1), 91–119. https://doi.org/10.1007/s11881-013-0088-6

Cameron, H. E. (2016). Beyond cognitive deficit: The everyday lived experience of dyslexic students at university. *Disability & Society, 31*(2), 223–239. https://doi.org/10.1080/09687599.2016.1152951

Department for Education and Department for Health. (2015). *Special educational needs and disability code of practice: 0 to 25 years.* London, England: Department for Education (DFE). Retrieved from www.gov.uk/

Fitzgibbon, G., & O'Connor, B. (2002). *Adult dyslexia: A guide for the workplace.* London, England: Wiley.

Giones, F., & Brem, A. (2017). Digital technology entrepreneurship: A definition and research agenda. *Technology Innovation Management Review, 7*(5), 44–51. Retrieved from https://ssrn.com/

Guerrero, M., Urbano, D., Cunningham, J. A., & Gajón, E. (2017). Determinants of graduates' start-ups creation across a multi campus entrepreneurial university: The Case of Monterrey Institute of Technology and Higher Education. *Journal of Small Business Management, 56*(1), 150–178. https://doi.org/10.1111/jsbm.12366

Guillies, W. (2015). *Kaufman foundation 2015 state of entrepreneurship address.* Kansas City, MO: Marion Kauffman. Retrieved from www.kauffman.org/

Halfpenny, J., & Halfpenny, C. (2012). *In their element: The case for investing in dyslexic entrepreneurs.* Leadhills, Scotland: Halfpenny Development Ltd. Retrieved from https://s3.amazonaws.com/

Higher Education Statistics Agency (HESA). (2019). *Higher education student data.* Cheltenham, UK: HESA. Retrieved from www.hesa.ac.uk/data-and-analysis/students

Hornsby, J. S., Messersmith, J., Rutherford, M., & Simmons, S. (2018). Entrepreneurship everywhere: Across campus, across communities, and across borders. *Journal of Small Business Management, 56*(1), 4–10. https://doi.org/10.1111/jsbm.12386

Hughes, S., & Scholtz, F. (2015). Increasing the impact of business simulation: The role of reflection. *The International Journal of Management Education, 13,* 350–361. https://doi.org/10.1016/j.ijme.2015.06.001

Jones-Evans, D., Thompson, P., & Kwong, C. (2010). Entrepreneurship amongst minority speakers: The case of Wales. *Regional Studies, 45*(2), 219–238. https://doi.org/10.1080/00343400903241493

Kendall, S. (2018). Supporting students with disabilities within a UK university: Lecturer perspectives. *Innovations in Education and Teaching International, 55*(6), 694–703. https://doi.org/10.1080/14703297.2017.1299630

Khajeheian, D. (2017). Media entrepreneurship: A consensual definition. *AD-Minister, 30,* 91–113. http://dx.doi.org/10.17230/ad-minister.30.5

Kuratko, D. F., & Morris, M. H. (2018). Examining the future trajectory of entrepreneurship. *Journal of Small Business Management, 56*(1), 11–23. https://doi.org/10.1111/jsbm.12364

Li, C., ur Rehman, H., & Asim, S. (2019). Induction of business incubation centers in educational institutions: An effective approach to foster entrepreneurship. *Journal of Entrepreneurship Education, 22*(1), 1–12. Retrieved from www.abacademies.org/

Logan, J. (2009). Dyslexic entrepreneurs: The incidence; their coping strategies and their business skills. *Dyslexia, 15,* 328–346. https://doi.org/10.1002/dys.388

Mawhirter, D. A., & Garofalo, P. F. (2016). Expect the unexpected: Simulation games as a teaching strategy. *Clinical Simulation in Nursing, 12,* 132–136. https://doi.org/10.1016/j.ecns.2015.12.009

McFarlane, J. (2016). Economic theories of entrepreneurship. In N. Arshed & M. Danson (Eds.), *Enterprise: Concepts and issues* (pp. 15–34). Oxford, UK: Goodfellow Publishers. https://doi.org/10.23912/978-1-910158-75-3-2880

Miller, D. (2014). A downside to the entrepreneurial personality. *Entrepreneurship Theory and Practice, 39*(1), 1–8. https://doi.org/10.1111/etap.12130

Nabi, G., Linán, F., Faycolle, A., Krueger, N., & Walmsey, A. (2017). The impact of entrepreneurship education in Higher Education: A systematic review and research agenda. *Academy of Management Learning and Education, 16*(2), 277–299. https://doi.org/10.5465/amle.2015.0026

Navalenny, B. A., Logan, J. M., & Carawan, L. W. (2018). The relationship between emotional experience with dyslexia and work self-efficacy among adults with dyslexia. *Dyslexia, 24,* 17–32. https://doi.org/10.1002/dys.1575

Neergaard, H., Tanggaard, L., Krueger, N., & Robinson, S. (2012). *Pedagogical interventions in entrepreneurship from behaviorist to existential learning.* Proceedings. Dublin, Ireland: Institute for Small Business and Entrepreneurship. Retrieved from http://www.isbe.org.uk/Award-Winning-Conference-Papers-2012

O'Byrne, C., Jagoe, C., & Lawler, M. (2019). Experiences of dyslexia and transition to university: A case study of five students at different stages of study. *Higher Education Research & Development, 38*(5), 1031–1045. https://doi.org/10.1080/07294360.2019.1602595

Pavey, B., & Adkins, P. (2010, August). *Dyslexia-Friendly entrepreneurship: What do dyslexic entrepreneurs say?* [Presentation at Inclusive and Supportive Education Congress (ISEC)]. Belfast, Ireland: Queen's University.

Ryder, D., & Norwich, B. (2017). What's in a name? Perspectives of dyslexia assessors working with students in the UK higher education sector. *Dyslexia, 24,* 109–127. https://doi.org/10.1002/dys.1582

Shirokova, G., Tsukanova, T., & Morris, H. M. (2017). The moderating role of national culture in the relationship between university entrepreneurship offerings and student start-up activity: An embeddedness perspective. *Journal of Small Business Management, 56*(1), 103–130. https://doi.org/10.1111/jsbm.12363

Smallbone, D., & Kitchling, J. (2019). Are anchor institutions the answer to the prayers of small business owners in the UK? In B. Dallago & E. Tortia (Eds.), *Entrepreneurship and local economic development: A comparative perspective on entrepreneurs, universities and governments* (pp. 33–52). Abingdon, UK: Routledge.

Smythe, I., & Everatt, J. (2001). *Adult dyslexia checklist.* London: British Dyslexia Association. Retrieved from https://cdn.bdadyslexia.org.uk/

Welsh Assembly Government. (2010). *Youth entrepreneurship strategy (YES) action plan 2010–15.* Cardiff, UK: Author. Retrieved from https://businesswales.gov.wales/

Welsh Government. (2019a). *Arfor.* Cardiff, UK: Author. Retrieved from www.rhaglenarfor.cymru/

Welsh Government. (2019b). *Supporting entrepreneurial women in Wales.* Cardiff, UK: Author. Retrieved from https://gov.wales/

Zulfiqar, S., Sarwar, B., Aziz, S., Chadia, K. E., & Khan, M. K. (2019). An analysis of influence of business simulation games on business school students' attitude and intention toward entrepreneurial activities. *Journal of Educational Computing Research, 57*(1), 106–130. https://doi.org/10.1177/0735633117746746

Conclusion

The Experience of Entrepreneurs With Dyslexia

Barbara Pavey, Neil Alexander-Passe and Margaret Meehan

Introduction

This book contributes to the discussion regarding the intersection of entrepreneurship, dyslexia and education. It looks at different perspectives, including the lived experience of entrepreneurs who experience dyslexia. These perspectives are contributed by entrepreneurs and academics from around the world. The structure of the book moves from understanding entrepreneurship to discussing dyslexia, then considers how these translate in school, higher education and the workplace. Personal perspectives and research add to an understanding of how individuals with dyslexia cope from school to work, and how they decide that entrepreneurship is the right approach for them to take in order to gain both emotional well-being and professional success.

The editors are grateful that the topic of entrepreneurship and dyslexia has attracted the interest of some of the most highly respected academics and researchers in their fields. At the same time, they are glad to have been able to offer an opportunity for new writers to approach this topic. Consequently, the chapters of this book can be seen to draw upon the works of a wide number of authors from different backgrounds and disciplines. Chapters include: biographical narratives, examinations of a range of contexts where entrepreneurs with dyslexia are at work, perspectives in current understandings of dyslexia, descriptions of the impact of schooling upon learners who experience dyslexia, along with the implications for entrepreneurship, and accounts of small-scale, qualitative research. All these provide a means of informing entrepreneurship study.

Chapter authors have sought to explore both the nature of entrepreneurship and the conditions that cause some individuals with dyslexia to choose an alternative to the regular working environment. First, they may choose to be self-employed, and, second, they may aim further, having a vision of growing a business beyond being a sole trader or practitioner. The reach of some entrepreneurs who experience dyslexia has extended to encompass a desire to effect change in society. In bringing something unique to the marketplace, they have sought to improve conditions generally, in addition to creating a niche for their own business development.

Some of the contributing authors experience dyslexia themselves. This has enabled them to bring their experience, as well as their knowledge and subject discipline, to a deep consideration of the topic. Other contributors describe findings about experiencing dyslexia at the same time as being an entrepreneur. From the evidence provided by empirical studies and collected across a range of sources, the chapters contribute information towards answering the key questions underlying the book's topic: Are individuals with dyslexia uniquely skilled to be entrepreneurs, and, if so, what should be educators' response?

Should We Rethink Disability?

Commencing with movements arising in the 1970s, the introduction of the social model of disability challenged traditional thought about disability. It moved debate away from the deficit-based medical model of disability, which focussed on individual lack and dependence. Instead, it offered a social justice view based on the belief that the members of a society should support one another. 50 years on, the understanding of disability in society has evolved; individual differences are recognised and acknowledged, and where these are disabling, they are supported through legislation and policy.

In considering this change, Valeras (2010) offers the concept of bi-ability in which individuals with invisible disabilities (such as dyslexia, asthma, diabetes and epilepsy) question the label given to them by society. Within the bi-ability perspective, individuals advocate for the abilities they can offer rather than allowing a focus on the difficulties or barriers they are perceived to have. They argue that they can, subject to the task, be classed sometimes as disabled and sometimes as able-bodied, depending on the circumstances they face. The pressure to disclose dyslexia can mean that opportunities are reduced due to a misconception of what someone with dyslexia can achieve.

Other terms, such as self-determination, are also being used to rethink disability, where the concept of empowerment has meant that rather than disability being seen as a lack, it embraces the concept of difference. Dyslexia is one of several differences, which, if embraced, can give rise to alternative perceptions and perspectives, which in turn can lead to innovative solutions. This outlook has congruency with the positive psychology movement, as described in this book. However, the challenge for both the workplace and education is to tap and utilize such abilities. The authors in this book champion the skills that individuals with dyslexia can offer, especially as entrepreneurs.

It should not be forgotten that giving up the term disability in favour of difference, risks minimising the specific obstacles with which individuals must contend. It is not easy for some to move from one perspective to another when their hindrances to learning are severe and long-standing; indeed, these characteristics provide the definition of disability. There may always be a difference between individuals' self-perception and externally imposed categories of description, but inclusive principles are intended to reduce the prejudices and denial of opportunity that arise from a dearth of awareness. Individuals who experience dyslexia are not a homogenous group; their nuanced learning needs may seem complicated and puzzling to educators, leading, especially in the past, to inconsistent and sometimes meagre attempts to meet literacy learning needs. In entrepreneurship, businessmen and businesswomen with dyslexia can render this difficulty inconspicuous or irrelevant. In their chosen setting and with control over their own business and communication methods, disclosure is no longer an issue, confirming the fundamental principle of bi-ability.

Is the Workplace Suited for People Who Experience Dyslexia, or Is Self-Employment and/or Entrepreneurship a More Viable Option?

The conventional workplace setting requires a narrow set of skills and abilities, which often focus on numeracy and literacy. Individuals who have struggled at school and who leave with few qualifications, when they experience undiagnosed or unsupported dyslexia, can find it difficult to progress in this context and may feel rejected or excluded from traditional workplaces. For modern students, paper qualifications are an entrenched gate-keeping mechanism that stretches from school-level assessments and achievement tests to university degrees. These mechanisms enable employers to apply them as a kind of sieve, screening out some and letting through others. Unfortunately, without such paper qualifications the choice of careers is limited.

Within economic restrictions, careers guidance services do their best to support students who experience learning difficulties and to help them to find opportunities for future employment, but most of these opportunities will involve further study or training of one kind or another, inevitably with a literacy work-load. Where careers guidance is the task of internal school staff, these professionals may not be knowledgeable about dyslexia or other learning difficulties. Although well-intentioned, they may perceive only deficits. This can result in young people being guided into careers and lines of work which are ultimately unsuitable and unsatisfying because they do not play to strengths, allow alternative modes of working, or offer opportunities for personal growth.

This is unfortunate for individuals who have less orthodox thinking and learning skills, such as individuals who are disadvantaged by dyslexia, unless they can find some way of working around the system. People with dyslexia have been shown to succeed in a very wide range of careers; in fact, any sphere may include successful individuals who experience dyslexia. However, if particular qualifications are needed, access to conventional careers may require the support made available through equality legislation.

For these reasons, the possibilities of self-employment and entrepreneurship may become more attractive. Early activities of an entrepreneurial type may prove positive feedback, and many a young entrepreneur has developed a business mindset through interactions with their schoolmates. However, entrepreneurial activity cannot be recommended in schools' careers contexts because of the risks involved. It would be thought irresponsible to suggest setting up a business where there are inherent risks, potential for failure and the requirement, often, for family financial commitment.

At present, many people with dyslexia struggle in traditional work environments, especially in the corporate world where the qualities valued within those organisations include working to tight organisational structures and filling roles that have narrow frameworks. Where they feel excluded from traditional workplaces, some individuals may turn to self-employment or entrepreneurship in order to work in a more natural, holistic way that suits them better. Some will be drawn to traditional trades, in which work is done with the hands and where the work is expected to be done to a high level of skill. Some people may take a deliberate self-employment approach; keeping their business small may allow them to remain beneath a threshold for tax or for other financial reasons. Self-employment may help solo workers to cope better with individual tasks because of the flexibility that might be applied to time pressures; their time is their own.

Furthermore, increasing their company to employ other craftspeople changes tradespeople's role to a managerial one, which is not the work that attracted them in the first place and which does not appeal to them when the business develops. This is the basis for the different conceptions of entrepreneurship, since a sole trader's company is limited in scalability and growth. Nevertheless, self-employment may still be a new business and will almost certainly require entrepreneurship of some kind. It remains to be seen whether new forms of business developed through electronic technologies will bridge this gap.

It is uncertain whether entrepreneurs who have dyslexia are driven to an entrepreneurial choice by natural ability and passion to do things their own way or are driven to do this because they are not a good fit in traditional work settings. Sir Richard Branson is said to have asserted just this, that he was unemployable, so had no choice but to set up his own business. In turn, this raises considerations about whether, since conventional educational experiences may not prove positive for learners with dyslexia, education policies need to change focus in order to equip students for future careers. This would presumably entail a move towards the kind of skills of collaboration and team-working, computer use and problem-solving recommended by entrepreneurship advisory groups. They are also the sort of skills which would allow learners with dyslexia to take a more prominent role in classroom activities without being disadvantaged by literacy difficulties.

Operating against this is the established understanding that low literacy and numeracy achievements are linked to poverty, through the lack of opportunities for disadvantaged learners. Education policy makers cannot disregard this on the grounds that some learners are able to overcome their educational disadvantage and build wealth and status through entrepreneurship. At present, the focus remains on a traditional, conventional curriculum, but it is possible to wonder whether the skills promoted and valued there are indeed the skills required for the future, as the nature of work, and workplaces, changes.

Can Higher Education (HE) Nurture Individuals With Dyslexia in Their Efforts to Become Entrepreneurs?

In Higher Education (HE) it is increasingly the case that employability, and information about the settings in which graduates find careers, contributes to statistics which feed into the university league tables. These tables are the rankings by which universities are judged. Teaching, feedback and assessment as well as student experience are important aspects which contribute to an institution's standing in university league tables. These in turn have an impact on student numbers and thus on the university's financial well-being. Consequently, embedding employability into degree qualifications has an impact on universities' standing and finances.

Research seems to indicate that although some characteristics of entrepreneurs may be innate, and these may align with certain characteristics of people who experience dyslexia, it is possible for talent to be fostered and trained so that students can become successful entrepreneurs. Individuals with dyslexia are going to find their way to entrepreneurship courses because of the knowledge, access and practical input that they provide.

However, evidence from this volume and from the wider literature suggests that without change the capacity of higher education to nurture entrepreneurship for learners who experience dyslexia is open to challenge. The drivers of inclusion and universal design include legislation and the shrinking of special funding for students with disabilities. Unless pedagogies are adjusted to take account of a wider range of learning requirements, then traditional content, skills, attitudes and methods within the subject domain may reduce and even hamper access for these learners. This threatens their ability to achieve well and consequently reduces the opportunity for their work to have good outcomes and reflect well upon the university.

People with dyslexia who have negotiated schooling with relative success, and who have managed to achieve the qualifications necessary to gain entry to a university, could be recognised as a small, select group. Nevertheless, statistics describing individuals with dyslexia at universities in the UK indicate a growing community, existing among a student group whose members may also have alternative, or co-occurring, learning differences. The challenge for HE educators, once students gain entry, is therefore to create courses that build on their strengths, and to support students in overcoming their learning barriers while reducing any barriers arising from traditional pedagogies. Students in HE generally know they have some skills to have reached this far, and it is the job of academic and professional staff to foster students' self-confidence and self-esteem in order that student entrepreneurs can progress to start-up. Specialist support professionals emphasise the importance of developing a working relationship with a student so that they can reach their full potential.

How Should We Account for a Higher Incidence of Entrepreneurs Experiencing Dyslexia?

The small-scale and qualitative studies, literature reviews, personal accounts and theory and policy explorations brought together in this book demonstrate that entrepreneurs who experience dyslexia, and people with dyslexia who are also entrepreneurial, can be found everywhere. For every single person who discloses their dyslexia there is probably another who is managing without disclosing it, and yet another who is carrying on with life and business without worrying much about their dyslexia. What is no longer in any doubt, confirmed by the accounts within this book, is that entrepreneurs with dyslexia can be found operating across a range of business settings. They identify opportunities, find new solutions, create, lead, delegate, build and turn over businesses, sell them on and then start something new. Entrepreneurship suits them.

The reasons for this good fit can be teased out from the accounts and studies described here. Authors have researched the traits and characteristics associated with entrepreneurship; people with dyslexia who have experienced these traits in action, perhaps observing them within family businesses, would be able to see the advantages in them. For a person who experiences dyslexia, these traits can be effective in contexts where interaction and information do not depend on written language resources. They represent areas where someone with dyslexia can operate more comfortably and build their skills over time. Add in the

strategies, preferences and motivating factors developed in the process
of a school experience which may not have been particularly congenial
and the conditions are created for some people with dyslexia to take
an entrepreneurial stance. Successful traits and characteristics can, with
experience, become strategies, perhaps even business survival skills,
gaining importance and viability that work well for entrepreneurs who
experience dyslexia.

Not all people with dyslexia become entrepreneurs, though many more
individuals may be entrepreneurial in their approach to life and some,
described as intrapreneurs, may take an innovative and entrepreneurial
approach to their work within an established company. With the
understanding that entrepreneurship can be taught, the issue of whether
an entrepreneurship tendency is genetically transferred retreats from the
foreground of discussion. The genetic and neurological characteristics
of dyslexia remain under investigation, with cumulative increments of
knowledge continually adding to the understanding of specific literacy
difficulties. In the meantime, governments around the world, as shown by
the chapters of this book, are seeing the advantages that individuals with
dyslexia can bring, helping to bring new approaches to problems that
conventional thinking may not resolve.

Is There Scope for Further Research?

The concurrence of entrepreneurship and dyslexia is not an easy area to
research. Logan herself concludes her study by urging caution because
of the possible complication of Attention-Deficit Hyperactivity Disorder
(ADHD) in establishing confirmed characteristics in entrepreneurs who
experience dyslexia; she calls for further research with larger numbers,
calling her own findings 'tentative' (Logan, 2009, p. 345). There are
issues about definitions of entrepreneurship, definitions of dyslexia and
the conceptualisations that are used in identifying entrepreneurs who
experience dyslexia. The indicators of dyslexia used in Logan's research
could themselves be scrutinised critically, since understandings of dyslexia
still vary. The ways in which dyslexia is identified varies enormously
in research, from the broadest question-based identifications (Hessels,
Rietveld, & van der Zwan, 2014), through checklists and descriptor-based
instruments such as Logan's (see also Chapter 2 and Chapter 8), to the
rigour of full psychological assessments mandated for access and resource
purposes (Chapter 13). Some respondents in the research self-identified

their dyslexia, if only because formal diagnosis was not widely available, for one reason or another, when they were young.

In interviews, respondents have tended to provide their backstories, their emotional contexts and the personal relevance of their experiences, in addition to answering the target questions; it has been pondered whether this might be a characteristic of a thinking style associated with dyslexia. This tendency creates its own research issues, providing more, and different, data than requested. In the context of some of the research described in this book, the issue is resolved by these detailed responses being taken forward for further examination so that respondents' contributions are respected fully. Research continues.

In terms of entrepreneurship education, there is more that could be done to improve access, opportunity and practice for potential entrepreneurs who experience dyslexia. The small-scale and qualitative research in these chapters, together with investigations of the topic's literature, shows no evidence of:

- university and college staff going into schools to work with school pupils, including pupils with dyslexia,
- learners, including pupils who experience dyslexia, attending 'taster' days for university business courses,
- support being focussed to help with entrepreneurship study,
- different admission regimes that would help applicants with dyslexia, for example presentations, portfolios, or transcriptions showing school progress and application rather than examination results,
- anything different at all being offered to pupils with dyslexia who have entrepreneurial interest.

Any and all of these could offer research potential through action research or the evaluation of effectiveness, adding to useful knowledge about co-occurring entrepreneurship and dyslexia.

Research into entrepreneurship may adapt following new approaches to entrepreneurship developing in the interconnected, electronic world. The goodwill and effort donated freely by entrepreneurs and students with dyslexia who agreed to be interviewed reflects those individuals' hopes and wishes that the difficulties they endured will be improved for their successors. Beyond understandings of co-occurring entrepreneurship and dyslexia, the variable which remains to be explored is the influence of environment. Consequently, there is room for further research, including personal narratives, enabling the concurrence of entrepreneurship and dyslexia to be better understood.

If there Is Concurrence Between Entrepreneurship and Dyslexia, What Should Be the Educational Response?

To summarise the present position:

- Discussions in the literature about entrepreneurship and entrepreneurship education lean heavily upon considerations of theory and definition.
- The nature of the pedagogical methods through which entrepreneurship is, or could be, taught is less frequently discussed than theory, definition and structure.
- The definitional perspective can depend on whether entrepreneurship education is designed to promote value development or venture development.
- Understandings of entrepreneurship education are complicated by the variety of purposes attributed to it, described as being by, with, about and through entrepreneurship. The nature of courses, and their contributory modules, is likely to vary accordingly.
- Where entrepreneurship education is focussed around value development, there is a strong relationship with personal and social development, sometimes known as 'lifeskills.'
- The Entrepreneurship Competence Framework (EntreComp) seeks to embrace and then settle the longstanding debates surrounding entrepreneurship theory and definition by offering a comprehensive model that seeks to address all the aspects of the subject.
- Entrepreneurship education as described in the EntreComp supports a 'Progression model'. Bacigalupo, Kampyis, Punie, and van den Brande (2016) note that this is not the same as a step-wise curriculum but is a model which allows for development and progress towards expertise through choice of pertinent learning outcomes.
- In this model, entrepreneurship education is seen as a potential means of curriculum reform.
- Discussions about entrepreneurship often lead towards a socially constructed view of entrepreneurship education, moving away

from traditional business studies approaches. However, academic validation rests with maintaining links to business studies and through that area to economics.

- Narratives of entrepreneurs are encouraged in the literature but so far they are not frequently found.

The question might be asked as to why entrepreneurship education matters, and particularly why it matters for entrepreneurial learners who experience dyslexia. It might be argued that an entrepreneur will find a way to be entrepreneurial, no matter how constrained. But the modern world of business is complex, and, in order to be successful, entrepreneurs need to be able to navigate the rules, regulations, habits, expectations and the language of the business world. Without this ability it would be difficult to grow a business, or a small business might remain small despite its potential for development. A person with dyslexia has extra difficulty in these areas; therefore, entrepreneurship education needs to be aware, and supportive, of dyslexia learning needs. The previous summary allows room for pedagogical developments of this kind.

To maximise the conditions for learners with dyslexia to achieve successfully within entrepreneurship education, it is first necessary to understand how they might approach entrepreneurship learning, and consider how this understanding can be employed in promoting a supportive pedagogy. In this way, student satisfaction is increased, entrepreneurial effectiveness is increased and the potential for business growth is increased. It is recognised that, '[d]yslexia friendly good practice is, in fact, good practice for all' (Mackay & Tresman, 2005), and so it is hoped that the chapters in this book will contribute to the process of helping potential entrepreneurs to achieve when they experience dyslexia.

Fortunately, much more is known today about how to help learners who experience dyslexia, through understanding their learning characteristics beyond the issue of literacy. Offering a good teaching and learning environment for students with dyslexia, of any age, is not a matter for support workers but for teachers and lecturers themselves. The humanitarian goal of minimising traumatic learning experiences is important, but there is also the issue of improving effectiveness in undertaking and growing businesses in a modern, interconnected world. Embracing educational practices that will improve access in study and practical training for would-be entrepreneurs is likely to be of benefit in their future businesses.

A learner who experiences dyslexia does not make expected progress in literacy skills and is hampered by being unable to remember literacy-based learning or maintain an expected rate of learning. In many ways, the learner's work may resemble that of a younger learner. It may include such things as letter reversals and confusions and vocabulary restricted to that which is known and safe but which does not reflect the learner's level of actual knowledge and understanding. Literacy skills do not become automatic as they do for learners who do not experience dyslexia, so literacy tasks cause higher levels of fatigue. Work may be produced more arduously and in smaller amounts than a teacher or lecturer expects. When the learner is taught something to correct this, or to add new knowledge, it is not retained easily. Educators need to recognise these characteristics and work to alleviate them.

Learners with dyslexia often try to hide their difficulties, and successes in non-literacy areas may cause others to believe that learners are not trying hard enough. They may avoid literacy tasks in a number of ways, or rely on friends to help them or to cover for them. Learners may fall further and further behind in their work since much of the curriculum relies automatically upon literacy for access. Working harder may only increase learners' difficulty as fatigue and distress come into play; these can make a learner manifest their dyslexia more severely than usual. Teachers and lecturers become frustrated and learners lose confidence. Educators need to avoid putting learners with dyslexia into the position of trying to hide their difficulties by being responsive to the educational difference.

Dyslexia may remain hidden until the literacy demand of higher education swamps students and leaves them unable to meet that demand; there are people being identified as experiencing dyslexia as late as the PhD stage. As learners become older they may react angrily to the situation in which they find themselves, and sometimes the burden of dyslexia can lead to depression and its consequences. One entrepreneur respondent with dyslexia told researchers, in seriousness, that it was important to continue with this enquiry because raising awareness of the issues could save lives. Educators need to understand the emotional impact of dyslexia and the associated, enervating impact of literacy-based work.

Multi-sensory methods, alternative ways of recording, seeing the big picture and small steps leading to that big picture work best for learners who experience dyslexia. All these things tend to require more time and more expense from educators, and these resources are not always available. Offering a good teaching and learning environment for students with dyslexia, of any age, is not only a matter for support workers, but also a matter for teachers and lecturers, through modifications to pedagogies. Any attempt to meet learners with dyslexia half-way, listening to what they say about their own learning and making content more accessible to them, is likely to help. For guidance, entrepreneurship educators can call on the principles of universal design for instruction, learning, or inclusion and Dyslexia-Friendly practices to increase access and engagement (Appendix One).

In terms of adjusting the format of courses for entrepreneurship, qualitative research indicates that practical, real-life experiences are necessary to channel the student-to-business start-up. Use of simulations and games can be less effective than business start-up laboratories and incubators; the latter are more 'hands on,' vocational and kinaesthetic. This preference for kinaesthetic activities is well documented in dyslexia literature, along with the processing difficulties that can accompany transmissive styles of input.

Following inclusive principles, universities are beginning to modify learning environments to engage different types of learners. This can mean:

- adding images to PowerPoint slides,
- choosing easy-to-read typefaces,
- reducing the amount of text on each slide,
- using colour to differentiate text,
- providing lectures on video, or otherwise electronically, to allow for individuals who need more time to process complex information,
- providing handouts in electronic format,
- avoiding situations where students are required to read a screen, listen to the lecturer, follow a handout and make notes all at the same time,
- showing learners the big picture and end point.

At the HE level, universities recognise that inclusion is necessary, but the process of change management depends on individual academics understanding, and being committed to, the actions required to effect this change. If, as the Welsh government initiatives seem to recognise, the entrepreneurs and business leaders of tomorrow will not always come from traditional pathways, there is likely to be an untapped source of business ability among people who think differently and have a non-traditional profile. It is to the advantage of both learners and educators alike to adopt proactive ways of facilitating learning for potential entrepreneurs who experience dyslexia.

Are Individuals With Dyslexia Uniquely Skilled to Be Entrepreneurs?

In discussing the intersection of entrepreneurship and dyslexia, the question inevitably arises as to whether individuals with dyslexia are uniquely skilled to be entrepreneurs. This is very similar to the question of whether people with dyslexia are inherently creative. While there are many with dyslexia in the creative professions, and similarly there are many entrepreneurs experiencing dyslexia in a range of fields, it can no longer be said that they are born with these skills. Where, then, did they learn these skills and abilities?

Entrepreneurs who experience dyslexia may talk about being undervalued at school and being judged as being lazy and unintelligent. Indeed, authors in this book have talked about their school experiences and the effect of these on their later life career choices. It has been argued that there has been a lack of identification and support for learners with dyslexia in mainstream education, and that they have suffered as a result. The evidence suggests it may be a reaction to what schools have *not* done that has created the environment for many people with dyslexia to develop coping strategies and defence mechanisms, fostering the core skills which are recognised among entrepreneurs and industry leaders.

It could even be argued that mainstream education nurtures entrepreneurship in individuals who experience dyslexia through negative experience, with a lack of screening and intervention, creating a difficult educational environment. In this case, learners with unidentified dyslexia may fail on an hourly basis but may also learn an extremely important lesson that they can fail and then move on and start again. This lesson has been found to be very important to people who wish to be entrepreneurs, as commonly a person's early business ventures may fail. It is only those who can learn from failure and bounce back, demonstrating necessary resilience, who will succeed in business as entrepreneurs.

This is a harsh process, perhaps akin to throwing a young child into a pool to sink or swim and is not a justification for good outcomes that may transpire later. Nevertheless, this is very much the experience of many with dyslexia in mainstream education; some will find a way to stay afloat while others will go under unless aided. Evidence from mainstream education indicates that those who quickly gain the skills to survive emotionally and educationally will do so by developing resilience, negotiating skills and creative skills to highlight their strengths and maintain their sense of self-worth. They may find their identity through extra-curricular activities or incidental and peripheral activities. People who do not manage such an accommodation may suffer all their lives from the difficulties and uncertainties caused by, and accompanying, their situation.

What part does dyslexia play, then, in an individual becoming an entrepreneur? Is it because of innate qualities, or could it be that because they have dyslexia and feel excluded from traditional work environments people turn to entrepreneurship to cope in the business world, so that 'doing it my way' is in fact the only way they can do it? Is it a case of survival? It could be argued, especially where entrepreneurs experience dyslexia, that they are drawn to entrepreneurship because it enables them to reformulate their lives in order to create uses for their undervalued abilities. Nevertheless, it must not be forgotten that dyslexia itself is not related to measurable indicators for characteristics associated with intelligence, that is, Intelligence Quotient scores. Neither individuals with dyslexia nor entrepreneurs form homogenous groups.

Conclusion

The chapters in this book call on current understandings of entrepreneurship and dyslexia, in order to move the discourse from journalistic accounts of famous entrepreneurs with dyslexia toward a more comprehensive exploration of Logan's 2009 finding, that greater-than-expected numbers of entrepreneurs are identified as experiencing dyslexia. Many of the chapters report small-scale and qualitative research studies and personal narratives, pointing out the importance of lived experience for lessons in entrepreneurial learning. Together, the chapters provide perspectives that aim to help individuals who experience dyslexia and who have entrepreneurial interests.

In response to the question of whether people with dyslexia are uniquely skilled to be entrepreneurs, the answer, as discussed in these chapters, would be a qualified yes. This is demonstrated by divergent patterns of thinking, use of non-literacy-based methods of information transmission and communication, enthusiasm for interesting stimuli, attraction towards new and wide-ranging outlets for a person's skills and interests and, of course, ingenuity in exploiting these in order to generate income. However, this potential would also need to be hedged about with caveats concerning experience, interest and opportunity. An entrepreneurial identity for someone with dyslexia would not depend solely upon inner characteristics but also upon environmental ones, including those inputs provided by entrepreneurship education.

While entrepreneurs with dyslexia may be discussed as a group within these pages, the individuals concerned have their own identities and dyslexia may not be the most significant factor that concerns or interests them. Nevertheless there may be some common factors associated with their journeys towards entrepreneurship. In the case of entrepreneurs who experience dyslexia, it is possible that their entrepreneurial characteristics relate to personal behaviours selected by them as effective in their youth and school years. Preferred behaviours become strategies. A person with dyslexia who has an entrepreneurial turn of mind, seizing or creating opportunities and using and re-using these strategies to good effect, can turn strategies into entrepreneurial skills.

An entrepreneur who experiences dyslexia is more likely to rely on their own skills and perceptions than on literacy-based interactions, employing other individuals and services to fill gaps in their own skills—which they recognise through their own experience. They focus their attention on the aspects of business that interest them and that they know they do well. For these reasons, there may be a whole different style of doing business for entrepreneurs with dyslexia, facilitated by advances in communications media. Employing bricolage in the interests of developing a business, rather than relying on written resources, may be the skill that successful entrepreneurs who experience dyslexia use very well. This difference of style may be an important characteristic for many entrepreneurs with dyslexia and may go some way to explaining a higher than expected incidence of dyslexia among entrepreneurs.

An understanding of this difference of style may help educators to shape their pedagogies in ways that are more helpful to learners who experience dyslexia. Teachers and lecturers can have a great deal of impact upon students' lives; it is only when a student begins to realise that they have skills of their own that they can develop the confidence that allows their abilities to flower. This demonstrates the importance of developing a working relationship with the student. Not all learners are the same, and some need more input than others; this is at the heart of inclusive practice.

Using the information that is available and drawing insight from the accounts that may be found in these chapters, practitioners can develop their own ways of making pedagogy accessible. The key factor in helping learners with dyslexia who have an entrepreneurial interest may be the willingness of educators to do so.

References

Bacigalupo, M., Kampyis, P., Punie, Y., & van den Brande, G. (2016). *EntreComp: The entrepreneurship competence framework* (No. JRC101581). Brussels, Belgium: Joint Research Centre, European Commission. Retrieved from http://publications.jrc.ec.europa.eu/repository/handle/JRC101581

Hessels, J., Rietveld, C., & van der Zwan, P. (2014). Unraveling two myths about entrepreneurs. *Economic Letters, 122,* 435–438. https://doi.org/10.1016/j.econlet.2014.01.005

Logan, J. (2009). Dyslexic entrepreneurs: The incidence; their coping strategies and their business skills. *Dyslexia, 15,* 328–334. https://doi.org/10.1002/dys.388

Mackay, N., & Tresman, S. (2005). *Achieving dyslexia friendly schools: Resource pack* (5th ed.). Reading, MA: British Dyslexia Association.

Valeras, A. B. (2010). We don't have a box: Understanding hidden disability identity utilizing narrative research methodology. *Disability Study Quarterly, 30,* 3–4. Retrieved from http://dsq-sds.org/article/view/1267/1297

Contributors

Editors

Neil Alexander-Passe experiences dyslexia himself, and has over the last 20 years specialised in the emotional experience of having a learning difference. He has published twelve books and ten peer review papers in the field of dyslexia, looking at correlations with mental health, creativity, parenting and marriage. He gained his PhD in 2018 investigating 'Dyslexia, Traumatic Schooling, and Post-School Success.' His current focus is with a 'bi-ability' theoretical model for dyslexia and the use of a 'post-traumatic growth (PTG)' concept to understand how many individuals with dyslexia can be successful 'despite or because' they experienced traumatic schooling as children.

Neil is the Special Educational Needs and Disabilities Coordinator (SENDCO) at a large secondary school in North London, and an Expert SEND Adviser for the UK's Department of Education (Standards and Testing Agency). Neil is Scientific Board Member for the *Asia Pacific Journal of Developmental Differences, Dyslexia Association of Singapore*.

Margaret Meehan, formerly a conservator and a researcher in inorganic chemistry, Margaret has worked with adults with Specific Learning Difficulties (SpLDs), particularly dyslexia, in several HE institutions for over 20 years. Initially supporting students with dyslexia who also experienced difficulties with mathematics and science, she went on to deliver specialist tuition to students with SpLDs, Autistic Spectrum Condition, well-being issues and medical conditions across all disciplines, and to manage specialist tuition for academic success in her university.

Margaret has published journal articles and books in the area of SpLDs and continues to research in this area. She is a qualified teacher of the Alexander Technique and a teacher of Jessica Wolf's Art of Breathing technique. Margaret is a former chartered chemist and chartered science teacher, senior fellow of the Higher Education Academy. She is also Scientific Board Member for the *Asia Pacific Journal of Developmental Differences, Dyslexia Association of Singapore*.

Barbara Pavey As an educator, Barbara Pavey has a wide range of professional experience. Trained originally as a primary teacher, Barbara has taught all ages from six to 60, through primary, secondary, further and higher education (HE). Following her academic degrees, she gained a post-graduate diploma in Special Educational Needs (SEN) and dyslexia, together with the qualification of Associate Member of the British Dyslexia Association (AMBDA). She has 40 years of experience in SEN, including teaching, administration and lecturing. On completing her doctorate in 2002, Barbara moved into HE, where she focussed on dyslexia and SEN specialism, training specialist teachers and SEN and Disability Coordinators (SENCos).

Barbara has an international reputation in the SEN and dyslexia fields through the Dyslexia-Friendly focus of her books and articles. Barbara continues to work and write in the field of SEN and dyslexia as an independent scholar and consultant.

Chapter Authors

Paul Adkins At the time of writing, Paul Adkins, now retired, was Senior Lecturer in business management and marketing, in the Department of Land, Farm and Agribusiness Management at Harper Adams University (England). His duties at Harper Adams University included lecturing in business and management, and his research interests included new enterprise development and management, entrepreneurship and dyslexia. Paul Adkins is the author of *Organisational Slack Resources: The definitions and consequences for business flexibility and performance*. He is Fellow of the Higher Education Academy and Member of the Chartered Management Institute.

Matthew Armstrong is a qualified nurse; he has worked extensively across the health care sector, with an interest in mentoring clinical students especially those who struggle with literacy and mathematics. As an entrepreneur, Matthew acquired a property portfolio which he developed and managed himself. As a business consultant, he worked with entrepreneurs to develop their business, going on to establish his own limited companies in recruitment and letting. Matthew is a Specialist Tutor for Swansea University, working with people who have an SpLD, well-being issues or medical conditions. Independently, Matthew is exploring new innovative business models in 'Serviced Accommodation.'

Gillian Conley is a full-time lecturer at Barony Campus of Scotland's Rural College (SRUC) in South West Scotland, with specialist interests in academic support, education, study skills and dyslexia stemming from having over 20 years of experience in working full-time in education. Within the farming community of Dumfriesshire, she has worked with individuals who had to learn and work using a variety of techniques to overcome tendencies associated with dyslexia. Gillian is passionate about education. As part of her ongoing research, she has developed a questionnaire which has been used to help profile and discuss the specific attributes of people in the agriculture industry who either have been professionally diagnosed with dyslexia or who have reason to believe that they experience dyslexia.

Angela Fawcett is a leading international researcher into dyslexia and other developmental disabilities, encompassing a range of theoretical and applied contributions to this field. Her approach is broad and interdisciplinary, ranging from child and cognitive development to educational screening and intervention, as well as development cognitive neuroscience. She is Vice President of the British Dyslexia Association, Former Chair and Director of the Centre for Child Research at Swansea University, UK and Special Envoy to the world for Dyslexia International. She is the former editor in chief of *Dyslexia: An International Journal of Research and Practice* from 2004 to 2010 and continues as executive editor. Professor Fawcett is Emeritus Professor at Swansea University and held the prestigious Leverhulme Emeritus fellowship, from 2011 to 2014, and is currently Research Consultant at the Dyslexia

Association of Singapore (DAS), and Honorary Consultant to the Dyslexia Association of Indonesia. She has contributed three of the major theories of dyslexia with her colleague Professor Rod Nicolson, eight screening tests for dyslexia, one authored book and eight edited books, in addition to over 80 publications in high-impact international peer-reviewed journals and over 50 contributions to edited works. She currently serves on the UK All Party Parliamentary Group (APPG) for dyslexia.

Eva Gyarmathy is a senior researcher at the Institute for Cognitive Neuroscience and Psychology of the Hungarian Academy. Her research interests focus on multiple exceptional gifted individuals, such as talent associated with SpLDs, Attention-Deficit/Hyperactivity Disorder, autism and/or social, cultural differences. She is a university lecturer for several universities.

As a psychotherapist, her activity directs toward the care of the profoundly gifted and multiple exceptional talents. She is a consultant to private schools that serve gifted children and adolescents who could not be integrated into the mainstream school. She founded the Adolescent and Adult Dyslexia Centre and the Special Needs Talent Support Council.

Deborah Hewes is Assistant Director, Publicity and Publications at the Dyslexia Association of Singapore (DAS). Deborah experiences dyslexia and is passionate about raising awareness about learning differences. All three of her children have learning differences and, as a result, she has spent most of the last 20 years supporting her children's academic careers as well as helping other families with children who have learning differences. Deborah's psychology honours degree thesis investigated 'Adolescents with learning disabilities: An investigation of academic self-concept, self-esteem and depression in International school students.' Her master's degree in SEN researched into 'Singaporean Entrepreneurs and Dyslexia.' Deborah is Managing Editor of the *Asia Pacific Journal of Developmental Difference*. In 2015, she edited the first book *Embrace a Different Kind of Mind—Personal Stories of Dyslexia* and in 2017 designed and published the 25th Anniversary book for DAS, *Clearly Different-Dyscovering the Differences*.

Nigel Lockett is Professor of Entrepreneurship at the University of Strathclyde and Head of the Hunter Centre for Entrepreneurship.

He is a senior academic, experienced manager, serial entrepreneur and community leader. To raise awareness of dyslexia, he blogs as *The Dyslexic Professor*. Nigel is currently Co-Investigator on the £7m GCRF RECIRCULATE project. Before joining Strathclyde, he worked as a professor at Lancaster University Management School and Leeds University Business School. In 2015, Nigel was awarded the prestigious National Teaching Fellowship for his outstanding contribution to enterprise in HE and leadership. He also has over 25 years of experience as a company director, with a track record in managing start-up, joint venture and social enterprises. His current research interests include knowledge exchange between universities and industry, academic entrepreneurship, entrepreneurial learning and the use of Customer Relationship Technologies by small to medium sized enterprises.

Louise Manning is Professor of Agri-food and Supply Chain Security at the Royal Agricultural University and has worked for over 35 years in the agri-food supply chain in a range of roles. Her expertise is in the area of food security and food integrity including food safety, food quality, food crime, policy and governance, social and corporate responsibility, personal development, resilience, risk assessment and mitigation strategies. Louise has carried out projects for government bodies, academic institutions and companies across the world. This work includes strategic risk analysis and mitigation for both corporate organisations and public bodies. She has published multiple peer-reviewed articles, authored book chapters and written and edited books in the subject area.

Roderick Nicolson is currently Professor of Psychology at Edge Hill University, Lancashire and formerly at the University of Sheffield. Working with Angela Fawcett, he has spent 30 years developing integrated theoretical explanations for dyslexia, from automatisation deficit (1990) to cerebellar deficit (1995) to procedural deficit (2007) to Delayed Neural Commitment (2018). Recently, he applied the insights of positive psychology to dyslexia, creating a new approach–positive dyslexia—which is aimed at allowing individuals who experience dyslexia to find, develop and celebrate their strengths rather than merely remediate their weaknesses, with one major theme being entrepreneurial success.

Geetha Shantha Ram is Director of SpLD Assessment Services, Director of English Language and Literacy Division, Director of Staff Professional Development and Head of the Research Committee for DAS. Formerly Assistant Director of the DAS Academy, Geetha has trained educators, parents and other professionals. She is a speaker at international conferences, such as the 2019 International Dyslexia Association conference in Portland, Oregon. She is an advisor for the Register of Educational Therapists (Asia). Geetha has a master's degree in English and is currently pursuing a doctorate in the area of giftedness and SpLDs. With over 15 years of experience supporting children and adults, Geetha provides an important service to people with dyslexia, helping them to develop their potential and their appreciation of their own unique gifts.

Maximus Monaheng Sefotho of the University of Johannesburg completed a post graduate diploma in disability studies with the University of Cape Town in 2016. In 2018, he edited a book, *Philosophy in education and research: African perspectives*, on which his workshops are based. Of particular interest is the inclusion of a chapter on the philosophy of disability: African perspectives. In the same year, he authored a chapter, 'Disability and inclusive employment through the lens of educational psychology' in I. Eloff and E. Swart (Eds.) *Understanding educational psychology* (p. 296–300). His work yielded a brainchild in the form of an envisaged Centre for Visual Impairment Studies, (as co-director) currently being developed as well as an advanced diploma in visual impairment studies envisaged to start in 2019/2020.

Poliana Sepulveda holds a degree in business administration from the University Center of Brasilia (2011), a certificate in coaching by the University of Cambridge, a master's degree in leadership and management from the University of Sheffield (2013) and a PhD from the Institute of Psychology of the University of Sheffield. Her main research area is positive psychology and work psychology. Poliana has experience in planning and implementing projects in companies in the area of people and talent management.

Robert Smith is currently Independent Scholar but was formerly Professor of Enterprise and Innovation at the University of the West of Scotland, based at Dumfries. Rob is a prolific writer and has published over 170 book chapters and journal articles on entrepreneurship in a variety of forms including rural, gender and criminal, as well as family business and policing. Rob has a keen interest in dyslexia and entrepreneurship and several of his publications relate to either this and/or farming and dyslexia. Rob's interest in dyslexia and other learning difficulties stems from his belief that he experiences dyspraxia and displays many of the tendencies associated with that condition.

Appendix

Appendix One

Comparison of Principles of Universal Design for Instruction and Dyslexia-Friendly Principles (Pavey, 2015)

Principles of Universal Design for Instruction (Scott, McGuire, & Shaw, 2003, p. 375–376, citing Shaw, Scott, & McGuire, 2001).	Principles of Dyslexia-Friendly Practice (Pavey, Meehan, & Waugh, 2010, p. 99–105, citing Pavey, 2007).
1. Equitable use—instruction is designed to be useful and accessible by people with diverse abilities. Provide the same means of use for all students, identical whenever possible, equivalent when not (Scott, McGuire, & Shaw, 2003, p. 375).	Input takes account of multi-sensory learning. Multi-sensory inputs are close together in stimuli and in tasks. Practitioners' talk time reduced; board-copying reduced; handouts available ahead of teaching.
2. Flexibility in use—instruction is designed to accommodate a wide range of individual abilities. Provide choice in methods of use (Scott, McGuire, & Shaw, 2003, p. 375).	Learners can use alternative means of recording, e.g. poster, tape, Information and Communications Technology. Practitioners know and use learners' preferred individual learning styles and challenge learners to use different learning styles in a manageable way. Practitioners know their own preferred individual learning styles and challenge themselves to move outside of their own comfort zone.
3. Simple and intuitive—instruction is designed in a straightforward and predictable manner, regardless of the student's experience, knowledge, language skills, or current concentration level. Eliminate unnecessary complexity (Scott, McGuire, & Shaw, 2003, p. 375).	Instructions clear, explanations repeated, timescales and length of work product clearly stated, subject-specific words linked to clear concepts. Input given in small chunks. New concepts are linked to previous concepts. Texts are given ahead of time for practice purposes.

Principles of Universal Design for Instruction (Scott, McGuire, & Shaw, 2003, p. 375–376, citing Shaw, Scott, & McGuire, 2001).	Principles of Dyslexia-Friendly Practice (Pavey, Meehan, & Waugh, 2010, p. 99–105, citing Pavey, 2007).
4. Perceptible information—instruction is designed so that the necessary information is communicated effectively to the student, regardless of ambient conditions or the student's sensory abilities (Scott, McGuire, & Shaw, 2003, p. 375).	Teaching uses diagrams and illustrations, bullet points and lists and colours for identification purposes. Text resources include a font which is clearly distinguishable, in shape and size, with rounded shape and two-story 'a.' Photocopies are clean and clear, text is in small groups, clearly separated. There are frequent headings, shown in bold, separate from the text; off-white or tinted paper is used. Diagrams and illustrations are used and give the same information as, or related to, text and are situated near relevant text.
5. Tolerance for error—instruction anticipates variation in individual learning pace and prerequisite skills (Scott, McGuire, & Shaw, 2003, p. 375).	Extra time is allowed for learners to finish written work if necessary. Learners' output is judged predominantly on quality and content. Judgements of laziness are avoided.
6. Low physical effort—instruction is designed to minimize non-essential physical effort in order to allow maximum attention to learning. Note: This principal does not apply when physical effort is integral to essential requirements of a course (Scott, McGuire, & Shaw, 2003, p. 375)	Assessment criteria are clearly stated, including those for alternative formats. Learners' output uses diagrams and illustrations, bullet points and numbered lists. Learners are asked how best they learn, changes in teaching acknowledge what learners say about how best they learn.
7. Size and space for approach and use—instruction is designed with a consideration for appropriate size and space for approach, reach, manipulations and views regardless of a student's body size, posture, mobility and communication needs (Scott, McGuire, & Shaw, 2003, p. 375).	Care is taken so that learners with possible dyslexia see and hear the teacher or lecturer clearly. Learners experiencing possible dyslexia have opportunities to work in a quiet area. Visual displays and pedagogical resources conform to text resource guidelines; learners who request tinted paper may have it.

Principles of Universal Design for Instruction (Scott, McGuire, & Shaw, 2003, p. 375–376, citing Shaw, Scott, & McGuire, 2001).	Principles of Dyslexia-Friendly Practice (Pavey, Meehan, & Waugh, 2010, p. 99–105, citing Pavey, 2007).
8. A community of learners—the instructional environment promotes interaction and communication among the students and between students and faculty (Scott, McGuire, & Shaw, 2003, p. 376).	Learners are allowed to ask questions. Rewards can be achieved by all the learners in the group.
9. Instructional climate—instruction is designed to be welcoming and inclusive. High expectations are espoused for all students (Scott, McGuire, & Shaw, 2003, p. 376).	Learners' reading aloud, or writing on a board, is voluntary. Learning tasks consider and deal with emotional issues; care is taken to protect learners' feelings and ensure that they are not teased because of literacy difficulties.

References

Pavey, B. (2007). *The Dyslexia-Friendly primary school: A practical guide for teachers*. London: SAGE.

Pavey, B. (2015). The UK's Dyslexia-Friendly initiative and the USA's universal design movement: Exploring a possible kinship. *Asia Pacific Journal of Developmental Differences, 2*(1), 39–54. Retrieved from www.das.org.sg

Pavey, B., Meehan, M., & Waugh, A. (2010). *Dyslexia-Friendly further and higher education*. London, England: SAGE.

Scott, S. S., McGuire, J. M., & Shaw, S. F. (2003). Universal design for instruction: A new paradigm for adult instruction in postsecondary education. *Remedial and Special Education, 24*(6), 369–379. https://doi.org/10.1177/0741932503 0240060801

Shaw, S. F., Scott, S. S., & McGuire, J. M. (2001). Teaching college Students with learning disabilities. *ERIC Digest*. Arlington, VA: ERIC Clearinghouse on Disabilities and Gifted Education. Retrieved from https://files.eric.ed.gov/fulltext/ED459548.pdf

Index

Note: Page numbers in italic indicate a figure and page numbers in bold indicate a table on the corresponding page.